Cook - Peary
1st
edition

RETURN FROM THE POLE

FREDERICK A. COOK

Return from the Pole

FREDERICK A. COOK

Edited, with an Introduction, by Frederick J. Pohl

Pellegrini & Cudahy NEW YORK

CONTENTS

n

↑

EDITOR'S NOTE

Dr. Cook wrote *Return from the Pole* in longhand, beginning it in 1930 and completing it in 1935 when he was seventy years of age. The author's Arctic adventures had passed repeatedly through his mind on the lecture platform, and this explains the reappearance of phrases, sentences, and even an occasional passage of several sentences used in the skeletal threading of the narrative in a few pages of his earlier book, *My Attainment of the Pole*. His family wish me to extend their thanks particularly to Miss Eileen O'Connor who typed the original manuscript.

Dr. Cook left several suggestions for a title—*At the End of North, Down from the Earth's Top, Where North Is South, Aftermath of the Polar Conquest*—but none of them seemed as satisfactory as *Return from the Pole*, which came out of a discussion I had with Dr. Cook's daughter and her husband.

Editing *Return from the Pole* has been a happy undertaking in which many people have been helpful and generous.

My reading on the subject of polar exploration was facilitated by the courtesy of the attendants at the New York Public Library. They assisted in procuring books from the Library of Congress and the Boston Public Library. Mrs. Helene Cook Vetter, Dr. Cook's daughter, spread before me the diaries, notebooks, and unpublished writings of her father. I am indebted also to Miss Helen I. Buck at the library of the American Alpine Club, and to the attendants at the Brooklyn Public Library, and the libraries of the Kings County Medical Society, the Explorers' Club of New York, and the American Geographical Society. Dr. Vilhjalmur Stefansson kindly placed at my disposal the resources of his splendid library of Arctic literature.

F.J.P.

RETURN FROM THE POLE

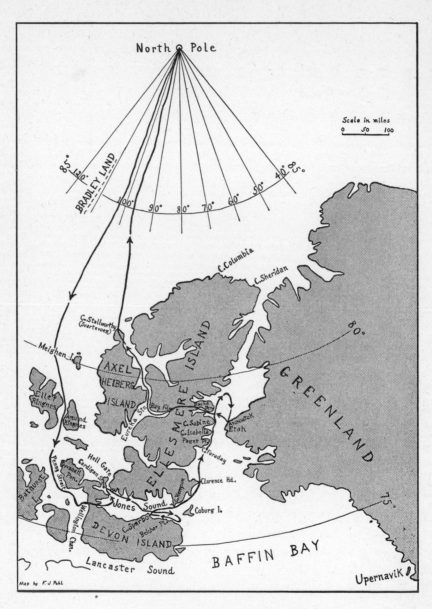

COOK'S ROUTE TO THE POLE

n

↑

CHRONOLOGY

1907

July 3   Cook sails on the *John R. Bradley* from Gloucester, Mass.

Aug. 27   Cook lands at Annoatok.

1908

Feb. 19   Cook and his party leave Annoatok.

March 21   Cook's supporting party turns back.

March 30   Cook discovers Bradley Land.

April 21   Cook records attainment of the Pole.

April 23   Cook begins his return journey.

June 13   Cook returns to sight of land north of the Ringnes Islands.

July 4   Cook starts to cross Grinnell Peninsula to Jones Sound.

July 6   Peary sails on the *Roosevelt* from New York.

August 11	PEARY reaches Etah.
Sept. 5	PEARY reaches Cape Sheridan where the *Roosevelt* is frozen in for winter quarters.
September	COOK and his two Eskimos establish underground winter quarters at Cape Sparbo.

1909

Feb. 22	PEARY leaves the *Roosevelt* for Cape Columbia and the Pole.
April 1	PEARY's supporting party turns back at 87° 47′ N
April 6	PEARY records attainment of the Pole.
April 7	PEARY begins his return journey.
April 18	COOK and his two Eskimos return to Annoatok.
April 21	COOK leaves Annoatok by dog team.
April 23	PEARY reaches land at Cape Columbia, and Bartlett reaches the *Roosevelt* at Cape Sheridan.
April 27	PEARY reaches the *Roosevelt*.
May 21	COOK reaches Upernavik.
July 18	PEARY sails south after the *Roosevelt* is freed from the ice.
July 27	PEARY arrives at Etah and questions Harry Payne Whitney and Cook's Eskimos about Cook.
Sept. 1	COOK, on the *Hans Egede* bound for Copenhagen, reaches Lerwick in the Shetland Islands, and telegraphs, "Reached the North Pole April 21, 1908."
Sept. 4	COOK arrives in Copenhagen.
Sept. 6	PEARY reaches Indian Harbor, Labrador, and announces, "I have the Pole, April 6, 1909."
Sept. 8	PEARY, after receiving news of Cook's claim, telegraphs from Battle Harbor, Labrador, "Dr. Cook has handed the public a gold brick."

n

↑

INTRODUCTION

The North Pole Controversy—
A Review of the Facts and Claims

The conquest of the North Pole had challenged explorers and stirred the imagination for centuries. Many daring men had tried and failed; some died on the great white wastes above Greenland. Then on September 1, 1909, the *Hans Egede*, a blubber ship, reached Lerwick in the Shetland Islands on its return to Denmark from Arctic waters and Dr. Frederick Albert Cook, who had come aboard at Upernavik in Greenland, announced by telegraph: "Reached the North Pole April 21, 1908. Discovered land far north." The world was thrilled. No word of the explorer had come out of the polar region since late 1907. Dr. Cook had conquered the Pole.

On September 6, 1909, five days after Cook's announcement and as he was being honored by scientists and royalty in Copenhagen, the *Roosevelt*, returning from the Arctic after more than a year's silence, reached Indian Harbor, Labrador, and Robert Edwin Peary, a rugged explorer who had failed in six previous polar efforts, telegraphed: "I have the Pole, April 6, 1909." It seemed now that Peary had failed in his twenty-five-year ambition to be the first man to reach the Pole. It had been a crusade with him since the age of twenty-eight (he was now fifty-three), when he wrote that the fame of Columbus would be equalled only by the man who stood "with 360 degrees of longitude beneath his motionless feet and for whom East and West shall have vanished, the discoverer of the North Pole." As he was preparing for his final and successful assault against the polar ice, Peary had declared in the presence of President Theodore Roosevelt: "The final and complete solution of the polar mystery . . . is . . . the thing which is intended that I should do, and the thing that I must do."

Two days after his first announcement, Peary, on September 8, sent a second telegram from Indian Harbor: "Do not trouble about Cook's story. . . . He has simply handed the public a gold brick. The above statement is made advisedly and at the proper time will be backed by proof."

Lincoln Steffens, an outstanding journalist of the day, wrote: "Whatever the truth is, the situation is as wonderful as the Pole. And whatever they found there, those explorers, they have left there a story as great as a continent. The Pole, discovered, is peopled with a human romance: it is a part of the epic of man. I suppose the controversy will last longer than that of Sampson and Schley; unless Peary can blow Cook into the air, it will go down all the ages. And even if Cook is found to have made some error in his observations, and didn't get there, there will still be a story. It is great. I am as excited about it as I haven't been about anything for years."

The centuries-old struggle for the Pole had been turned into one of the most dramatic controversies of the twentieth century. It was no longer a question of whether man could reach the Pole—but did Dr. Frederick Albert Cook, a lone wolf, reach the Pole? When Peary made his "gold brick" charge, there was little inclination to examine the evidence scientifically. Because opinion was about equally divided, the press intensified the dispute. Cook made his account exclusive to the New York *Herald*, while Peary's went to the New York *Times*. Both papers sold their stories widely, each favoring its own man.

But as time went on encyclopedias and atlases accepted Peary as discoverer of the Pole and Cook was stripped of character and reputation. However, as I read the manuscript of *Return from the Pole* and went back to study the evidence presented by both parties, there appeared to be many reasons why Cook's claim should be taken seriously.

Before he made his dramatic dash for the Pole, Dr. Frederick Albert Cook was known as a daring explorer and a good physician, a founder and president of the Explorers' Club in New York. The youngest of four children, he was self-made, having supported himself from boyhood when his father died. Born in 1865 in Hortonville, near Callicoon Depot, New York, he attended rural school and labored at farm work and country jobs until he was fourteen. Lacking money to buy a sled for winter coasting, he cut young trees and built the best sled in the region. Geography fascinated him and he loved to roam the Catskills. In Port Jervis, he managed two years of high school, but when he was sixteen the family moved to Brooklyn and young Cook sold vegetables in Fulton Market and attended night school. With a hand printing press, he earned enough money to buy a milk route. By rising at 1 A.M. each morning to make his milk-route rounds, he was able to study at Columbia, attending the College of Physicians and Surgeons for one year, 1885-86, and later, University Medical College. He had been practicing medicine only a few months when, in 1891, he answered an advertisement: Robert E. Peary, a civil engineer attached to the Navy, wanted a surgeon for his North-Greenland Polar Expedition.

Peary was impressed by the young doctor, and Cook was impressed by Peary. Peary was rugged and daring, driven by ambition for discovery and fame. He was eleven years Cook's senior and had already had a career that pointed to big adventure. Born in Cresson, Pennsylvania, in 1856, he had gone to Bowdoin College in Maine, and then as a naval engineer surveyed in Nicaragua.

Peary's 1891 Expedition went into the far north, and at the end of 130 miles on the first trip northeast over the Greenland Ice Cap, Dr. Cook "was the first to volunteer to go on." Peary found him "always helpful and an indefatigable worker" and admired his "unruffled patience and coolness in an emergency." In the ethnological field, Peary said, Cook "has obtained a large mass of most valuable material concerning a practically unstudied [Eskimo] tribe." He was also grateful for Cook's skill as a surgeon. Peary's leg was broken by the spokes of the steering wheel of the *Kite*, the expedition ship, when ice jammed the rudder. "Thanks to the professional skill of my surgeon Dr. Cook," Peary wrote, "my complete recovery was rapidly attained."

Dr. Cook returned to the North in the yacht *Zeta* in 1893, and again in 1894 in the *Miranda*. He was organizer and commander of both groups, the latter the largest scientific expedition which had ever sailed to the Arctic. When the *Miranda* struck an iceberg off southern Greenland, and everything seemed hopeless, Cook traveled ninety miles through rough waters in a small open boat and returned with a rescue ship.

For the next three years Cook practiced medicine in Brooklyn and hankered for polar exploration. Then he joined the Belgian Antarctic Expedition (1898-99) as surgeon, photographer, and anthropologist. Again he distinguished himself as a man who had the rare qualities of patience, stamina, courage, and imagination needed for exploration. Roald Amundsen, first mate of the expedition's ship *Belgica*, was impressed by Cook. "He was beloved and respected by all . . . upright, capable, and conscientious in the extreme. . . . He, of all the ship's company, was the one man of unfaltering courage, unfailing hope, endless cheerfulness, and unwearied kindness. . . . His ingenuity and enterprise were boundless. . . . He was quiet and reserved, but the success of the whole Belgian expedition was due to him. . . ." Later, during the Cook-Peary dispute, Amundsen said, "Cook is the most reliable man I ever met. I would trust no other man as I trust him."

The South Polar expedition resulted in Cook's first book and it brought him considerable fame as an explorer, scientist, and writer on exploration. His *Through the First Antarctic Night* (1900) is much more than an exciting narrative of exploration; it is an important study of the psychological effects of spending a winter in polar darkness. But Cook was concerned with more than exploration and the psychology of darkness, and in a section on "The Possibilities of Antarctic Exploration" he stressed the economic importance of the resources of the Antarctic—ichthyological, ornithological, and mineral.

His book finished between calls on patients in Brooklyn, Cook was eager to be off again, challenging the cold, windswept polar wastes. In 1899, Peary had reached 85° 51′ North. Now he was ready to try again, and Cook sailed with him in 1901 on Peary's auxiliary ship *Erik*. The expedition failed.

Soon thereafter, Dr. Cook married Mrs. Marie Fidell Hunt,

widow of a Philadelphia surgeon. This was his second marriage; his first wife, whom he had married while he was a student, had died just as he was beginning medical practice.

Leaving polar exploration for the time to Peary, Dr. Cook made, in 1903, an unsuccessful attempt to climb Mount McKinley, the highest peak in North America. The mountain was inaccessible from the southwest and west, but he would not give up the challenge. Three years later, in 1906, Cook was back again. His first try failed, and after all but two of his companions had given up and returned to the safety of the valley, Cook reported that he and Edward M. Barrill, leaving one man at base camp and traveling light, found a way up a northeast ridge with slopes of 60 degrees. Dr. Cook stated that "from the upper slopes, we saw that there were several miniature ranges running up to two main peaks about two miles apart, to the west a ridge with a saddle, to the east a similar ridge, with one main peak to the southeast. This peak was the highest point." He spoke of the "ridiculous ease" of the ascent from 16,300 feet to the highest peak at "20,391" feet (actual height is 20,270 feet), aside from breathing difficulties and physical weariness. He described the sky above the summit as looking very dark. From the 18,400-foot level he told of seeing the ice-blink (whiteness in the sky near the horizon caused by the reflection from an ice field) from 200 miles away, north of the St. Elias group. All this, in time, would enter the Cook-Peary controversy.

When Cook returned to New York from Mount McKinley, he learned that Peary had reached 87° 6′—a new "farthest north"—and was now organizing with the support of President Roosevelt an elaborate expedition, his final effort to conquer the Pole. Cook listened to the talk, read about Peary's plans in the newspapers, kept his own counsel, and busied himself with medicine and writing *To the Top of the Continent,* an account of his assault on Mount McKinley. In May, 1907, he published in *Harper's Weekly* an article entitled "Why Not Conquer the South Pole?"

"The Boreal Center," he wrote, "has managed to hold public interest. The Austral point has been neglected." Why? "Great enterprises depending upon popular acclaim for financial support drift with public opinion in narrow grooves. . . . To the South Pole, to the new fairy land of scientists! This should be the foreword of coming explorers. It is a problem peculiarly adapted to American dash, and it should be achieved under the Stars and Stripes."

But Dr. Cook had his eyes on the North Pole also. He lunched, early in 1907, at Holland House with his millionaire friend, John R. Bradley. Bradley wanted to go north on a hunting trip: would Cook accompany him? Cook suggested, instead, that they go to the North Pole—Bradley sharing the honor with him.

"Not I," said Bradley. "Would you like to try for it?"

"There's nothing that I would rather do; it's the ambition of my life," Cook replied.

Thus the stage was readied for a great drama. Peary's one ambition was to reach the North Pole; so was Cook's. But while Peary publicized his plans to get support, Cook, with the aid of Bradley, planned quietly, without fanfare. He would go north on a hunting trip with Bradley, and if conditions were favorable would remain to make a dash for the Pole the following year. Cook explained there was no need for the huge sum Peary was planning to spend. He would not make his winter headquarters in a ship frozen in as near the Pole as possible; he would not need a relief ship to come up the next year to bring him back to civilization. Instead, he would travel southward across the frozen bays of Greenland by dog team. "I will cross the inland ice to Cape York. I shall cross Melville Bay to Upernavik. Once a year a blubber ship takes blubber from Upernavik. I can pay passage from there to Copenhagen."

And so the plan evolved. Bradley had his boat ice-sheathed with three inches of white oak, the bow and stern steel-plated. When the *John R. Bradley*, with Captain Moses Bartlett in command, pulled away from Gloucester, Massachusetts, on July 3, 1907, it was believed that Dr. Cook and Bradley were off to hunt bear and walrus in the polar region.

The trip north was leisurely. They stopped for hunting trips ashore and in Arctic waters. Bradley was impressed with Cook's qualities as a man. "Cook never complains, never swears, don't care whether his hair is long or short, don't care whether his shoes are tied or not, but just keeps plodding along." On August 27, Cook landed at Annoatok, some fifteen miles above Etah, Greenland, where he found conditions ideal for his winter base —a logical place for a take-off since he had no ship for winter headquarters farther north. Eskimos, in anticipation of Peary's return, had laid up large stores of meat and trained a great number of sledge dogs. Cook put ashore from the *Bradley* tons of pemmican, sugar, tea, coffee, canned goods, hickory wood for sledge building, hardware, iron, steel, copper, cooking utensils, 150 feet of stovepipe, 10,000 boxes of matches, various scientific instruments, a canvas boat to carry a sledge across open water, bales of biscuits, 120,000 cans of food, 150 gallons of alcohol, barrels of rice and flour; and for trading with the natives, guns, knives, beads, and trinkets.

When the *John R. Bradley* brought its owner back to the States, Cook and one white companion, Rudolph Francke of Hoboken, New Jersey, remained behind in the Arctic. Not until Bradley arrived in New York in late fall, 1907, with a letter from Cook to the Explorers' Club was the full extent of his plan known. "I find that I have a good opportunity to try for the Pole, and therefore, I will stay here for a year. I hope to get to the Explorers' Club in September 1908 with the record of the Pole. . . . Here's for the Pole with the flag."

Reaction among Peary's friends to Cook's announcement that he was in the Arctic poised for a dramatic dash to the Pole was one of indignation. Peary had made several attempts to reach the Pole; he was now readying for another—an expedition that had been widely publicized and had received official blessings. Perhaps Herbert L. Bridgman, secretary of the Peary Arctic Club, expressed the sentiments of the Peary group best of all. "The fitting out of the *Bradley* by stealth, while within the prescriptive rights of the owner, invited remark among men who respect honor and observe fair play. . . . That his [Peary's] men, methods, and reasoning should be appropriated and the long struggle finished before he had his fair and final opportunity is a transaction upon which the American people will render just judgment." In a statement prepared for the editor of the New York *Times*, Peary charged Cook with surreptitious preparation for his expedition and accused him of locating at Annoatok for the purpose of using Eskimos and dogs assembled there in expectation of his own arrival. This action, Peary wrote, was "one of which no man possessing a sense of honor would be guilty." Although Peary was confident Cook would fail, he was not at all happy with the thought of Cook in Annoatok.

Unaware of the storm he had created back in civilization, Cook wintered in the Arctic, hunting and trading with the Eskimos. Drawing upon the skill he had mastered as a boy in the Catskills, he built his tough, light hickory sledges. It was his plan, conceived after reading of the explorations of Sverdrup, to cross Ellesmere Land, a route that went through game country, and thus to live off the land until he got to land's end, for the dash across the ice of the polar sea.

On February 19, 1908, Cook left Annoatok with ten Eskimos,

eleven sledges, and 105 dogs. He instructed Francke to guard a valuable collection of blue fox furs ($10,000 worth, Cook said later), and to wait for his return until June 5, 1908. If he had not come back by then, Francke was to leave Cook's stores with a trusted Eskimo and go south with the furs and some ivory. After traveling more than 400 miles overland, Cook started out on the ice from the northern end of Axel Heiberg Island for the Pole. The last of his supporting party left him on March 21, and he went on north with two Eskimos, two sledges carrying 800 pounds apiece, and twenty-six dogs.

The *Roosevelt*, carrying Peary to the Arctic, cast off from a pier at 26th Street, East River, New York, with Captain Bob Bartlett, nephew of Moses Bartlett, in command, on July 6, 1908, a month after Cook had expected to be back in Annoatok from the Pole. An excited crowd watched. Dr. Cook was in the Arctic, and unreported. Could the indomitable Peary—a man past fifty who had already lost eight toes in polar exploration—reach the Pole? The next day at Oyster Bay on Long Island Bartlett dressed ship and Peary welcomed President Roosevelt aboard. Teddy's benediction was "Bully!" No explorer had ever left America with more flourish.

The *Roosevelt* reached Etah in August, and Peary, learning that there had been no word from Cook since March 21, when the last of his supporting party turned back, took over Cook's supplies, posting the following notice: "This house belongs to Dr. F. A. Cook, but Dr. Cook is long ago dead and there is no use to search for him. Therefore, I, Commander Robert E. Peary, install my boatswain in this deserted house." Francke, Cook's lone white companion in the Arctic, was ill with scurvy, and Peary consented to let him go back to the States on his auxiliary ship *Erik*, but only if Francke would give him the 200 blue Arctic fox skins and the narwhal tusks and walrus ivory belonging to Dr. Cook. Francke wrote: "I was compelled to accept the terms to save my life." (Later, John Bradley, who had left Francke in the Arctic with Cook, said Peary sent him a bill "for $100 for sending Francke home 'for humanity's sake.'" And Cook, after he had come out of his long silence in the Arctic, stated, "One narwhal tusk worth to me at least $1,000 was polished and sent as Peary's trophy to President Roosevelt.")

On September 5 the *Roosevelt*, edging slowly north in the Arctic ice, reached Cape Sheridan, anchored in shallow water, and was frozen in for the winter as Peary's headquarters.

Peary hunted with the Eskimos, prepared sledges, and studied plans. On February 22, 1909, he left the *Roosevelt* with seven white men, one Negro, fifty-nine Eskimos, 140 dogs, and twenty-three sledges carrying 500 pounds each for Cape Columbia where he took off over the ice for the Pole. Bob Bartlett, the last of Peary's supporting party, turned back on April 1, at 87° 47′ N., 130 geographical miles from the Pole. Peary and his best dog driver, the Negro Matthew A. Henson, and four Eskimos disappeared toward the North and the Pole.

Now the miles of windswept polar ice held the destiny of two ambitious men. One was believed dead; the other had just set out, determined to reach the Pole.

Then on April 18—seventeen days after Peary had taken leave of Bob Bartlett and struck out over the last 130 miles, Dr. Frederick Albert Cook and his two Eskimo companions—Etukishook and Ahwelah—were seen a few miles away struggling toward Annoatok. "Human beings could not be more unkempt," according to Harry Payne Whitney, who went out to greet them. "They were half-starved and very thin, terribly dirty, and Dr. Cook, like the Eskimos, had long hair reaching to his shoulders." (Whitney, a millionaire sportsman, had come north with the

Peary party and remained during the long winter to hunt with the Eskimos.) Cook told Whitney that he had reached the Pole, but pledged him to secrecy: he wanted to get back to civilization and make the announcement himself. If Peary returned, Cook authorized Whitney to tell him that "Dr. Cook said he had been beyond Peary's previous 'farthest north.'" Cook also pledged his two Eskimo companions not to reveal to anyone that they had been to the Pole. Whitney was convinced Cook had reached the Pole.

Cook said that it had taken him thirty-six days to cross the polar ice to the Pole. On March 30 at 85° N. he discovered land to the west, which he named Bradley Land, and which he described as 1000 feet high, extending for fifty miles from 84° 21′ N. to 85° 11′ N. He reached the Pole on April 21, recorded the event in his diary, and made observations. He was exuberant. The day before "when he had looked at his sun glass and seen that they were only one day's journey from the 'great nail'," Cook jumped and danced like a medicine man, according to his Eskimo companions.[1] When he reached the Pole, Cook said: "My spirits were high and I shouted like a boy. The Eskimos looked at one another, surprised at my gaiety."

Cook started back on April 23, but the weather turned bad. The ice began to jam and crack and drift. Two months later, exhausted and starved, he reached land, miles from the point of his planned return. He made slow progress, lived off the land, and in September reached Cape Sparbo on Jones Sound where he spent the long winter night in a cave. When conditions permitted, he resumed the slow march homeward, reaching his base at Annoatok on April 18, 1909. . . . Almost fourteen months to the day from the time he had left it.

On that day Peary, on his return from the Pole, was ap-

[1] Maurice Francis Egan's "The Witnesses for Dr. Cook," *The Rosary Magazine*, Vol. XXXV, No. 5, November, 1909.

proaching land at Cape Columbia. He had reached the Pole on April 6, worn, haggard, and in "a daze" after four days of sleeplessness. It had taken him thirty-seven days to cover the 413 miles from Cape Columbia to the Pole.

Cook remained only three days in Annoatok, then set out by dog team for the 700-mile journey to Upernavik to catch the blubber ship for Copenhagen. He had planned to take two Eskimos and two sledges, but one Eskimo fell sick. This necessitated cutting down the amount of luggage, and he left his instruments and original records of astronomical observations and some other property in Etah with Whitney to carry back to New York.

On April 23, sixteen days after he left the Pole, Peary reached Cape Columbia, rested two days, and arrived at the *Roosevelt* on April 27, in spite of the two days' rest, only two days after Bob Bartlett. He prepared to depart for New York as soon as the ship could be released from the ice. Nine days before reaching Etah on July 27, he was told by Eskimo hunters that Dr. Cook had returned from the Pole. Until this moment, he had believed Cook dead, and that he, Peary, had been the only man to reach the Pole. When Peary arrived in Etah, Whitney told him Cook was back and that Cook had told him to "tell Peary that Cook had gone beyond Peary's farthest north." Peary made no comment and Whitney said Peary asked him no more questions. Then Peary called in Cook's Eskimo companions— Etukishook and Ahwelah—for questioning by George Borup, an Eskimo-speaking member of Peary's party. "We pretended to know they had been far north and tried to make them admit they'd been ten or fifteen marches out to sea," Borup wrote later. The Eskimos told contradictory stories, refused to admit they had been very far from land ("four marches" at most) or that they had been at the Pole. The next day, Whitney said later, Cook's Eskimos came to him and asked "what Peary's men were trying to get them to say. Peary's men had shown them papers, but the Eskimos declared they did not understand these papers." It was on the testimony of the Eskimos whom Cook had pledged to secrecy that Peary would later base his "gold brick" charge.

When Peary left Etah, he refused to permit Whitney, who was returning on the *Roosevelt*, to bring Cook's records, scientific instruments, and other property aboard. "The Commander will not permit Mr. Whitney to bring any of Dr. Cook's effects aboard the *Roosevelt* and they have been left in a cache on shore," Matt Henson, Peary's driver observed.[2] Whitney, with the aid of Bob Bartlett, separated Dr. Cook's property, put it in boxes, and cached it in the rocks. The cache was never recovered, and Whitney observed on his return to the States: "It may be remarked that ten years ago Peary did with the explorer Sverdrup, who was cruising in Smith Sound, what he had done with Cook: he refused to bring back any of Sverdrup's letters and records."[3]

In August, as the *Roosevelt* moved across Baffin Bay, Cook boarded the *Hans Egede* for Copenhagen. He told Captain Schonbye that he had been at the North Pole with two Eskimos, and that he had pledged those Eskimos to secrecy. Peary on the *Roosevelt* and Cook on the *Hans Egede* were on their way to the first cable and wireless stations where they would make their historic announcements.

Cook reached Lerwick in the Shetland Islands on September 1, filed a brief story to the New York *Herald*, telegraphed the Brussels Observatory—"Reached North Pole April 21, 1908 . . ."—and his wife, vacationing in South Harpswell, Maine—"Successful and well." Cook did not know that Peary

---

[2] Matthew Henson, *A Negro Explorer at the North Pole*, page 178.

[3] "Whitney Believes Both Peary and Cook Reached the North Pole," *Boston Herald*, September 29, 1909.

had reached the Pole and was now on his way home on the *Roosevelt*.

The news thrilled and stunned the world. It seemed incredible, a newspaper writer said, that a man who "did not start for the Pole with a procession of brass bands" could have got there. But as Ernest Ingersoll, naturalist and explorer, observed, Cook "would have been more widely known had he not been so shy, modest, and seemingly unconscious of heroism." Peary had tried for the Pole six times and failed, and now Cook had beaten him, reaching the Pole in a spectacular unpublicized dash across the ice pack three months before New York gave Peary a rousing send-off on the *Roosevelt*. The fact that even now, on September 1, 1909, there was no news of Peary increased the tension.

When Dr. Cook arrived in Copenhagen on September 4, he was greeted by the Crown Prince of Denmark, entertained by the King, questioned by scholars and scientists, interviewed by 100 journalists who had rushed to the city from many countries to get the full story. There was general acclaim, but some were doubtful. They recalled that in the past there had been exploration hoaxes.

W. T. Stead, dean of the journalists present in Copenhagen, acted as chairman at the historic newspaper interview.

"Doctor, would you say you really think, so far as you are able to judge, that you have discovered the North Pole?"

"I think so."

"You have set your foot right on it?"

"Oh, I couldn't say that. I got to where there wasn't any longitude."

"What does the Pole look like?"

"Ice."

"You made a dash to the Pole?"

"It was simply that—a dash. We did not try to carry all the

heavy instruments that others carry. Therefore, there is nothing so scientific about the achievement. We traveled as lightly as possible, and made fifteen miles a day . . ."

"Impossible!" someone interjected.

"Danish miles, yes. English miles, no," Cook replied.

There were many more questions: "Do you consider yourself a competent man to take down records?" . . . "Doctor, are you a Christian?" But Cook handled himself well. E. Fountain Hussey, a reporter, was impressed: "It is afterward that the simplicity of his manner, his pleasant directness, the probability of what he says, come back to mind and make it harder to believe that he lies than that he tells the truth."

Professor Torp of the University of Copenhagen interviewed Cook and reported: "Dr. Cook stood the test perfectly, although the examination was of an intricate, scientific character. There was not a detail or question put before him to which he failed to reply in the most satisfactory way. As there were certain questions of a special astronomical nature with which I myself was not sufficiently acquainted I called in our great astronomical scientist, Professor Stramgren, who put an exhaustive series of mathematical, technical, and natural scientific questions to Dr. Cook, based particularly on those of his contentions on which some doubts had been cast. Dr. Cook answered all to our full satisfaction." [4]

Mr. Stead found Cook "a naïve, inexperienced child, who sorely needed someone to tell him what he ought to do in his own interest. It was pathetic to see his efforts to readjust himself to the busy, bustling new environment of modern civilization." Before it was known that the *New York Herald* had sent instructions to offer $20,000 for the rights to Cook's story plus an exclusive interview, Cook asked only $3,000. *Hampton's Magazine* offered a guaranteed and bonded $100,000 "for ex-

[4] *Current Literature*, October, 1909.

clusive rights for magazine and publicity service." Another newspaper publisher sent a blanket agreement to double what anyone else offered. A European syndicate declared itself ready to pay more than $500,000. Dr. Cook, for some unexplained reason, turned down the three largest offers and sold his story to the *Herald*. Stead declared: "It is enough to make one weep! But as he used to say plaintively, 'I am not out for money.' . . . He certainly is about the last man whom any business firm would send out for money. . . . Everything that a clever rogue would do instinctively if he wished to hoax the public Dr. Cook did not do."

On September 6, two days after Cook had reached Copenhagen, Peary on the *Roosevelt* reached Indian Harbor, Labrador. He had not yet heard of Cook's announcement. "I have the pole, April 6. . . . Arrange expedite transmission big story . . ." Peary telegraphed the *Times*. And to his wife: "Have made good at last. I have the old Pole." Mrs. Peary, by coincidence, received the message at South Harpswell, Maine, at the same telegraph station where Mrs. Cook had received the message from her husband.

In Copenhagen, journalist Philip Gibbs was standing beside Dr. Cook when he was handed the message: ". . . I am bound to pay a tribute to his cool nerve. He read the message on a bit of flimsy, handed it back, and said: 'If Peary says he reached the Pole, I believe him.' " Dr. Cook cabled the New York *Times* "Glad Peary did it. Two records are better than one." Another journalist heard him say: "I hope Peary did get to the Pole. His observations and reports on that region will confirm mine."

When Peary was handed a copy of Cook's announcement on September 8, he said, as quoted in the *Herald*: "I am the only white man who has ever reached the Pole." Then he telegraphed his charge: "Cook's story should not be taken too seriously. The Eskimos who accompanied him say that he went no distance North. He did not get out of sight of land. . . . Cook has simply handed the public a gold brick . . ." Peary contended that Cook had hidden out until enough time had elapsed to make his claim to the Pole plausible.

Peary supporters shouted: "Cook is a fraud. . . . He must offer proof that he reached the Pole. . . ." But there was little, if any, inclination to question Peary. His expedition had been publicized as no other had; it had been blessed and encouraged by high government officials and businessmen. Peary was the sentimental favorite in the race, and his announcement that he had reached the Pole "immeasurably gratified the world."

Offer proof? Cook would do it just as soon as he had in his hands the records he had left in Etah with Whitney. But then he learned that Peary had ordered Whitney to leave the records and instruments on the shore at Etah. When Peary was criticized for this action, his friends said that he was within his rights; that Dr. Cook was a fool to have separated himself from his instruments and observations; that he should have taken them with him on his 700-mile journey down the Greenland coast.

It was charged that Cook had manufactured the story of pledging his two Eskimos to secrecy as an afterthought. But he had witnesses. Captain Schonbye, of the *Hans Egede*, reported a conversation with Cook aboard ship in August: "He told me that he had definitely told the two Eskimos and Panikpah [the father of one of his companions] to tell nothing whatever about the journey." However, the Eskimos must have told their fellow tribesmen, for members of the Stolberg-de Quervain Expedition said that they had heard from Eskimo sources in the Arctic weeks before Cook's public announcement, that "one Dr. Cook" had discovered the Pole. Knud Rasmussen found that many natives knew the story of the two Eskimos who had been at "the Great Nail."

Rasmussen reported: "I have not met the companions of Dr.

Cook, but I am informed by trustworthy members of the same tribe, that the expedition had, on the whole way out, comparatively very favorable ice and good weather. The ice got better and better the farther out they went. How far they have been, they have, of course, not been able to decide; but they have said that their journey across the ice fields away from land was so long, that the sun appeared, reached a high point in the sky, and at last did not set at all, and it was almost summer before they reached land again.

"Further, they have said that it was autumn before they decided to camp for the winter, before they would try to return to Annoatok. The Eskimos, being very experienced in finding their whereabouts by means of maps, have themselves shown me on my own map the route of the expedition toward the North Pole, and the winter camp at Jones Sound, which district is not quite unknown to them, owing to their dangerous bear hunts in that region. . . . The Eskimos stated decisively that they were very much astonished when Cook told them that they had now reached their goal, [North Pole] because the place was not at all different from the other ice over which they had traveled. For several days they had asked Cook to return, but this was because they had an impression that they were so far from land that they could never get back to their home. So it is sure that the travelers were not compelled to turn back because of ice hindrances, but only because they believed the goal was reached. . . .

"It was the Eskimos' opinion that Cook had been at the Pole, and that he, according to the statement of his companions, during the whole journey had shown unusual strength and energy. The Eskimos expressed great joy that the Pole had at last been reached, as the many expeditions have used up the best men among them. At the same time, they spoke with real pride of their two countrymen; they were perfectly sure that Cook never would have reached the Pole if he had not had the benefit of their skill as dog-drivers and hunters. . . ." [5]

Etukishook and Ahwelah told their fellow Eskimos stories that contradicted what they told Peary, Donald B. MacMillan, and other members of Peary's expedition in 1909, and MacMillan again in 1918.

Since the stories told by the Eskimos to Peary, MacMillan, and others was the principal evidence upon which the "gold brick" charge was based, it is important to know that the Eskimos gave different accounts to MacMillan in 1909 and in 1918. MacMillan was present with Peary and Bob Bartlett when Borup, Peary's Eskimo-speaking aide, questioned them in Etah in July, 1909. The following table points up the contradictions:

Dr. Cook's Eskimo boys are reported by

Peary, Bartlett, MacMillan, Henson, and Borup to have said in 1909:	MacMillan to have said in 1918:
They went two marches out on the polar ice. (Four marches, as deduced from later statements by Peary.)	They went one march out on the polar ice.
They proceeded beyond this point.	They did not proceed beyond this point.
They spent one night at the first camp.	They spent two nights at the first camp.
They marched north to about ninety miles from Axel Heiberg Island.	They returned south, having been at most about twelve miles from Axel Heiberg Island.

[5] Rasmussen's statement appeared in *Politiken*, Copenhagen, October 20, 1909, and was translated from the Danish for *Rosary Magazine*. The statement is dated September 25, 1909.

They returned to Axel Heiberg Island west of where they left their cache.	They returned directly to their cache on Axel Heiberg Island.
They remained there four or five sleeps.	They did not stop to sleep there.
They took nothing from the cache.	They took everything from the cache.
They went south to about (as they pointed out on a map) 80° 30'.	They went south to about 79°.
They went out about forty miles from Axel Heiberg shore.	They followed the west shore of Axel Heiberg about five miles from shore.

Dr. Cook returned to New York in late September, 1909, and was triumphantly received in Brooklyn. He started a lecture tour, but the demand for "proof" became so pressing that he gave it up, announcing on October 18 that he would devote himself to preparation of statements and records which he would submit to the University of Copenhagen. He secluded himself in Bronxville, and on November 8, 1909, according to Walter Lonsdale, Cook's secretary,[6] Cook was told of a conversation overheard in Washington between "two well-dressed men."

"Soon you will hear of his coming out in the papers saying he has been robbed of his North Pole data. . . . Even if he does get his data on board ship, it will never reach Copenhagen, for the man who carries it will be doped, or the express company that ships it will have no safe that cannot be cracked. . . . Ah, the old man has planned it all right."

Previously, Lonsdale reported, Cook had received from an "Anonymous Samaritan" a copy of a telegram Peary was alleged to have sent the editor of the *Times* "requesting the edi-

[6] *Travel Magazine*, May-June, 1910.

tor to meet him and assist in issuing damaging reports against Dr. Cook." Also, Lonsdale said, "Cook was followed by spies in Bronxville."

Then, on November 24, Lonsdale reported he and Cook left Bronxville, "and realizing we had shaken off shadowers, Cook said: 'Lonsdale, here is a chance of getting away unnoticed, and I'm going to take it.'" They went by circuitous route to Pennsylvania Station, and Cook said goodbye: "Now I will be able to get some sleep. I will . . . write Wake [H. Wellington Wake, his lawyer] under the name of Fred Harper telling him my plans."

Before his sudden change of mind, Cook had planned to sail for Europe on the *Cedric* with Mrs. Cook, taking one copy of the data he had assembled and sending another copy with Lonsdale on another ship. Lonsdale sailed for Copenhagen on November 25 with his copy of the data, and a few days later Mrs. Cook received a letter posted in Toronto from her husband. She was to meet him in Europe: "If the hounds are still pursuing you, put my original records in a safe deposit box and leave the key with Wake; if they are not following you, bring the records with you." Mrs. Cook sailed on December 4, taking the original data.

On December 9, after it was learned that Cook had left for Europe, the New York *Times* published an affidavit, dated November 7, and signed by George H. Dunkle and a Captain Loose, stating that they had manufactured the records. The two men had come to Cook and offered to work out the astronomical data backwards, starting from Cook's conclusions. Cook said he soon learned that the men were trying to make him look like an ignorant person incapable of taking observations as well as trying to trap him into presenting falsified records, and, as a result, he dismissed them. *The Independent* [7] said that this "last

[7] December 30, 1909.

and most skillfully arranged plan for his exposure was a most ludicrous failure, for the series of observations manufactured by Captain Loose and brought forward in New York after Dr. Cook's report had been deposited in the safe at Copenhagen, were not included in the evidence submitted to the committee."

The University committee stated that Cook's records did not contain "any original information which can be regarded as proof" that he reached the Pole. Dr. Cook was not surprised; his original records had been left on the shore at Etah by Peary. The verdict, he observed, which was a "neutral" one "which carried no implication of the non-attainment of the Pole, but which was interpreted as a rejection, helped to stamp me in the minds of many people as the most monumental imposter the world has ever seen."

Monumental imposter? What was it based on? "Who's the Liar?" asked Casper Whitney in *Collier's*: "No language can be strong enough to condemn these efforts to prejudice the public's mind and to blacken the character of Dr. Cook. . . . While Peary's experience and standing contribute to make his word suffice, Cook has earned no such position, and must prove his claims." [8]

George Kennan, who had spent two years in Siberia under conditions similar to those in the Arctic, published in *The Outlook* [9] a series of statistics designed to prove that it was impossible for Cook to have remained alive on the polar ice for eighty-two days with only the food carried on two sledges: he would have had to have 5,000 pounds of dog food. But then, Kennan wrote, "Dr. Cook might have started with only half this quantity and might have lessened his consumption by gradually killing his dogs." Which is nearer to what Dr. Cook did.

[8] *Collier's*, October 16, 1909.
[9] October 2, 1909.

The Independent,[10] in an article by E. Fountain Hussey, who had interviewed Cook at Copenhagen, attacked Kennan's tabulations and showed that with Cook's specially designed sledges, it was possible to carry enough food to have survived the long stay on the ice. Now *The Outlook* urged its readers to reserve judgment. *The Living Age* [11] found Dr. Cook "too rhetorical," whereas Peary's "have the old Pole . . . have nailed the Stars and Stripes to the North Pole" was "excusable and even likeable." It was hard, the magazine continued, to accept the assertion by Dr. Cook that he made the journey from Etah to the Pole in two months, "though it is fair to say that on the final dash Peary went faster." The same magazine quoted *Punch* on the *Herald's* use of Dr. Cook's story of his conquest of the Pole:

> In rival type it almost looked
> As if the whole account was Cooked!

and

> If it is true that you achieved
>   The dash across those dismal floes
> In isolation unrelieved
>   Except by stuffy Eskimos,
> Let me, although a mere land-lubber,
>   Anoint your head with oil of blubber.

Now Cook's past was examined for evidence. It was asked: "If he lied about the Pole—why not about McKinley?" From Edward M. Barrill, Cook's companion on the ascent, an affidavit was procured stating that he and Cook falsified their claim of having reached the top of McKinley. It was big news. However, an investigation by Roscoe C. Mitchell, a former New York *Herald* reporter, revealed that Barrill had said he had

[10] November 11, 1909.
[11] October, 1909.

been offered $5,000 to deny Cook's story of reaching the top of McKinley. Mitchell reported that the editor of the Seattle *Times* "told me he would have been willing to pay $5,000 to $10,000 for Barrill's statement. . . ." Mitchell was also told that a Tacoma bank passed $1,500 in bills to Barrill. Barrill's affidavit, warned *The Nation*,[12] "is not conclusive evidence of the falsity of the Doctor's story; for, certainly, a man who signs a sworn statement that he had been a voluntary participant in the concoction of an elaborate and swindling falsehood cannot be accepted as an unimpeachable witness when he swears that he had lied."

Cook stood on the record of the observations he had made in *To the Top of the Continent*, declaring that in time the account of his observations would prove his claim to McKinley. Since then several men who have mastered McKinley have corroborated some of the details Cook described. There are two main peaks as Cook had said, the one to the south the higher. He reported that he ascended a knife-edged arète, a northeast ridge, and that the final stages were easy. All the explorers who have ascended the mountain have described and used a knife-edged arète, a northeast ridge, with some slopes of 60 degrees, above which they found vast ice fields between rocky ridges leading up to the summit, with easy slopes above the snow fields that do not require any particular mountaineering skill, except knowing how to breathe at such altitudes. In 1910 two miners, Peter Anderson and William Taylor, like Cook, found the final ascent easy; from a camp 4,500 feet below the summit, they scaled North Peak carrying a fourteen-foot flagpole which they planted in bare rocks on the summit, and returned to camp all in one day. They were called liars until their flagpole was seen on the summit three years later.

Belmore Browne in 1912, and again in *The Conquest of Mount*

12 October 21, 1909.

McKinley, 1913, published a photograph of a "Fake Peak" (not the summit of McKinley, but a peak 8,000 feet high and twenty miles away) which he submitted as the peak which Dr. Cook had photographed and published in *To the Top of the Continent* as the McKinley summit with Barrill holding a flag. Some think that Browne's "Fake Peak" and Cook's "Summit" are identical. Ernest C. Rost in 1914 declared that there were six points in which the photographs differ, and so also, later the same year, did Edwin Swift Balch in *Mount McKinley and Mountain Climbers' Proofs*.

The attack on Cook's character reached its height in 1911 when Congress was holding hearings on a proposal to recognize Peary as the discoverer of the North Pole, and when Herbert L. Bridgman said that friends had subscribed $350,000 "to see Peary through."

Dr. Cook returned again to America on October 29, 1910, and secluded himself at the Palatine Hotel in Newburgh, New York, to write the story of his conquest of the Pole for *Hampton's Magazine* for $4,000.

The first installment of "Dr. Cook's Own Story" appeared in January, 1911, as Peary was attempting to convince a Congressional committee that he had discovered the Pole. It was billed on the cover as "Dr. Cook's Confession." After Cook had OK'd the proofs and signed each galley, and had departed to rejoin his family in Europe, the magazine "made insertions and eliminations, which distorted Dr. Cook's story in a vile manner," Miss Lilian Eleanor Kiel, editorial stenographer for *Hampton's*, testified before Congressmen. "We cut through the galley proofs and inserted what has been known to the world as Dr. Cook's confession of 'mental unbalancement.' The 'confession' was dictated to me by a subeditor. . . . Dr. Cook was on the ocean to Europe to get his wife and children. I then thoroughly believed that the 'confession' was authorized by Dr. Cook, and

I was horrified later to find that he knew absolutely nothing about it."

I have been unable to find any record of what actually were the spurious insertions into Dr. Cook's original account, but there are various sentences in what *Hampton's* published which make his story appear as an admission of mental instability. There were statements like the following:

"After mature thought, I confess that I do not know absolutely whether I reached the Pole or not. This may come as an amazing statement; but I am willing to startle the world, if, by so doing, I can get an opportunity to present my case. By my case I mean not my case as a geographical discovery, but my case as a man. Much as the attainment of the North Pole once meant to me, the sympathy and confidence of my fellow-men mean more."

"I shall try to open the most secret chambers of my mind, and show my mental processes during the past several years, how my ambitions, my discouragements, my thoughts, my illusions, played their part in this drama of my mental life; and prove how inevitable, psychologically, as I see it now, was my triumph and my tragedy."

"Whatever the results may be, whether I shall be believed or not, my whole aim in coming back is to prove, if possible, that I did not premeditate a lie for money, and that willingly or consciously I did not do anything to disgrace America. I have come back with the intention of telling the truth as far as is humanly possible for anyone. I shall bare my soul to friends and foes. With all the fervor of yearning in me, I want to be able to live again among my own people, to be able to walk on the streets of my city, and to find Americans willing to shake my hand, and to have them say, 'Cook may have unconsciously lied, and may have deceived himself, but he did not deliberately try to deceive others.' I have not come back for money. My chief reason for giving my story to the world through *Hampton's Magazine* was to insure its being read in its full content."

"For the position of suspicion and disgrace in which I find myself, I blame no one excepting myself. I want it to be understood now that I do not intend to enter into any controversy with Commander Peary, and that my feeling is that Commander Peary deserves the honor of a notable achievement, which was the result of sacrificing life work. I have never questioned Commander Peary's claim to the discovery of the North Pole. I do not now. I did not consciously try to filch an honor which belongs alone to Commander Peary."

"It was a thing," Miss Kiel said, "if he had not been a strong character, which might have turned his brain; but he was heartbroken, and he refused to look at the magazine."

"Imagine my amazed indignation . . ." Dr. Cook wrote. "Imagine my heart-aching dismay when I found the magazine which was running the articles in which I hoped to explain myself, had blazoned the sensation-provoking lie on its cover—'Dr. Cook's Confession.' I had made no confession."

The press shrieked: "Dr. Cook Admits Fake!" "Dr. Cook Makes Plea of Insanity!"

The victim wrote: "I felt impotent, crushed. In my very effort to explain myself I was being irretrievably lost. I was being made a catspaw for magazine and newspaper sensation. . . . But misrepresentations do not make history."

In a calmer frame of mind, Cook wrote in *My Attainment of the Pole*: "History demonstrates that the book which gives the final authoritative narrative is the test of an explorer's claims. . . . Men who have sought the truth of the claims of discoverers have sought, not abstract figures, but the continuity of the narrative in the pages of the traveler's final book. . . . Figures must inevitably be inadequate and any convincing proof that can exist is to be found only in the narrative account of such a quest."

As Dr. Cook rested his case with the verdict of time, Peary was unable to persuade Congress, even with the backing of the President, the Secretary of the Navy, and the National Geographic Society, that he had discovered the North Pole. In the end, the words "discovery" and "discoverer" were stricken from the bill which had been introduced at the request of the Geographic Society.[13]

It was impossible for Peary to prove that he had been at the Pole. Expert computers from the Coast and Geodetic Survey, employed by Peary, made computations of his work, and came to the conclusion that Peary's march on April 7, 1909, may have carried him to within a stone's throw of the Pole. For proof that Peary reached the Pole, Donald B. MacMillan, a member of the expedition, said: "I know that Admiral Peary reached the Pole. . . . The character of the explorer . . . is always the best evidence of his claim. . . . We have his word."

Testifying before the Congressional Committee in January, 1911, the month the first installment of "Dr. Cook's Confession" appeared in *Hampton's*—and after he had procured a ten-month postponement of the hearing—Peary offered Congress only his word. He said that the only inspection of his instruments ever made by the Geographic Society had taken place "after dark" in the baggage room of the railroad station where he had his trunk.[14] The inspection was brief and perfunctory. Was there any check on the accuracy of the instruments? he was asked. "That I could not say. I should imagine that it would not be possible to make tests there." He had taken "no observations for

[13] *Congressional Record*, March, 1911, page 4223.
[14] The record of the hearings appears in *Congressional Record*, 64th Congress, 1st Section, Vol. 53, No. 44, pages 2793-2852.

longitude at any time on the trip" and had made no observations for compass variation.

Peary was asked why he had taken only his sledge driver Henson on the final dash to the Pole. Wouldn't another member of the expedition have been a more informed corroborating witness? Peary answered: "The Pole was something to which I had devoted my life, a thing on which I had concentrated everything, and in which I had put money, time, and everything else, and I did not feel that under those circumstances I was called upon to divide with a man who, no matter how able and deserving he might be, was a young man and had only put a few years in that kind of work, and who had, frankly, as I believed, not the right that I had to it."

Peary was recognized as a great Arctic explorer. He received medals at home and abroad—in most cases not for discovery of the Pole, but "for Arctic services" and "for Arctic explorations." Dr. Cook, too, had his supporters. The Chautauqua Managers' Association, carefully investigating Dr. Cook's claims before it engaged him as one of its lecturers, concluded that "the North Pole has been honestly reached by Dr. Cook 350 days before anyone else." Rear Admiral W. S. Schley wrote on January 7, 1911:

> Dear Dr. Cook:
> I have never varied in the belief that you and Civil Engineer Peary reached the Pole. After reading the published accounts daily and critically, of both claimants, I was forced to the conclusion from their striking similarity that each of you was the eye witness of the other's success.
>
> Without collusion it would have been impossible to have written accounts so similar, and yet in view of the ungracious controversy that occurred since, that view (collusion) would be impossible to imagine.

While I have never believed that either of you got to within a pinpoint of the Pole, I have steadfastly held that both got as near the goal as was possible to ascertain considering the imperfections of the instruments used, and the personal errors of individuals under circumstances so adverse to absolute accuracy.

Again, I have been broad enough in my views to believe that there was room enough at the Pole for two; and never narrow enough to believe that only one man got there.

I believe that both are entitled to the honor of the achievement.

Very truly yours,
W. S. Schley.

After the dramatic year of 1911, the fury of the controversy abated. Although Peary got credit for discovery of the Pole on maps, in encyclopedias and in dictionaries, writers, scientists, and explorers continued to examine the evidence in an effort to find out: Did Cook discover the Pole? Did Peary reach the Pole? The evidence for the claims of both parties is still inconclusive.

Between 1911 and the publication now of *Return from the Pole* some important facts have been developed; the most important, so far as Peary's claim is concerned, are errors in his books, proven inaccuracies in his "discoveries," and almost incredible speeds and distances on his return from the Pole.

In Peary's book, *The North Pole*, published in 1910, there are contradictions: the distance from Cape Columbia to Cape Sheridan is ninety miles on page 193 and seventy-three miles on page 326. Peary gives three different dates for his crossing of the 84th parallel northbound—March 18 (page 7), March 11 (page 232), and March 14 (page 235).

By 1916, the U. S. Navy Hydrographic Office had removed

five of Peary's reported "discoveries" from government charts: "Peary Channel," which Peary described as a waterway running across Greenland from east to west, and which Rasmussen showed did not exist; "East Greenland Sea," which the Danes proved was high land; "Crocker Land," "Jesup Land," and the soundings which Peary claimed to have made in 1909. It was Cook who first questioned the existence of Crocker Land. In his dramatic dash to the Pole, he reported, he had found no land where Peary charted Crocker Land. Forty-two years later, in 1950, A. G. Anderson, head of the U. S. Navy Hydrographic Office, stated: "Crocker Land, which Peary thought he observed . . . is now generally believed not to exist."

Major General A. W. Greely, an Arctic explorer,[15] became a "reluctant" Peary doubter: "When Peary returned, I believed he had attained the Pole and as an American rejoiced. However, after reading his various and rather conflicting accounts I reluctantly came to believe that he had failed. . . . Geographic and Arctic experts . . . told me that they concluded that he had failed. These adverse judgments were somewhat based on Peary's incorrect reports in former expeditions. . . . Peary's photograph of the North Pole ice, which you reproduce, is strong evidence as to the impossibility of making over that ice the unparalleled distances stated by Peary."

Captain Bob Bartlett had left Peary 130 geographic miles, or 150 statute miles from the Pole. Bartlett's ability to make correct astronomical observation of position was beyond question. Peary, then, had 150 statute miles to go over an unbroken trail to the Pole; this required at least 160 miles of travel, since roughly 10 per cent must be added for detours around and over pressure ridges and deviations in directions. From what he conceived to be the Pole, he made two excursions at right angles to each other, one to a point ten miles away, and the other eight

15 *The Independent*, October 17, 1925.

miles away, so that he covered thirty-six extra miles at the Pole.
On his return from the Pole, which he left at 4 P.M. on April 7,
Peary said he reached Bartlett's camp on the evening of April
9. Thus he covered 150 statute miles (plus extra distance for detours) in fifty-six hours, with time out for rest and sleep. He
either traveled seventy-five statute miles a day for two days or
he never came near the Pole. William E. Shea pointed out that
from Peary's own written record he must have traveled seventy-
one geographical miles on April 8. "Is it plausible?" Shea
asked.[16] The 150 statute miles to the Pole from Bartlett's camp,
plus the 36 miles at the Pole, and the return 150 statute miles,
with a modest 10 per cent added for detours, made 370 statute
miles in eight days—April 2 to April 9—at an average of forty-
six miles a day. Shea insisted 30 per cent should be added for
detours and estimated a minimum of fifty-seven statute miles a
day. "This Peary claimed to have done over a course that both
he and Ellsworth [a later Polar explorer] described as infernal." [17]

Fridtjof Nansen, an expert on the Arctic, estimated his own
best day's march on level ice fields at twenty-five miles a day.
Even at this speed "the dogs . . . are beginning to get tired."
Such testimony, experts observed, not only denied the argument
of Peary supporters that Cook could not have reached the Pole
in his recorded time schedule, but cast grave doubts on Peary's
claim to have reached the Pole.

Regarding speeds and distances, Peary testified before the
House Committee:

MR. ENGLEBRIGHT: What was your best day's travel in your
Arctic trip, either going or coming?

CAPTAIN PEARY: The best day's travel was on the second
march on the return from the Pole.

16 *The Independent*, June 12, 1926.
17 *The Independent*, August 22, 1925.

MR. ENGLEBRIGHT: How far did you go?

CAPTAIN PEARY: Fifty geographical miles, estimated.

Matthew Henson, the Negro sledge driver, did not agree with Peary. On arrival in Labrador in September, 1909, Peary had said: "You must understand that there is no riding in sledges when you go to hunting the Pole. If the man with the sledge is able to walk beside it, without any further work than the driving of the dogs, he considers himself lucky. The man with the sledge must bend over handles, guiding it away from the rough places, lifting it by main strength over them sometimes, reducing the strain on the dogs or sledge wherever possible. . . . The nearest thing that I can think of to sledge driving is breaking up virgin soil behind a plow drawn by horses and oxen." [18]

But a year later Henson described Peary's condition during the final dash to the Pole. He was sleepless during the four days from April 2 to 6. "We marched and marched, falling down in our tracks repeatedly, until it was impossible to go on. Peary was in a continual daze." On the return Henson said: "One of the sleds was fur-lined and Peary rode on it during the entire journey. After two marches back on the return journey he was practically a dead weight."

Dr. Cook, traveling light, estimated his speed on his best day at twenty-nine miles.

On the basis of an examination of all the evidence, including the intimate, detailed account of Arctic conditions in *Return from the Pole*, I believe Dr. Cook reached the Pole. Why?

1. Dr. Cook said he knew he had reached the Pole when the shadows of one of his Eskimos on the level ice were of equal length at each hour for twenty-four hours. One of the photographs he made near the Pole corroborates his statement: the shadows of an Eskimo seated on a sledge show that the sun was

[18] *The Independent*, June 12, 1926.

at an angle of 12°, the altitude of the sun near the Pole when he said he was near there.[19]

2. Dr. Cook said he did not find land at the position Peary charted Crocker Land; later exploration by Donald B. Mac-Millan revealed that Crocker Land did not exist. This is evidence that Cook went north over the polar ice for at least 100 miles beyond where Peary quoted the Eskimos as saying he turned back.

3. Beyond the 86th parallel, Cook reported extensive ice fields with few crevasses and little or no crushed ice thrown up as barriers. Cook is thus a witness for Peary, who on his return said this very condition made possible his extraordinary speed in his final dash to and from the Pole.

4. At the Pole, Cook reported no land, only drifting ice. Before this there had been three theories: ice, land, and open sea. Thus Cook's was the first published record of what does exist at the Pole—drifting ice.

5. Cook, returning from the Pole, said he had been carried by the drift of the ice to the west of the northern end of Axel Heiberg Island and saw Ellef Ringnes and Amund Ringnes Islands to the south and what he thought was Axel Heiberg Island to the east. Vilhjalmur Stefansson in 1916, at the latitude and longitude given by Cook, saw the previously unknown Meighen Island in the direction Cook reported sighting land to the east.

It seems probable that what Cook actually saw was Meighen Island. In *My Attainment of the Pole*, giving his position at latitude 79° 32′ north and longitude 101° 22′ west, "in Crown Prince Gustav Sea," Cook wrote: "To the east were the low mountains and high valleys of Axel Heiberg Land, and between us and the land lay fifty miles of small crushed ice and impassable lines of open water. . . . The land to the south was nearer. Due

---

[19] "Mending Near the Pole" in *My Attainment of the Pole*, facing page 282.

south there was a wide gap which we took to be Hassel Sound." In *Return from the Pole* he says: "Land appeared far to the east and far to the south. . . . When the observations were placed on the map, I guessed the land to the east to be Heiberg Island, the land to the south, Ringnes Land. This, after further investigation, proved to be true." The words "proved to be true" can refer only to the two Ringnes islands, the land to the south, in which direction Dr. Cook was drifting. It cannot refer to the land to the east which he was unable to approach. After he had learned from Dr. Stefansson's explorations of the existence of Meighen Island, he maintained that nothing he had ever said could be construed as a denial that he had seen Meighen Island. He became convinced that the land he had seen to the east was actually, the as-yet-undiscovered Meighen Island.

Dr. Cook wrote that he was drifting to the east, and wishing to return to Axel Heiberg Island where his caches of food lay, he compensated for what he believed to be an eastward drift by traveling slightly to the west of south. Actually, as he subsequently discovered, he had been drifting to the west, and so, with error of assumption plus actual drift, he widely missed his goal. Peary in 1909 was fortunate in that he advanced northward and returned where the ice of the polar sea was held near the shores of Grant Land (northern end of Ellesmere) with a minimum of lateral drift. Dr. Cook, farther west, was unfortunate in being caught in a drift to the west. The fact that his account of his return from the Pole told of this hitherto unknown westward drift, with consequent delay of a year at terrible risk in reaching civilization, is perhaps the strongest argument for Cook.

6. Some years later, Donald MacMillan, a member of the Peary expedition, found two of Cook's depots, one of them 400 miles from his base, thus indicating that Cook had traveled at least halfway from Annoatok to the Pole.

One of the best arguments for Cook's attainment of the Pole was made by Thomas F. Hall [20] in 1917: "To accept Peary's version one must first be convinced that Cook decided to abandon all his caches of provisions that he had provided along his return route, and with an apparently aimless purpose, wandered a year in a previously explored country to inevitable destitution, possibly for all he could have known, to starvation and ignominious death; that he voluntarily marched 500 miles away from his caches of supplies to crawl into an underground den at Cape Sparbo. Can a sensible intelligence accept this version? Would such a proceeding on Cook's part result from anything short of downright hopeless imbecility? . . . If we do not accept this version, then there is not left existing a scintilla of outside evidence tending even to show that Cook's version is not true."

Why had Cook disappeared for fourteen months? Had he returned in June, 1908, as he planned, he would have been absent, Hall contended, "a long enough time for plausibility. Why instead make an insane excursion around by Sparbo?"

It is possible that someday Cook's claim to the Pole will have further supporting evidence. He said he discovered "Bradley Land" at 85° 16′ N. and recorded the event in his diary: "We noted many curious land mirage[s] of clif[f]s and mountains invested of glacial walls and pinnacles, but signs of land of this kind had been seen so often without noting other positive evidences of land on closer approach that I did not at this time credit our eyes. At noon however we saw actual land to the west. It was an ice-sheeted country about 1000 feet high and about 60 miles away. What we saw of its coast ran almost in a straight line from N. to S. for 30 miles and at both ends the coast line fell off quickly and was lost in steel-colored haze which soon obscured the entire outline."

[20] *Has the North Pole Been Discovered?*, pages 344-5.

Verification of the existence of "Bradley Land" would be conclusive evidence that Cook traveled far north on the polar ice. Sir Hubert Wilkins, in his flight to the Pole, was unable to locate "Bradley Land." But in one of his later flights at a longitude less than a dozen miles to the west of the eastern edge of Bradley Land as located by Cook, Wilkins reported that at "about the latitude 85°" a cloud forced his pilot to descend from a 7000-foot altitude.[21] "Because we seemed to be getting quite near to the ground long before our altimeter indicated that we were near ground level, I decided to go on down close to the surface in order to check the instrument. We were still, I believe, about 500 feet above the ice when our altimeter registered about 1500 feet above sea level. It was lucky for us that we could observe the surface, for if we had needed to be guided by the instruments alone—what with the compass swinging and the altimeter more than 1000 feet in error—we might well have flown right into the ice."

Could it have been that instead of his altimeter being "in error," his plane was close to the surface of "Bradley Land"?

I vividly recall my reactions to the Cook-Peary controversy: my initial acceptance of Dr. Cook's announcement of his success, with pride that an American had been the first to reach the Pole; the excitement of the drama that began with Peary's "gold brick" charge; the shock of the cumulative charges of fraud made against Dr. Cook; my growing doubt that he had reached the Pole, because of my assumption that a man against whom there were so many accusations was probably dishonest. Then through the years there came a reaction, the feeling that something about the story as it had come to me was not right; but I had no moving desire to study the facts until I read *Return from the Pole* and realized that the experiences Cook recorded

21 *Thoughts Through Space*, pages 128-9.

were in some ways unparalleled in Arctic annals. Only a man
of extraordinary power of observation could have described so
vividly the animal, marine, and vegetable life—the Arctic dawn,
the waking of the ravens and rats and foxes, and the first impact
of light. I then re-examined in great detail all the records I could
locate and I found Cook's claim had strong supporting evidence.

But what about Cook's later life—his spending five years in
prison for fraud? After 1910, Cook traveled, lectured, and
wrote, made an anthropological expedition to Borneo, served as
a geologist in Wyoming, and then became an oil promoter in
Fort Worth, Texas. There, in 1923, he was sentenced to fourteen years and nine months in a federal penitentiary and fined
$12,000. He had been convicted of using the mails to promote
"worthless" stock in the Petroleum Producers' Association, of
which he was president. Others convicted with him received
sentences of up to five years. Cook had written the promotion
literature and follow-up letters. The case received wide publicity. After "a quarter of a century" of ignoring activities of
oil-stock swindlers, *The Literary Digest* said, the federal government decided to prosecute, and singled out the company
headed by the conspicuous Dr. Frederick Albert Cook, who
some people thought of as Munchausen, Cagliostro, Titus Oakes,
and Ananias all rolled into one. Dr. Cook insisted that he was
innocent, and had sold the stock in good faith. Some weeks before the indictment, after watching a gusher burn, Cook wrote
in *World's Work*, apparently with a clear conscience, "I was
wondering if all this roaring fire wasn't sent as a kind of warning to the fake promoters—the meanest men in the world. . . .
I don't believe that the man who would willingly defraud the
public and take from investors . . . the money which they
have so carefully saved, without giving them a fair return, deserves much better an end than might be typified by this flaming
gas well."

In sentencing Cook in November, 1923, Federal Judge John M. Killits delivered a "blistering rebuke" which reminded *The National Oil Journal* "of a cheap brawl in which the victor, after having knocked his opponent successfully to the ground, stamps the prostrate form." His appeal denied, Dr. Cook went to Leavenworth in April 1925, with no time allowance for months spent in jail. He was an exemplary prisoner, assisted in the hospital, organized a night school, and edited *New Era*, the Leavenworth Penitentiary paper. He struck a note of hope, urged convicts to learn useful trades. He was paroled in March, 1930.

The oil lands of Dr. Cook's company, declared almost value-less by the government, were bought by an oil company at the U. S. Marshal's sale, and one parcel, purchased for $10,000, brought in millions while Dr. Cook was still in Leavenworth. "I was tried and convicted for overstating potential values in prospective oil fields," Cook wrote to *Time* magazine in 1936. "It is also a fact that the potential oil lands which I had acquired were not fully tested and were stamped as practically worthless by the prosecution. It is a fact, and this has not been reported by those who have tried to defame me, that some of the lands under question have since produced wealth of millions, far beyond the wildest assertions which I made in literature and letters of the company.

"The court record of my trial gives the following evidence. The following facts were admitted by the Federal Bank Examiner:

'(1) Dr. Cook was the largest cash investor in the company and held no promotion stock.

'(2) Dr. Cook had drawn no salary or commissions or profits of any kind.

'(3) The books of the company balanced with no indication of embezzlement or missing funds.'

"I have never in my life taken a penny that did not belong to me, and I am convinced today, as I was in 1923, that my judgment in regard to every phase of my oil development was sound."

Between 1930 and 1935, Dr. Cook wrote *Return from the Pole* and declared: "Before I die I must clear my good name." He suffered a cerebral hemorrhage on May 3, 1940. Two weeks later President Franklin D. Roosevelt pardoned him, restoring his civil rights. He died on August 5, 1940, in New Rochelle, New York. Peary had been dead twenty years.

Dr. Cook was a brave man with strength of spirit. Early in the Cook-Peary controversy, the *Review of Reviews* commented: "So many and so great are the incidental discomforts of fame that only bold men of good digestion and strong nerve should even try to make their way along the thorny path of ambition toward the goal of pre-eminence and popular note."

Friends, who believed in him and knew what he endured, thought his was the saddest case of its kind in history. His tragedy paralleled that of Columbus. He was rejected, despised, imprisoned, and neglected. Columbus turned to divine support; Dr. Cook relied upon the innate sense of justice in men and, appealing to the future, wrote *Return from the Pole*.

FREDERICK J. POHL

Brooklyn, New York
1951

n

↑

AUTHOR'S NOTE

The theme of this narrative starts as an aftermath of the polar conquest; it deals with the return journey. Within two months after leaving our base camp on the Greenland shores, while yet in fair vigor, we reached that elusive area on the earth's top designated as the North Pole. This success was the primary object of the expedition. Perhaps in serious history this attainment will always be the climax to ages of poleward pioneering. But to the men who first walked about the polar axis the reaching of the Pole was but the beginning of a most desperate adventure.

To us there was no climax until by our own efforts we proved to ourselves that we could survive and return in good health to our respective homes. This return journey close to the magnetic meridian,[1] between the geographic pole and the Magnetic Pole, gives title and substance to this book.

FREDERICK A. COOK

n

↑

1

TO THE END OF NORTH

In the shadow of the unknown at the top of the globe there is an area over which, when we travel north by compass, we go south on the map. The needle of the compass points not to the geographic pole but to the Magnetic Pole. This center of magnetic attraction is located northwest of Hudson Bay, on or near Boothia Felix Peninsula,[2] the most northern extension of the American continent. Magnetic north ends there. Geographic north ends at the North Pole, located in the mid-area of a deep, ice-covered circumpolar sea. Here all meridians of longitude meet. The distance between these two poles is 1,200 miles, and along this expanse of land and sea, north by compass is south underfoot.

This region, though moderated by a marine climate, is perhaps least advantageous to all forms of land life. It is a frigid desert of rocky islands, separated by wide ocean channels but cemented together and to the North American mainland by salty sea ice. During the long winter of nine months the desolate expanse is swept by stormy zero blasts. In the brief summer of three months it is misty and foggy and chilled with frequent snow storms. The summer snow, however, melts rapidly and serves as rain to hardy plants.

For months during the coldest season there is no direct sunlight. The gloom of the long Arctic night is there a foretaste of death to all living things. The long Arctic day, however, with its nightless months of cheer, gives double life and double power to all life that can survive. Excepting only glacier-covered areas there is no large part of the earth's surface where life is less abundant. Desert doom and icy desolation are stamped on all the midlands from Pole to Pole of this frozen north world.

And yet there is contrast. Not all is doom and death and frozen crystal. Where the battle of life is hardest there the joy of living is also greatest and perhaps most enjoyed because of the ever-present threat of icy termination.

The urge to live, the contest to survive, the inherent primitive genius of men to overcome seemingly hopeless conditions is here noted as a most glorious passion of existence. Hunger and cold, if not too long continued, clear the brain for action as nothing else can. This is the most profound lesson which Arctic experience has to deliver.

To all men in all places the make and break of daily

events give spark and time to the engines of life. In the narrative which follows, events were mostly the results of our own acts. We had to fight continuously a battle of life against famine and frost. It was, in a way, trench warfare. To escape the wrath of polar blasts, we got into ditches and crevices, under rocks and snowbanks, seeking the protective cover of Mother Earth. As we logged daily events, failure and success in devising means of subsistence became a means of transmission to indicate the power of life—or the coming silence of death.

When as a boy I wandered through the north woods from home to school, the thrill of the wilderness fascinated me. The joy thus attained became an urge, a power to generate ambition and new courage to venture further and further into the unknown. To me nature was a never-ending school of delight. How the zest of budding plants, the call of baby creatures of the summer wild linger in memory, later to bespeak the goodness of life! How the silence and glory of a winter in timberlands, with its four-paw tracks of furry animals in snow, speak in thought and action! Then, as now, every plant, every bug, every fish or other animated creature had a means of expressing the joy of living. These messages were not in words but in a sign language that every day I tried to learn. The voice of the wild thus became a lifelong study.

In going from the lowlands to mountain tops and noting there the dwarf and desert-like life with its hardy tenacity, there came the ambition to visit the hot deserts of the tropics and the snowy wastes poleward. What did plants and animals and humans do where there did not exist trees for protection? I reasoned that the forest best mothered all life. I had yet to learn that the feathery crystals of snow could blanket and protect plants and animals.

Dire need for food and clothing kept before me the hardship of poverty, but I managed to live as other boys did without luxuries, pioneering in the foothills of the Catskills. As I passed out of the country school into a university still with abject want as my best driving force, I was able to find work to pay tuition expenses.

Graduation was for me a declaration of independence but I soon learned that education is a lifelong job. I had acquired only an academic system with a desire to study. Poverty with opportunities was still in my favor. I volunteered and was accepted as the physician of an expedition, without salary, for a voyage of exploration poleward. In one way or another, either as staff scientist or as leader, I became associated with seven expeditions poleward[3] from 1891 to 1907. Accumulated experience with augmented ambition now culminated in an expedition with the sole purpose of reaching the North Pole.

Since the polar quest is in effect a prelude to the subject matter of this book, it will be necessary to outline this part of the journey to place us where this battle for life against famine and frost begins.

In the final dash for the Pole, we left northwest Greenland, February 19, 1908, at sunrise. The airline distance to our chosen destination at the Pole was 700 miles. I had spent the winter with its long night at Annoatok,[4] the northernmost village of the northernmost people. Rudolph Francke, who assumed duties as camp director, was my only civilized companion. My two Eskimo companions who, with me, in this dangerous adventure battled for the privilege of living,

were savage boys of twenty years, from these most northern
Eskimos. Other men of this wild folk joined our polar expedition and remained as helpers and dog drivers to the end of
known land. The route ultimately selected made necessary
a detour to the west which lengthened our polar journey
200 miles, but this choice gave us a tour through promising
game lands.[5] It did indeed enable us to feed ourselves and
our dogs from musk oxen and bears secured en route for
half the polar distance.

We expected to return along the same way, and to better
ensure a regular food supply we left caches of food and
equipment at accessible points of land every fifty miles. But
an unkind fate denied us the privilege of coming back by
this route to take advantage of the cached stores. Because of
this mishap, our return was delayed for a year, a year during
which we lived like the wildest of wild men, subsisting without outside aid—on meat, mainly raw, of animals secured
by a hand-to-hoof and hand-to-paw contact. To escape
death from intense cold we huddled like animals in rock
caves and dungeons of ice and snow.

The north end of Heiberg Island, the poleward limit of
known land from our position, was reached in mid-March.
Thus far, though traveling during the feeble light of the
coldest season, with temperatures ranging from 50° to 83°
below zero, we enjoyed the luxury of full stomachs. But
henceforth the aspect of life was to be different. We were
at the shore of the mid-polar sea. Our destiny was 520 miles
beyond, over an unknown moving sea of ice where no life
could be expected to augment our food supply. The main
supporting party of Eskimos now arrived, with four men
and fifty-four dogs, pulling four heavily loaded sleds. I ad-

vanced fifty miles over the rough, broken ice of the circumpolar sea. From there, after a careful study of our prospects,
I decided to continue the journey with but two sleds drawn
by twenty-six dogs, driven by two men. The other two Eskimos went back to join the others en route to home lands
in Greenland. We now had material to afford a scant subsistence for eighty days. With this we must win or fail. We
were to be in a region beyond all human help and perhaps
beyond all animal life.

And what a lifeless desert of floating damnation we invaded! With an average speed of about fifteen miles daily,
we advanced over drifting miles of ice, suffering the torture
of steady zero weather ranging from 36° to 63°. Eating
mainly dried meat and tallow, camping in domes of crystal,
shelters of snow flakes, with snow for a bed, ice for pillows,
mere existence became more and more a desperate challenge,
but we steadily advancd toward our goal. From a position
300 miles below the Pole, we discovered land a long distance to the west. One hundred and fifty miles further along
we reached what looked like land-adhering ice. Continuing
over moving masses from one to ten miles in diameter and
from ten to fifty feet thick, we at last reached an area upon
which the earth's axis should be located.

Our methods of determining position were with the sex-
tant and accessory instruments like those used by shipmas-
ters. The latitude, after a test of observations for two days,
was apparently 90° with longitude zero. Though no nautical observations can be absolutely accurate, we believed this
position to be the North Pole.

This position, also indicated by dead reckoning from the
last known point of land, was verified by a measurement of

the length of shadows. Our shadows were the same length
for every hour of the twenty-four-hour day. Only at the
Pole or very near it can shadows be of equal length for
every hour, because only there is the sun of nearly equal
altitude at all times of day when above the horizon.

Now we were at the earth's top—the North Pole, the axis
around which our world turns. But what a cheerless, what
a hopeless spot to have aroused the ambition for conquest
during ages! There was here no land, no life, nothing to
mark the center of desolation, the floating icy crust of the
sphere. We were the only pulsating creatures in a dead
world of ice.

We had reached the North Pole, the end of north geographically, and had lost east and west. It was here south in
every direction, for in theory and in practice from the polar
axis all is south. It was indeed south as we looked down over
the globe along every meridian, since all meridians come together here. There is no longitude and, therefore, no time as
measured by the clock. But since we still used the compass
which, pointing to the Magnetic Pole, is not influenced by
the geographic pole; also since we still used the chronometers
rated from the longitude of Greenwich, England, we were
still in the same working condition we were before making
allowance for the changed positions.

Everything we said and did here was questioned by us,
and will be by others. With conditions as above reported,
all seems unnatural. Under long-continued physical and
mental strain, with food, shelter and habits of thought abnormal, the observer must himself become subhuman or a
superman to envision a world so new that the mind is slow
in grasping the strained perspective.

The test of our attainment of the Pole is not to be rated by any claim for pinpoint accuracy but by a report upon the physical conditions about the top of the globe. Our observations are the result of the first actual visit, the first journey to pierce the Boreal Center. We were at the Pole on April 21 and 22, 1908. No one claimed to have been there before.

In my published accounts the utmost detail of the local polar environment is given. In substance these data do not fit any previous theory. The absence of land, the absence of life, the absence of icebergs, the general sea, air and other terrestrial conditions which I placed on record as a picture of the polar surroundings all have since been confirmed from over the Pole by the combined observations of the air service of Byrd, Amundsen, and Nobile.

For a quarter of a century efforts were made by R. E. Peary and his friends to discredit this first polar attainment and to advertise Peary as the discoverer of the North Pole, but the Pole was never lost and, since it is an imaginary axial point around which the earth turns, it can never be discovered. Peary came a year later, and reported conditions much like my report first published in September, 1909.

The North Pole, then, for which we seek a positive description, is in its environment a negative area, an ill-defined frozen sea. It is a deep sea, covered with broken and ever-breaking fields of salt-water ice. This endless expanse of moving, drifting, shifting ice, ever covered with snow, under the drive of air and ocean currents, expands outward and disrupts along the outer edges of the circumpolar reaches. The process of upbuilding and that of disruption combine at all seasons of the year to produce perhaps a rather even system of pack making and breaking. This in-

cludes an area of about 3,000,000 square miles. The top of
the globe is, therefore, covered by what is designated as a
mid-polar sea, studded farther south with some rocky islands
and surrounded by the great continents of the Northern
Hemisphere.

There is no land to mark the core, or the stem, or the axis
about which the earth revolves. Here the temperature for
ten months is below the freezing point and for much of the
time below zero. During the two months of summer, snow
and ice melt, but there is some freezing and some melting at
all times of the year.

Thus far we had made steady progress and had been rea-
sonably successful in all of our efforts to get over the difficulties while traveling over the top of the globe, but now in
returning our luck was soon to change. For over a year we
were to become terraqueous creatures with only such shelter and such food as creatures of the wilds can find. So
greatly did our experiences now differ that the dash to the
polar axis was in effect but an introduction to a continuous
battle for life against famine and frost for many long
months. In an air line, from our Greenland camp to the Pole
it was but 700 miles. This distance was for me to be extended to a walk of 4,000 miles over land and sea with the
shadow of death daily on the horizon.

2

CARRIED ASTRAY

At the time of our polar achievement, the elation of success did not linger many days. We had worries. Many serious dangers were promptly to engage our attention. To the Eskimo boys the poleward journey was a failure. No new hunting grounds had been found. To them the long quest over a lifeless desert such as we had covered was the waste of a moon in an important season for gathering meat.

Though unschooled wanderers, they had much natural intelligence. The Eskimo does not believe in a round earth. To him all the world is flat. He somehow has grasped the idea that white men have driven a nail into the earth somewhere up north, where the sun hides at night, and that this iron peg has fallen into the earth and become lost. Hence the Eskimo boys called the Pole the Big Nail (Tigieha). Since iron is more valuable to them than gold, they were interested in the search. But now the nail had slipped, as they believed, into the earth under a deep sea, their polar curiosity was lost in the hopelessness of further search.

To go as quickly as possible back to land to an area where we might find living things to eat was now to be a life-and-death struggle for three hungry men. We were alone, all alone, far from land, far from life—far from other human beings. This loneliness was so oppressive that tears came more easily than conversation, as we now back-trailed over icy seas of despair.

Thus beset, under anxious premonitions of impending danger we turned our backs to the position of the Pole and began the long return march. The weather for days had been fairly clear, with the thermometer a little above or a little below 40°. The humidity was high. The barometer dropped as we lowered degrees of latitude. Soon we were made to realize that we had before us a battle for life, with almost all the forces of nature against us. We felt this hard existence might quickly end in death. The weather suddenly became warmer, a sure signal of trouble on the polar pack. The light wind was gathering force. The sky was clear and the air was free of frozen crystal. In a few days, as we went homeward at top speed, the sky lowered and darkened. The barometer became unsteady and the thermometer dropped to a level near zero. A day or two later the ice of the frozen sea began actively to jam and crack, and overslid in huge pressure ridges, leaving in other places wide open lanes of water. This early change of weather we knew to be a bad omen for our immediate safety. The entire horizon of pack-ice over which we walked and drove our dogs was now drifting with some speed. Neither the direction nor the miles of daily shift of this movement could be accurately appraised. Allowing for some drift, we were setting a course to reach land where we had left it fifty days earlier.

It was difficult to hold a straight course in any direction. Many detours were necessary to cross from floe to floe over newly fractured ice fields, often separated by wide spaces of open water. With cloudy weather in fogs and mists, no sun appeared to afford an observation for position to correct our uncertain course. We would perhaps have gained time and distance if we sat down for needed days of rest, but our food supply was too limited to permit mental ease with good judgment. Dogs were eating dogs and eventually we must eat the canine survivors if the delay continued too long. Duty to ourselves and to our draft animals then seemed to force daily marches as far as failing strength would reach.

Homeward progress was thus slow. Days passed, weeks passed, in a dull routine of life-sapping monotony.

Our later methods of life will be better grasped if, as we go along, a brief introduction to my companions is here set down. Though widely separated in earlier fields of activity, we were to each other by no means new acquaintances. In 1891 among the first and most enduring savage friends were the parents of the young men who at that time were mere infants—not long out of the mother hood which serves as the Eskimo cradle. As years went on [6] I renewed this acquaintance with the boys and with their relatives and friends. Mutual confidence and trust was, therefore, long established between us. They called me Doto. Though the men were twenty, one seemed much older because of his steady nerve and his slow, mature method in thought and action. His name was Etukishook—I called him Etuq. The other was quick, dramatic and youthful in mind, rapid and unreliable in activity. His name was Ahwelah—I called him Wela. Both were well schooled as hunters, as every savage dependent upon meat for food must be. The art of chase to them was a profession, an art of life which requires a well-developed brain and an evenly developed body. All of this will appear as our battle for life against famine and frost got increasingly harder. When we envision the Eskimo in the light of a primitive artist, his vocation is a study in the progress of mankind within the working plans of all later generations.

My Eskimo companions were ill at ease, though on the whole more contented and less worried than I. With them, periods of intense excitement alternated with spells of suspended emotions and frozen passions. Aside from ourselves and our dogs, we had not seen a living thing for nearly two months. To me this lack of life over the great reaches of space covered was intensely depressing, but to them all about was alive. Even storms and cracking, driving ice represented living energy. When the spirits of the air or the gods of the sea were at war, humans must suffer. To elemental catastrophe they were stoically resigned, to watch and wait for better harmony. Physically they lived even now in a promising world. They saw almost daily distant indications of seals, birds, bears, and land. They could smell and taste land breezes, and hear sounds of weird animation when to me all was the frozen nothingness of an endless expanse of lifeless sea.

There was little change in the daily routine of our existence as we sought a footing over turning, twisting levels of the disrupting pack. Without knowing it we were being carried astray over a floating world of mystery. Our chief interest was in each other. Perhaps in this dull and long-continued line of travel, hunger and thirst, with desire for accustomed home companionship, were not to be unsatisfied longings—ever uppermost to force conversation, thought, and action. At this particular period, thirst was the most pressing passion.

How we craved for water! Necessity had enforced the habit and capacity of desert camels. It had been necessary to drink enough at the beginning—or at the journey's end—to last until the precious liquid was again accessible. There was water, good fresh water everywhere, but none to drink. Indeed our visible earth was all water. Except the smeary liquid of the briny deep all was rock-like strata of crystal. Water, ever plenty of it, but nothing to quench our thirst. We could ease the burning tongue or moisten the parched throat by eating a handful of snow warmed in the gloved hand. But this did not satisfy the bodily craving for liquid to take the place of blood-fluid oozing from the lung and from the skin as a result of great contrast between the blood heat and the coldness of the air.

Though the heavens were continuously screened under a gray gloom by either low fogs or high mists, indicating steady, warm, humid atmosphere, the thermometer in May remained near zero. Having been accustomed to very low temperatures for a long time, mere zero air to us seemed warm and hard to inhale. The increasing activity of the pack-ice made the entire horizon wobble and crack and rumble. There was in this some symphony of sound and rhythm of motion. The lilt of the frozen sea has in it music to ears in a humor for gladness. But we were submerged in sadness when restful hours for sleep became possible.

Still setting a course for the land where we left it in March, daily I became more and more convinced that our sense of direction was faulty. There was no sure means to correct our plotted course. We could make allowances for detours and for estimated wind drift, but the ice under our feet was all adrift. The direction and the speed of this drift changed too rapidly to estimate how much we were being carried astray.

For nearly two months the sky was too much obscured to permit an observation of the sun from which we could deduce a nautical position. In the meantime our food and fuel supplies were running low. Men and dogs had been on three-quarter rations for a month. More than half of the dogs had been eaten. Starvation was now a daily outlook as we searched over the breaking pack along a misty horizon for land, or something that might indicate a hope of obtaining game animals. The torture of the nothingness of this dead world of drifting ice drove us to the verge of madness.

While thus in a darkness of despair, to prevent an epidemic of suicides, I figured we must do something to celebrate. It was June 10, my birthday. I never had less hope, less cheer to put into a celebration, but I gave each a pocket knife and served an extra cup of hot tea with a double slab of pemmican. The weather on this day was hazy. The temperature was only a few degrees below freezing point, but the air was wet and cold. Half starved, we were more uncomfortable in this moderate cold than when the air had been 70° below zero, but somehow there was the will to cheer up. This feeling was transmitted to the half-dead dogs. They sniffed the air and began to howl in a chorus. I did not know whether the dogs cared to join the celebration of forced gladness, or if it was a protest for more food, or if the dogs were giving voice to the dead they had eaten— whatever the dog spirit was, their howl was noise the same as music to our ears so long senseless in the silence of the Arctic desert.

The next day, as we arose from our bed of wet ice, we felt better. The weather was colder and clearer. Some cheerful color was lined on the cloudy skies. Onward we marched to a destiny which to me at times indicated sure death, but the Eskimos and the dogs were periodically in better spirits. For a few days longer we helped to push and pull the sleds over ice much broken, thus aiding the limping dogs.

At last the clouds parted, the horizon appeared—land appeared far to the east and far to the south. The mere sight of land brought shouts from men and dogs.

But it was strange land:

Where were we in this weird world of drifting ice? When the observations were placed on the map, I guessed the land to the east to be Heiberg Island, the land to the south, Ringnes Land. This, after further investigation, proved to be true. For two months we had been carried adrift toward Alaska. We were now in a position making it impossible to go homeward by back-trailing our northern route. What to do next was the subject of serious consultations.

We had realized for some weeks that under present conditions our earthly time was short, that we would sink into an

icy grave if fortune did not favor us soon. Fortune now favored us by a new outlook over a strange land. The sight
was in itself cheerful by contrast to our previous experience.
But could we survive until we reached some rocky shores of
solid earth? Could we find animals or anything else to eat
on this land? It was picturesque to look at, but death-dealing
in its icy severity. A smoky sky indicated a wide expanse of
open water to the east all about Heiberg Island. There was
a water sky [7] behind us. A retreat to the north and east to
our food stations along the trail followed from Greenland
poleward was, therefore, effectually barred to us.

We had a canvas boat with which we might have caught
our destiny over the open sea, but young ice was still forming and this would cut the canvas of the boat like a knife.
We must, therefore, abandon all hope of a return to Greenland along known game lands. The sea ice was drifting
south. The season was so far advanced that the channel ice
of the American Archipelago was breaking and escaping in
Atlantic waters. Our only recourse, it seemed at that time,
was to go south with the drift. We understood that this decision would long delay our return but it offered the hope
of immediate subsistence, even if later all which life implies
must blend with ice tragedy of the End.

The primary object of our expedition had now been accomplished. We had been over the top of the globe, had
seen and recorded the physical conditions about the North
Pole. For three months we had walked over the drifting ice
which sheets the sea of the earth's top. With imperfect aids
to guide our sense of direction, we had invaded the twilight
of the unknown. Now, as we envisioned a return to solid
earth, where gladness was to free us of frozen emotions, the

brain was fired for action. Since our food supply was nearly exhausted, there was grave danger of starvation, of death by freezing, of slow ending of life by disease, when real happiness should begin to be an enduring inspiration. This shadow of death was to hang over us for many long months and our eventual escape from this impending doom represents the real theme of this book.

n

↑

3

BACK TO LAND

While thus trying to appraise the prospect of living, we were traveling and drifting nearer and nearer to the least attractive land. Far to the east above low clouds we got an occasional glimpse of rocky peaks separated by glaciers. The land ahead was in low hills, so much eroded by frost and storm that it seemed to offer no practical nook for plant or animal life. However, we saw only poleward slopes. Behind us was an area of 3,000,000 square miles of jammed pack-ice, extending over the top of the globe. No breathing life, no rooting plant had there been seen by us. All to the north was seeming death, where only ice grows. The land facing the top of the earth offers a cheerless frozen expression, but on earthly bodies with slopes facing south, there it should be different. We had come from a region which could not be worse. We were headed for a region which should be better. At any rate, all human life, all that the job of living implied, was to be gained by progress southward, toward the Magnetic Pole. Life to us was ever sweetest when death was nearest.

In our desperate efforts to get to land quickly, we had overestimated our strength. Beads of perspiration gathered on long unwashed faces. The dogs were as eager to reach land as we were, but their dripping tongues and forced breathing betrayed failing strength and overheating. Utter exhaustion, due to overwork and underfeeding for man and beast, was now a serious threat. Would we, could we, make a landing? Even a vigorous, well-fed sled team has great difficulty in crossing the jammed ice of the pack edge near land.

Selecting a big field of heavy ice, we halted for a breathing spell. Then it was discovered we were on the drifting pack of a fast-moving stream. The movement was toward shore, into an opening which seemed like a bay, but because of the steady southward movement of the pack, we concluded that we were entering a strait between two large islands. After a short rest we could see that this was true. In the strait we knew that the ice would be broken and jammed, making our position dangerous. We had been too long without sleep to be able to fight such a battle and, therefore, we could not risk the adventure at that time, not even with rapid progress to a new Promised Land in our favor.

Watching carefully the relative motion of the drifting ice

as against the land mass, we soon were able to determine the line of the land-adhering ice and the drifting pack. With our glasses we saw blank spots on this land ice and this aroused a fever heat of excitement—because the spots were thought to be seals. Our position, however, changed rapidly and, seeing from different angles, we concluded the spots were either algae-covered rotten ice or streaks of earth from land-slides. While thus engaged, it was noted that the shore line was not as far off as we had figured it. There was a wide belt of low ice-covered land extending toward us. The line of demarcation between land and sea had for us been hidden by a seemingly equal level and similar snowy cover, but now we saw a few rocks and some low sandy banks not more than five miles away. And the ice in that direction was of such an unbroken character that on it we could make rapid progress.

In our weakened condition it took hours of hard work to force a way over landward ice. There was deep snow with a weak crust which would not hold us or the sleds or the dogs. This surface condition makes most tiresome traveling. Eventually we found ourselves ashore without knowing just when we passed the dividing line between land and sea. We found ourselves ashore on a gradually rising slope. At last we were on land! The dogs, completely exhausted, sat down and gasped for breath. We threw ourselves across the sleds and allowed weary eyes to close for a few moments. All were too near the weariness of the end of life's mission for an expression of happiness. Of just how long we resigned ourselves to this bodily ease there is no record.

When feeling returned, all arose at once in rapt attention to the appearance of a new world. But still we were too tired, too thirsty, too hungry, too nearly famished in mind and body to enjoy the life-conserving event. Not far away there was a dull gray spot surrounded by dirty snow. We moved to this place, and there our feet were electrified by the gritty feel of dry sand. We looked at each other with wonder out of cavernous eyes.

Wela said: "Noon-ah-me ash-you-kay" (Land it is; of this there is no doubt). Etuq smiled with a savage gladness more expressive than words. I was too glad and too much engaged in thought to talk. To us these were impressive moments.

The dogs sniffed the air, pushed their noses into the sand, eyed the horizon, wiggled their ears, wagged their tails, and then, after about a dozen turns each, they too lay down to figure out the new environment. All, men and dogs, were then silent with eyes swinging from heaven to earth for some time, as if in meditative prayer.

The sun was warm. The air was soft. There was not a breath stirring, no creaking ice or oversliding motion of the pack was heard or felt. For a brief spell we now had no wants except the desire to get close to Mother Earth.

Now we longed to lie down lovingly and sleep for a day, with reverence to enjoy the sweetness of dry Mother Soil! But subconsciously there was the urge to move onward for a place where there were some signs of animal life which would provide means for subsistence. The call of hunger will not long yield to the desire for aesthetic enjoyment. We were now awakened to new glories and this awakening in turn forced rapid thinking to ensure self-preservation.

Our position was just about midway between the geographic polar axis, which we had left on April 22, and the

Magnetic Pole. The ice-covered sea which had served for us as solid earth had been a frozen desert, but the land as we now saw it after the first pleasing impression was, on further study, a depressing Arctic Sahara of sand, rocks, and snow, offering no plant and no animal life. This north end of land was in effect the end of life, the end of hope for living things. And what strange contradictions! We still went north by compass but we were ever headed south for the end of south, or the center of attraction to the needle at the Magnetic Pole. The sun did go from east to west, not over the zenith but around the horizon.

It had been more than three months since sunrise; another two months must pass before sunset. We had seen no stars for months, but the moon came up in daytime. The ice water between the floating icy rocks of water gave off clouds of steam like boiling water. The snow burned the face by reflected glitter from the sun. What a world of paradoxes! All was queer. We were queer ourselves, but not queer enough to set aside prudence. We knew that if we did not bestir ourselves to find something to eat, the darkness of death would overtake us before the coming darkness of the winter night.

Though anxious to start and ready to go in quest of food to a more promising terrain, there was something on the horizon in every direction to add mystery and new problems. The very danger of our position became weirdly fascinating. Though delay implied death, the brief moments of indecision aroused satisfying emotions. Not long before, we had seen five suns all at once.[8] On this day we saw both the sun and the moon at the same time, and both in weird duplication. Behind us there was the surprising picture of a range of mountains inverted, and some isolated islands—mirages of land where we knew there was only sea over which we had walked during the passing days. The very air was charged with madness. There was illusion, delusion, and misconception in all that our troubled eyes perceived. Could we ever escape this frozen damnation, the misery of this miserable world?

The only definite thing was the little beloved patch of gritty sand under our feet. The horizon was hazy, and changed every minute with our changing mood. Now there was the aspect of gladness, again there was the outlook of sadness. We could not decide, under these conditions, whether our location was a small island which might be awash at high tide or an extensive low land. In the uncertainty of this perverse appearance, we believed it unsafe to camp. Further along to the right, as we were facing homeward lands, there was what appeared like a more definite elevation which we reasoned should be a hill, or at any rate an island of more definite topography. Could it be possible that all the surface was in reality so indefinite, or were our eyes failing under the strain? We must find some place to rest and recuperate.

A few minutes later visibility improved. Yes, we were on an island—a vague, shapeless uplift, a sand dune or an elevated submarine bank, perhaps unworthy of a place on the map. A distant view was still impossible. Our general surroundings were under a high fog. The mystery of the enforced obscurity was to us a torture. The sea ice at high tide had been pressed upward over the gradual slope. A long tongue of thick land-adhering ice reached seaward for some distance, beyond lanes of water and more mist.

Heretofore we camped anywhere on ice adrift, so long as it offered good snow for a bed, but now we suddenly feared being carried further astray. We must get anchored to some land where there was a chance to find animal life for food, or resign ourselves to ending it all in starvation. Wela said he was too tired to move. Etuq said it might be well to lie down and dream, to await a clearing of the air. Under these conditions we decided the desolate isle would serve for a brief resting place. Some crevasses were seen not far away. We were in a region where we might expect seals in narrow lanes of water near land. Meat to us was of greater value than gold.

So we camped on the Isle of Mystery. The silk tent was set up and pegged down on sand. The dogs were tied to the ice edge. Four ounces of dried meat and tallow were served to each man and the same to each dog. The dogs ate snow as usual for a drink. We drank snow water. This was the full meal, and we had only a scant supply to hold life in bodies for a short time longer. Death by starvation was painfully near.

Because of utter exhaustion we could sleep in short naps, like a hungry bear waiting for his next meal. The urgent call of long unsatisfied hunger, however, agitated our bony bodies. Resigned, peaceful sleep had become a lost habit with us. In a few hours, worry opened my eyes to the awareness of our immediate danger.

I felt the still voice of death coming up out of the cold east from my couch of sand and snow. Lifting a heavy head from a block of ice serving as a pillow, and turning weary, disheartened eyes at my companions, expecting to find them at ease in that sleep which precedes the end, I found them also awake and looking anxiously at me. There was hunger in their faces, but it was hunger with hope and a smile. To me, in the depths of abysmal gloom, this smile, though distant and half sad, gave renewed vigor to the pathos of our fate.

We had long suffered, but together we had learned to extract joys from zero's lowest. Together we had invaded the coldest regions, with temperatures as low as 83° below zero. Together we had wintered through the long night with its blood-bleaching effect, and the long summer with the thrill of double days and double-living emotions. Coming thus through troubled months of sadness and gladness, we knew each other as few people do.

And yet the momentous question: Is this to be the end? could not be escaped.

Wela, a little hysterical, first in smiles and then in tears, said, "Doto, we trust you as our big brother. Find a place where we may expect bears and seals, and after that it matters not how long it takes, we will find food while you direct the way home." Etuq said, "Yes, if we are to live, we must put the life of other animals into us."

Again I looked at my companions, endeavoring to form judgment as to their power to withstand further hardship. Both were pygmies, twenty years old, five feet high, with yellow skins—typical in size and color of other Eskimos. But in five months their faces had acquired the change and aging of a generation of hard living. Reflecting sun-glitter from the snow had burned their faces. Our work under insufficient water and food had wilted their bodies. The faces were wrinkled and colored like winter-tried russet apples. I took notes in detail of physical conditions too lengthy to present

here. Though the skin was wrinkled, it was not flabby but
tightly adherent to what was left of the tissue which
badly padded the protruding skeleton. The conclusion was
reached, mainly from the pulse and muscular rigidity, that
there was ample reserve vigor to endure a few more weeks
of hard adventure.

We still had eleven faithful sled dogs, all like ourselves in
a deplorable state of semi-starvation. These were the survivors of a pack of twenty-six. The others had been eaten.
We loved these thin, ragged-looking warriors of better days.
Though the offspring of but half-tamed wolves, these animals had been to us thus far life-savers. Each dog was to one
of us a personal friend. They looked discouraged and neglected and this failing team power was most discouraging.
For weeks the dogs had carried their tails low and whined
in muffled voices when a fighting noise or vigorous howl
was the called-for expression. When an Eskimo dog fails in
voice and quits fighting, life is no longer worth living.

Our earthly possessions were few. All, however, must
now be appraised to estimate the capacity to extend life.
While thus gloomily engaged, we noted that the weather was
clearing for a promising start. We were dressed in ragged
suits of fur. There were no extra garments or patching material. The deerskin sleeping bags were too old to use and
must soon be fed to the dogs. The same was true of the foot-
wear and the mittens.

We had a tent made of Shantung silk but the strain of
snow-charged winds and the burn of the ice-reflected sun
had weakened the fiber. There were two sleds made of tough
hickory and this material, as was to be learned later, was our
greatest asset. We were depending upon two rifles, with

about a hundred rounds of ammunition for weapons to acquire food. One was a Remington 22, the other a Sharpe
rifle, forty-five years old. A few tins of dried meat and tallow, which we called pemmican, represented our last supply
of food. This would not keep us alive for more than a few
days. To secure water we must melt snow or ice. We had
710 matches. There was a blue-flame oil lamp but the fuel
was about all used. We had aluminum dishes, pocket knives,
some good steel saw-knives, and a mending kit to repair sleds
and clothing.

As a floor covering in the tent, we were using a folded canvas boat. This list of equipment was now to represent our
total wealth, and by judicious use of this material we must
live or die.

There were no other human beings, not even savage Eskimos or Indians, in so far as we were able to judge, within
600 miles of us. We could, therefore, entertain no hope of
early relief from others. The immediate outlook was blue,
the ultimate future was blank.

We could, however, rest with half-open eyes—and that
was much.

How often the restful glory of the end and the darkness
of death merge to give a satisfying emotion to those who
must pass into the great divide of the Beyond! This thought
lingered with some pleasure of relief as troubled eyes opened
and closed to a life of semi-death.

In this spirit of mingled misery and hope, we turned from
side to side in the tent. There was not a word of conversation, but anxious faces expressed much in that dead silence.
The silk tent was a mere gauze. Through it we could see
and feel the doom of a very cold and lifeless world.

Unexpectedly we heard a sound. Heads turned. Eyes rolled. Ears reached out. We had been half dozing but a gunshot could not have surprised us more. Not a word was said. Another sound came, followed by a series of soft, silvery notes—the song of a creature that might have come from heaven. I listened with rapture. I believed I was dreaming. The enchanting song continued—I lay entranced. I could not believe this divine thing was of our real world until the pole of our tent gently quivered. Then, above us, I heard the flutter of wings. It was a bird—a snow bunting trilling its ethereal song—the first sound of life heard for many months.

We were back to life! Tears of joy rolled down our emaciated faces. If I could tell you of the resurrection of the soul which came with that first bird note, and the new interest which it gave in our subsequent life, I should feel myself capable of something superhuman in powers of expression.

With the song of that marvelous bird a choking sense of homesickness came to all of us. We spoke no word. The longing for home gripped our hearts.

We were hungry, but no thought of killing this little feathered creature came to us. It seemed as divine as the bird that came of old to Noah in the ark. Taking a few of our last bread crumbs, we went out to give it food. The little chirping thing danced joyously on the crisp snows, evidently as glad to see us as we were to behold it. I watched it with fascination. At last we were back to life! We felt renewed vigor. And when the little bird finally rose into the air and flew homeward, our spirits rose, our eyes followed it, and, as though it were a token sent to us, we followed its winged course landward with eager, bounding hearts.

Only half-dressed, we had gone out of the tent to drink the air-charged thrill of the winged harbinger. Our world of desolation now was a land of fire. Nerves tingled. Muscles pulled for action. The haze of air and the maze of brain departed together. The frontier of a new horizon was for us now apparent.

The sun was in the south. The birds went south. Land was under the sun, and to it we moved with a rapid pace. The dogs, with ears and tails up, whined for speed, but the ice became more difficult for travel as we neared the shore. At last we set foot on land, real big spreads of snow-free earth with actual rocks of sandy crystal in the distance—not the rock-like strata of floating frozen water which so long had served as an insecure footing. Here was the first real earth we had touched in many long months.

Near by there was not a rock, nor a blade of grass, nor a sign of life of any kind. But it was land, Mother Earth. We sat down. The dogs pawed the ground. The joy of children digging into the sand of the seashore was ours. We were back to land, but the ring of the bird's voice was still in our ears, and where birds sing there must be life. How our hearts thrilled!

n

↑

4

A BEAR TO THE RESCUE

But what a scene! To the north was the grinding mass of pack-ice. In all other directions seen over sea ice, under and through thin clouds of moving frosty mist, was land. Here we must begin life. What a cheerless outlook! As we went along, we searched the barren land and found some rocks not even covered with black lichens on the south. Returning to the tent we were sadly disappointed because we had seen no possible source of food. While sitting down on the sleds to discuss our prospects of living, a little bird, probably the same we had seen before, lighted on some ground-soiled snow. Again this little bunch of feathered delight lifted us to the apex of happiness.

I wonder if ever such a bleak island in a desert of death had so impressed men before as a paradise. This impression was of short duration, as were all our pleasures.

The next day was cloudy and cold. The horizon was not clear enough to pick a definite line of march. We must, however, go somewhere. There was urgent need of more rest, but to lie down meant starvation. The dogs understood this as well as we did, for they were beginning to howl and fight and sniff the air for game odors and land delights. We packed up and went south over some very rough land-packed ice. Progress was slow. The sleds were light and had little load to carry but the animals were too weak to pull. Where the going was hard it was necessary for the men to push and pull and encourage. One dog collapsed from sheer exhaustion. We put him on a sled to ride but he died later. The Eskimo boys, savage-like, better withstood starvation. They now rose to a higher mental level with important reserve physical powers. I sank to lower animal depths like the dogs, where food and more food was my immediate desire.

Coming out of one fog bank and passing into another, I found nothing hopeful, but the dogs sniffed the air, turned their little sharp ears forward, while the Eskimo eyes bulged with eager anticipation. Ahead was a dark mist indicating open sea. Into this we pulled with double effort. As we did so, we saw the vague outline of a land. The shore-line ice offered good traveling. On this we moved southerly with some speed. After a while we saw a track, the track of a tiny four-footed animal. The dogs stopped and nosed the footprints. We fingered the impressions. They were fresh tracks of a lone tailless rat, the lemming. It was headed seaward. We passed onward, crossing many other lemming tracks.

Further along we saw an old bear track. Now we were surely in land of the living and we began to look for a camp location. In the meantime a storm was gathering in the north. A strong wind was on our backs which pushed us along at good speed. This wind soon changed to a half gale in gunshot rushes. The tent could not stand against this. The snow was too soft for a snow house. We were compelled to seek shelter behind some huge rocks tumbled down from some high cliffs not visible to us.

Here we suffered the torture of an icy Hades. The temperature was not low, only a few degrees below the freezing point, but we could not keep warm. The wind carried drift snow which cut like a knife. Nothing sheltered us. The rocks did break the wind but the driving snow came from everywhere. We lay down among the dogs to get a little of their heat, spread the tent and the canvas of the boat over and allowed the storm to expend its force. Soon we were buried warmly under the snow but it was necessary to push out a hole for ventilation from the bottom and another hole out of the top to prevent death as a result of the accumulation of our own breath and that of the dogs.

We remained in this packed position for twenty-four hours. There was no food accessible to eat. The dogs chewed part of the silk tent. Men and dogs ate snow to quench thirst. At last through the peep-hole we saw a bit of blue sky. I got out by wiggling like a worm and came out of the top of the heap. The wind had ceased. It was dead calm. But all earth had a midwinter aspect under a new cover of snow. Gone were all signs of summer. The air was brisk and frosty. In looking about I now saw much land, but only a few precipitous cliffs were free of snow. I called for the

Eskimos to pull out our few belongings. Fortunately they were all securely lashed to the sleds, which simplified our search in the digging. In a half hour we were again afoot with easy going over hard storm-driven snow. Another calamity was left behind. But other dangers were ahead, all unexpected and all presenting tortures which often brought us to the verge of death when the end of life seemed easier than the fight to live.

As we now walked southward along a wide channel packed with grinding pack-ice, no other footprints, no other signs of life were seen. To the west there was a continuous line of coast, a few hundred feet high in gradual slopes, mostly blanketed with snow. To the west there was also continuous land, somewhat less snow-covered with some bare, dark cliffs. We were traveling during hours considered night but the light was blinding from snow-glitter. At about the time when the sun was west, we came to the end of the channel. From here the land to the west took the form of low islands. Due south there was no land. Southeast was an island with sharp rocky peaks.

Now for the first time since approaching land I was able to place our position definitely on the map. The island to the southeast was North Cornwall. The channel through which we had come was Hassel Sound. Our Greenland home was 600 miles east, but impassable ice, open water, and a water sky in that direction made the way eastward seem impossible. While we were trying to decide which way to go and what to do, the dogs howled. Our empty stomachs grumbled, and we reasoned that they gave voice to the same feeling. The entire field of sea ice at about this time slowly separated from the land. We selected a small block of floating ice to serve as a raft, placed on this our dogs, sleds and equipment, and paddled over to the main pack. On this we drifted southward. Keeping the dogs harnessed to the sleds, we moved rather westward whenever ice with a workable surface appeared. Cornwall was rough-looking rock that we did not care to strike. Now we were en route somewhere by two systems of transportation, one by the natural drift of the ice, the other by our own leg use. Surely some favorable destiny should be before us. After all it seemed good to live even if the chill of death was stiffening our bodies.

As the ice upon which we were adrift went south the water behind us quickly filled with smaller ice pieces out of the north and west. It was now desirable to find an old field of thick ice to serve as a secure resting place while we passed the milling smash of the drift against Cornwall Island. For our famished bodies there was urgent need of more rest and more sleep, but no safe resting place was visible.

We had passed several bear tracks interesting to us but too old to interest the dogs. Noticing this we thought the poor creatures too near the end by starvation, too tired and weak to retain a hunting instinct. With human ego we considered that our wolfish instincts were better than the wolf propensities of the dogs, but we were soon to change our minds about this.

Another track was crossed. The huge footprints were old but we urged the dogs to follow the indicated course of the animal. One old master hunter among the dogs now assumed leadership and he dominated the two teams. The excited canines disobeyed the drivers and sought to manage their own method of approach to something which they got out of the air. Wolflike, some with noses down, others with noses up, they began the chase. Realizing that a hunting creature sees through the nose, we gave them their own choice of headway, and they took a course at right angles to the old tracks. In that direction ice was piled up in huge pressure ridges dangerous for the safety of our sleds and equipment. But a depleted larder was also dangerous. The dogs rushed onward with a union of action. The sleds bounced like rubber balls. To delay the reckless speed, we sat on the sleds and dragged our feet the better to steer the sleds from bad bumps. As we neared the rough icy uplifts we could see that it was impossible to cross with sleds. We tried but failed to turn the dogs from their chosen line of dash. Trying to manage the dogs, we worked until out of breath, but they managed us with plenty of breath to spare.

The first pressure line proved that we were right. It was impossible to cross. The ice was piled in huge blocks twenty-five feet high. The dogs sat down, quivering with nervous excitement, noses up, heads together, with curved tails doubly curled. Now it dawned on us that perhaps the dogs had a scent and a purpose in their disobedience. Wela took the field glasses and mounted the highest block of ice. He stood there for some time searching the horizon. The dogs eyed him. We watched him. There was absolute silence, but all were ready to jump. Wela came down with some animation but said nothing. The dogs understood him. They jumped into their traces. Then Wela pointed one finger of a bared hand along the ice ridge. In a second the sleds bounded along at a dangerous speed. Again we sat on the sleds and dragged our feet to halt the mad pace. The wolf spirit was in those half-starved dogs now with such force that our lives were endangered.

Suddenly the dogs halted, sat down, and looked up at a big hummock of ice. The pressure ridge made an abrupt turn at that point. We now knew what this meant. The dogs were directing us, with positive nose intelligence.

Etuq took the glasses and mounted the hummock. He came back quickly and pointed southwesterly. A bear was coming toward us. The wind was in the bear's direction and, as trained hunters, we should approach the bear out of the wind. We took a course accordingly. The dogs obeyed the order for a little while but their noses were turned easterly. In the meantime Wela took a rifle and Etuq passed the other to me, but I asked him to keep it and do his best.

In a few moments we passed a break in the line of the obscuring ice ridge. The dogs stopped. They saw the bear. We saw it—the bear saw us, and was heading our way at full speed. There was no water between us. The bear was hunting us. Why not let him come? We moved out of sight behind a hummock. Etuq went forward and lay down in imitation of a seal to bait the bear as a decoy.

But the dogs jumped and wanted a part in the play. We released their traces and they shot out like arrows. In a few minutes they stopped Bruin and encircled him. The bear was hungry and so were we. Only the victor in this case could live.

The dogs were thin and bony; the bear was lean and lonely. We were all hungry and desperate. The dogs were too weak to fight and they knew it, but they kept Bruin turning while one at a time nipped the bear's haunches. During the progress of this entertainment, mere man was out of the picture. The Eskimo boys now knew the bear was ours. They approached slowly. Wela shot. The bear fell. The dogs withdrew and sat down to await the next move. We gathered the traces and led them back to the sleds. Again they sat down with heads lovingly together but restful and satisfied. Soon we brought the sleds to the scene of the bear fight. During our absence the bear had come back to life, had risen, had made a few turns, and had decided to quit in our favor. Gladness gleamed from eyes of dogs. The peace of wealth and happiness was in our hearts.

Though the dogs had worked with desperation, we ourselves had an easy battle, but the excitement in our weakened condition had sapped too much vitality. We lay down on the sleds for a rest. The dogs ate snow and then also curled up for a rest. All slumbered for a few moments. Wela was the first to get up and move about. He got out the cutting knives, keened the edges, and went out to look at our wealth of food. Returning in a few moments, he asked the direction of home. I pointed east. Etuq now went out with Wela to prepare for a feast.

It is a native custom of the Eskimos to direct the head of the bear homeward before the body is cut up. This is done to allow the parting spirit of the bear to carry the message of his death to the folks at home. As the bear's body was now turned over for dissection, the head was directed eastward. A message had been sent to loved ones, and this made the boys happy.

Too tired to start a fire to cook the meat, we ate slice after slice of raw steak, also passing to the dogs piece after piece as fast as they could eat. No broiled porterhouse steak ever tasted better. Long-continued hunger had thus fitted us to the habits of carnivorous animals. Men and dogs ate raw meat with equal relish.

The dressed meat was placed back into the warm bear skin. A sled was set over the precious supply so that the dogs would not mess it up while we slept the sleep of the well-fed. In a few hours we awoke hungry, and again we filled up to full capacity. We kept this up for two days, and then this old world of trouble looked better.

Now life had to us a different meaning. We were tired and stiff and dull-witted as overfed gluttons always are. The dogs were so full they could only roll. Their thin legs were as yet too weak to carry the overloaded paunches.

An early march was impossible, but the ice upon which we rested was drifting southward in the only way that progress was possible. We also knew that an active pack is usually a good place to find game animals. So we continued to rest adrift on a moving sea of ice in peaceful slumbers while our bodies gained new strength. Burning bear fat, we made a fire in a dish, using bits of canvas as a wick. Over this we melted snow and drank liquid purity to our hearts' contentment. With plenty of meat inside, ice water was to us a greater blessing than any of the colored waters we call tea or coffee or wine.

Now that the immediate danger of starvation was lost in the new delight of our well-filled stomachs, I had time to plan our future.

Our destination, indeed all which the love of life implied, was 600 miles to the east on the Greenland shore. A direct return in this direction was now impossible. For me Greenland was but a stopping place en route to New York. Whatever our future desires could be, at present only one course was open—that with the drifting ice to the south. We had now in an active ice stream passed North Cornwall. Grinnell Peninsula was coming over the horizon. The ice was jamming into Penny Strait. Beyond was Wellington Channel, which led into Lancaster Sound, where we could hope to meet whaling ships. And thus for me a means of transport to Europe seemed accessible. To the Eskimo boys this route was exciting, for in this region their granddaddies had hunted and lived long ago. The distance to us at this time did not seem long.

In an air line it was only 200 miles. There along the coast would be found Eskimos and among them life would be interesting even if the return homeward would be delayed for a year. To the boys there was the lure of adolescent pals and marriageable girls. While both had sweethearts at home, because of the scarcity of women these girls might be mated to others before they returned. To me there was not only the opportunity of reaching the Scottish whaling ships but also the possibility of finding there the Canadian customs ship with my old friend Captain Bernier in charge, on which there would be the chance of going to study the Central Eskimos. Altogether our outlook now was rather pleasing. With full stomachs and good digestion, the cold future was full of promise. But what a life of exploring excitement was aroused in us as we saw new lands rise over the drifting ice!

As this plan of the course of our travel was being worked out and discussed with Wela and Etuq, the outline of a great new land loomed over the ice to the southeast.

This strange world of land and its possible life now excited our attention daily. The pack-ice about was all in motion but the drift and pressure were uneven, so much so that we were unable to make much progress by our own means of travel. Efforts were directed towards holding a safe position in the driving pack on heavy pieces of ice which would withstand the jam of the pressure as we neared the rocky shores. To the east there was continuously a smoky dark sky indicating much open water. It was June 20. The air was delightfully warm. The thermometer was 10° above zero. A sharp northwesterly wind was blowing rather steadily, and a shifting barometer indicated storm. With bright sunshine there was heat in the snow-glitter. We had eaten bear meat rather steadily for several days and this overeating made our bodies burn with heat from within. Under these conditions even ice seemed warm.

On the next day, the sun was to be brightest and thereafter, sad to our hopes, we were on the slide for the winter, for the sun would henceforth descend daily.

The sun is highest in the Arctic, as elsewhere, on June 21. It should be midsummer, but not until late in July or early August do we reach a season when the long midsummer day delivers continuous thawing heat. The ice, however, begins to rot early. Rust-colored lines filled with sea algae were seen eating into the surface ice. Occasionally there was a temperature above the freezing point, but not often on the sea. On land the season was much further advanced. The black southerly slopes of land now coming in view were almost all free of snow. The land was not yet near enough to see any green vegetation, but we guessed from the looks of the shores that plants were reaching out and that birds were nesting. "What will we find to eat on these strange lands?" was now in the look of three lonely faces.

We slept much—there was little else that we could prudently do. Leaving one on watch, two slept on the sled. We seldom pitched the tent or erected a shelter because the drifting ice was too uncertain in its security. New birds were coming over the horizon daily—gulls which indicated a nearness to open water, also some snow geese were in evidence. The dogs sniffed the air and eyed the flying creatures, with a growing interest, though like ourselves the poor overworked canines were in need of sleep and rest. They dozed and rolled and played in the snow, pushing their hot noses in the white chill.

We were drifting on the pack-ice and continuously looking for better positions. The land coming over the ice in the southwest appeared like a group of small off-lying islands. Beyond was Bathurst Island, a huge mass of unknown earth and rocks. To the east, Grinnell Peninsula was rising higher and higher and ever more promising as an Arctic oasis.

Etuq said, "On this land we will find musk oxen, reindeer, and Arctic hare." Wela, being bird-minded, promised ptarmigan, ducks, and geese. In another day or two we expected to be able to go ashore to see what this wonderland had in store for us. There were bear tracks and seal resting-places near our camp. Surely a Promised Land could not be far off!

Though the ice seemed to move fast, we were not nearing the unknown lands with the speed which our anxiety demanded. We spent long days of anxiety in entering the ice-jam of Penny Strait. At last we decided to leave our secure position on big ice of the middle of the pack and try to get nearer to the land to the east at the risk of trouble. Here only a few miles from the shore two big white wolves came out to look us over. They were not in a fighting mood nor were our dogs eager for trouble. The wolves howled; the dogs answered. Canine noses and tails went up in the gladness of wilderness friends. The wolves came continuously over the rough ice to within a hundred yards. Our dogs jerked the traces excitedly but we had pegged the sleds to the ice to prevent a wreck of our equipment. Wolves and dogs talked matters over. It was a beautiful picture with a thrill in every stir. After a while the wolves slowly headed back for the land. It was then deemed best to camp for a sleep in our position to enable the day's excitement to subside. We did not want the wolves, and the wolves seemingly did not want us.

n

$\uparrow$

5

WHERE NORTH BY COMPASS IS
SOUTH UNDERFOOT

We now entered an ice-jam—a grinding mill in which the rocks of a narrowing channel and up-striking rocks of off-lying islands served as saw-teeth of a huge destructive power to the ice on which we were trying to float south. We were derelicts for four days in this dilemma. Land at times was near, but escape from the drifting ice to shore for most of the time could only be attained at too great a risk to life. Furthermore, we had meat. There was more in sight, in bears and seals. We needed above all things time to rest and recuperate from the awful physical drain of our recent experience. Unexpectedly the outlook became less favorable. Our hopes proved to be too much in advance of workable progress. There was recuperation but not much rest. In the ice-jam, aiding us by a southward movement, it was ever a problem to keep from being jammed ourselves.

The tides were unusually active. Winds came in steady blasts from the north. Misty fogs and heavy clouds obscured the sun. In dull gray light, with blue-gray spirits, we fought for the privilege of keeping afloat on ice being smashed on all sides. On the whole the troubles were not particularly new to us, but the changes came too suddenly and too fast. If we had been encumbered with heavy equipment, we should probably have gone down as others had done in similar predicaments. Our nothingness was here a great advantage—a mere back-load of supplies and camp equipment, ten dogs and two sleds. All could be quickly divided and packed from one piece of ice to another. There was plenty of meat, but this we could leave behind if necessary. There was accessible fresh water on the ice, food in prospect, and the ice could not quickly separate and leave us, to drift away over dangerous ice-free waters. Yes, there was trouble, plenty of it, but not of the kind to greatly worry us. Unlike other Arctic explorers who died of scurvy and cold going north, we were adrift to the south where the worst region was to us a Promised Land, where hope offered better days.

In this trend of conversation I said to Etuq, "What say you?"

He replied, "Yes, we have lived where foxes die. Perhaps we will not die where foxes live."

There were fox tracks and bear tracks and even a few reindeer tracks on the ice. These above all things interested the Eskimo Nimrods. Looking at Wela for an expression, he said, "Yes, where bear eat, there we also will eat."

A week had passed since we saw the first of these rocky frozen islands through which our destiny must be sought at great physical expense and risk. It had been a short week of agitated hope and realized joys. We had made much progress, not in miles but in courage and muscular strength. Our bodies were still thin, so thin that except for mere walking at a steady gait the new muscles now put to use seemed to need oil to slip on other working tissue. The skin was no longer flabby or tight as it had been for months. It now began to have the old sense of a velvety touch with a subsurface life and freedom of action. In the dogs we noted a similar change, but they ate about ten pounds of meat a day—too much to afford freedom of action. We ate about five pounds. The long-empty stomachs could take more but our digestion was not as quick as that of the wolfish canines. Eating nothing but meat, mostly raw,[9] our recuperation was immensely satisfactory. If we were to survive, this new courage and new energy were the combination which must see us through.

Perhaps, after all, the vigor of life is most appreciated when, as with us, the shadow of death is often near. How we felt the urge to live at this time! How often we said, "It is good to eat and feel the thrill of good digestion," and yet what had we to eat! Only what the wildcat, the fox, the wolf and other carnivorous prowlers find in the wilds.

But we had the basic needs to keep going—food, shelter and the capacity to find subsistence as we went along. Yesterday we secured a seal and a bear. The bear was stalking the seal, so we bagged both. Our camp was in a silk tent in the center of an old solid field of blue ice about thirty feet thick, a square of about 50,000 feet. This for the present was for us a safe home while we drifted in rising, falling twists of jammed ice. We were located in the lee of a hummock about fifteen feet high. The entire field was thicker and higher than the level of other ice about. This gave us an outlook with some temporary guarantee of safety while we were being taken for a ride somewhere.

We had prepared a camp-fire. It was successful and this brought gladness to our frozen souls. Our supply of coal oil had become exhausted about a week ago. We threw the burning equipment away as excess baggage, because it was not useful for any other purpose. When all is frozen, fire is vital, not as a means to get warm, but to melt snow or ice to secure water. In the Arctic winter man may go without food for a week, but without water the body quickly cools for the end. But now in the brief summer we could find pools of water on the ice of the sea and on land. We could eat the meat raw and, therefore, fire was not so vital to our existence. But fire brings cheer. Hot food stimulates. With the means at our command, a camp-fire was extremely difficult to maintain. We tried many makeshifts without success. There was time as well as material for experiments. Hunger mothers inventors and in our position must mother three slipping lives. Surely our longing for a hot soup could devise a cookstove on melting ice. It did, and now we had the pot boiling.

We still had some pemmican, enough to keep alive for several weeks if all our efforts to find game failed. The big tins of some of the used material had been saved as a flooring to sit on wet ice. Under the edges of this tin flooring, we laid some strips of wood. In the center we built a fire. We started with some dry grass which we had earlier used in mittens and boots to keep hands and feet from freezing. Then we added some dry moss which was over a part of our kit sack. Over this we laid thin strips of fat. Soon the grass and moss served as a wick and by feeding blubber slowly we kept up a nice small fire which melted the ice below very little. The fire was housed from the wind by blocks of ice. A tin box served as support for the kettle. In the kettle we had first placed some ice from a small iceberg, for now about all the snow, and all sea ice, was salty. As the ice melted we placed in the pot some liver with soft parts of the mouth and head of the seal. To the Eskimo, liver, tongue and nose as food serve as a sex stimulant. We did not need a sex agitator, but we did need the fire of a fighting spirit. And this pot of hot stuff fired us for troubled days to come.

It will be difficult for others to understand that in the midst of our hardship there were brief spells of glory. All was not torture. Comfort and all that it implies must be regarded as relative to other conditions of accustomed life. We had pleasure and good feeling at times when all the world about was a shining gloom of mystery. Our experience of this day was of this type. After a fill of hot broth and hot bite of liver and seal head, all of which had the aroma and taste of cod liver oil, we crept into our silk tent and into our sleeping bags with the superiority feeling of soldiers after a successful battle. Sheltered from wind and ice and shivering moisture, we rested and dreamed of a world of goodness and prosperity. And why shouldn't we? Had we not by our own efforts become masters of our own destiny?

In the course of five or six hours the wind eased so suddenly that we woke up. The sun for a brief period flooded the distant unknown of rocky islands. A beautiful purple blue poured a liquid of intense light over the grinding pack. While we were thus admiring the splendor of the strange environment, the entire mass of the jam of pack-ice became agitated. It was high tide. The ice had room to spread and move. Each individual piece of ice suddenly acted as if gifted with life. All turned and rose or sank. There was oversliding and turning and cracking ice everywhere. Our own square began to groan and twist. Something was soon to happen. Would activity help us by a more rapid drift or were we again to be jammed into the narrowing channel faster than ever? The outlook was exciting, but along land the small crushed ice gathering there in a wide band made escape landward impossible. We must remain harbored on the big old square of solid ice as long as possible.

A few hours of anxious, watchful waiting followed. With the glasses we spent a good deal of time on the hummock to study the trend of the drifting jams. The huge pieces of ice were being milled like grain under stone. There was hazard, there was peril in every move that we could make, and yet we realized that soon we must move over the slipping, turning, angular masses.

While thus ill at ease, with the uncertainty of indecision, we stripped the heavy bones from the bear and seal meat and packed the choice parts. We fed the dogs all they could eat and arranged all our belongings in lashed units to be most easily handled over the wobbling surface on which a resting place could be found.

Suddenly our square of ice fractured into three parts with cracks close to our camp. We were probably aground on a reef or submerged rocks, but there was not time to ascertain the cause of the smash. The pieces tilted. Other ice in seeming mountains—piled upon our camp square. There was another solid acre to the south. To this we must betake our belongings promptly, but there was some water and broken fragments of unsafe ice in a direct route. By making a half-circle detour to the east we were able to keep on safe and workable fields. In an hour we were again on an old square which we thought would afford at least temporary safety while we watched the ice along land for a line of escape from the increasing damnation.

On this field we had a hard battle for three days, not so much because of the danger of disruption, or of being anchored in a jam, but of a slow drift with frequent interruption. Progress was slow. Our camp square was a hard, rock-like expanse of safe blue ice with no snow on it. The surface had no hummocks to shield us from the wind. There was no near uplift to serve as a watch tower. The big issue now was that of a water famine. There was plenty of meat, plenty of seal blubber for fuel. We could make a fire but there was no drinkable water. The temperature remained close to the freezing point, now melting, later freezing, but in a few hours again pools of water were on the ice. All the water was salty. We had not been in quite this position before. The milky-colored recongealed ice of the tops of hummocks or bits of icebergs, or snow of the upper drifts, had always been found to give us good water. Now all water was bad—salty—nauseating.

The wind was rather stiff with a biting edge, not because of extreme cold but because of the humidity-saturated air. We were able to keep comfortable even on wind-swept wet ice. Our equipment was well suited to this emergency. When the sun was not obscured by clouds, we could spread our sleeping bags on the sleds and thus enjoy rests. The tent was anchored to the ice in the same way that the dogs were anchored, by cutting holes in the ice floor in the Eskimo manner. With a mere pocket knife, Wela could cut down two angular holes meeting an inch or two below the surface. This served as a ringbolt. It is a simple device which saves many lives on ice in a storm. The tent was thus held down by four lines while blocks of ice held down the floor extension. Inside we had a waterproof floor cover. On this the folded canvas boat made a cushion, and at this time we also had two bearskins. Our camp was thus a joy in nearly all kinds of weather.

But how could there be comfort without water? For two days we made a meat broth of the least saline water. On the next day a small iceberg came into view. Etuq said he thought he could figure out a way to get some of this fresh-water ice. Wela joined him. In an hour they were back, each carrying huge pieces of ice. We soon melted some and drank to the joy of living. The supply of fresh frozen water was now ample for several days. Another agitating problem had been solved, but what was the prospect of our escape from this jam?

Under great nervous expenditure in trying to make southward progress we managed somehow to live, but it was a hard drive. Man is not a marine animal. We were trying to become conditioned to a supramarine existence like that of the bear. How we hungered for land and a solid footing! It takes strong souls to endure the risk and slow pace of this jammed pack, and we were a long way from being in the vigor of full strength. Something must happen to change our hard lot, but what could happen unless we risked life to force issues? The boys eyed the land with a love for home. To satisfy them even at the expense of delay we must find a way to reach shore.

Etuq saw a green patch and he said, "The flowers are in full bloom. All the animals are now nursing their young. Let us see the creatures and rest on shore for a day."

n

↑

6

YOUNG CREATURES

OF THE WILD

Strange how baby animal struggles interest all mankind. Here we were with a battle for life before us which we knew might end in death, but with all our troubles we were eager to see and feel roots and leaves and flowers of desert plants. When we observed a bear, a bird, a seal, or any form of land or marine life we wondered why or how the seed sprouts or the babies of the wilds survive in this frozen world. How does Nature bring forth and nurse its young along shores of waters ever icy? The source of this phase of human interest is to me an unfathomed mystery. It is, however, an inquisitiveness which furthers the art of living and, therefore, the problems of life's beginning should be in the baseline of the architecture of thought. This perhaps explains the lure of the baby world for us.

We had seen rat tracks, never in great numbers but tracks indicating small groups, all along the shores washed by the circumpolar sea, in snow, in sands, but never on the pack-ice. Far from land the little footprints thrilled us as an indication of life in regions where moving, living things were least expected. In Greenland we had seen very few indications of rodents, but now as we were heading for the American mainland the tracks became more frequent and more numerous. In so far as I was able to determine, we had to deal with but one kind of rodent, the lemming—a tailless bunch of steel-blue fur, light in winter, dark in summer, but always a neat dainty little creature, feeding mainly on roots of grass and other plants, eating sparingly at times of the sea life washed up on shore. It burrows underground for shelter and is supposed to hibernate in winter. Wela said this ice-rat was good to eat but very difficult to secure. Etuq would not eat it, but he must see its nesting place and see the rat babies.

The baby incubator of the Arctic works overtime when the sun's heat begins to be felt in the first weeks after the long night. We were now near the end of the breeding season for almost all polar life, and therefore little rats should soon be in evidence.

While drifting along shore at some distance, we passed a patch of tundra aglow with moss flowers, with green grassy slopes higher up. Etuq said, "Here I will find my rat babies."

Wela was not interested. He had tried and failed to catch and to trap the little things too often to waste any more time. To Wela the polar rat had been so elusive that the adventure did not seem promising; but we were now a family unit, and by the harmony within that union our world must be determined. We were co-defendants in a self-determination where interdependent manhood of a high order was important. My first duty now was not so much immediate self-protection as it was to secure future advantage in the form of aid of two savage boys trained in character and understanding; and therefore, to them nothing attainable was denied.

We were now adrift on a pack that did not drift. The ice was too broken and too irregular to offer us a promising route over it. Somewhere ahead the frozen stream was jammed against land. We were but a short distance from the shore of a land which looked enticing as a land for game. Though we had some meat on the sled, the Eskimos were hungry for a tour of inspection. We went ashore, my chief thought being to rest, to feed up, and to mend our sled, our boats and outworn clothing; but we discovered a baby paradise which was to inspire and thrill us for months to follow.

In seeking to find a landing place over shore ice we sought the level of an old field pushed far up on land at high tide. This gave us an easy route, for to land from ice under great pressure such as that from which we debarked is always a difficult and dangerous task. Here we saw several seals, but they also saw us and promptly disappeared with a splash into the water, between open cracks. This sight of seals was to us a demonstration that we were entering a region where we might survive, for the seal is to the Eskimo his breadfruit. Where seals can be secured, an Eskimo will withstand any seasonal hardship.

The upper slopes of the land were obscured by misty clouds, as all Arctic land is likely to be for much of the time at this season of the year. Near by were huge granite boulders decorated with black lichens along the faces exposed to the south. The effect was not only picturesque but enticing as a color study. The rock was old gold in color with some darker strata in a rusty hue with just a dash of red. Over the top and to one side in a depression along crevices was a lace-like drapery in black and straw color. The scene gladdened our frozen hearts.

Even the Eskimo has an eye for beauty, but he seldom gives it abstract expression. His appreciation of the glory of Nature is most likely to be expressed in the place selected for camp or in the area where he delights to wander in his quest for what life has to offer. We are likely to look upon the savage as a mere animal in quest of food, but he is artistic in all his handiwork, while all his habits, customs, tales, and traditions are based upon a sense of the dramatic, with the ancient philosophy of progenitors much more in daily use than with us.

This trend of thought was brought to my attention daily as I observed the manner of behavior of my two respected companions. The very purpose of our mission here was not to hunt and kill animals but to see and understand the babies of the animal domains.

Moving into an area among the most picturesque of the lichen-covered boulders, Wela said, "Oo-yax-w" which means rock town. But to him it was a reminder of a home town in Greenland, near which he was born, a desolate but picturesque area on the south shore of Inglefield Gulf where seals, walrus, and narwhal are abundant.

Etuq said, "No, it is more like Karnak, where the great
spirit brings forth the young of every kind of life. There I
as a boy sought the baby nests. I will do the same here."

The dogs were tied in two groups to rocks. Together we
started off over the desert wind-swept earth. There was little
snow and but little vegetation in the immediate vicinity. No
glaciers or mountains were visible. Excepting a few lemming
tracks, there were no signs of moving life. The temperature
was near the freezing point, at about 35°, but to us it was
warm. Nearing the end of June, the season—judged by that
of Greenland in the same latitude—should be farther advanced. Was the summer late or was the land a sterile waste?

These important questions entered our conversation. Over
the first gravel bank we came to a pool of water. It was not
clear crystal water such as we had sparingly used before, but
it was natural land water a little muddy. Lying down on
some flat rocks, we drank the turbulent liquid with the relish
of famished desert folk. And, camel-like, we did not move
away until we had an overload of drinks inside. Then we
fetched the dogs and gave them the same luxury.

How we loved that land! And yet the first appearance
was that of a picturesque desolation. The Eskimos separated,
wandering farther and farther into the unknown—Etuq going north to find the patch of green seen the day before
from the pack; Wela going southeast to find something, but
having no idea what to look for. I went back to camp with
the dogs and there began to mend our outworn equipment.

As the hands found work, the loneliness and silence of
this seemingly dead world engaged the head until my heart
hungered for some kind of sentimental appeal. I looked at
the dogs rather steadily as they turned in the sun to better

feel the feeble heat. I had thought that they were asleep, and perhaps they were, but every few moments one would rise, sniff the land air, and then sit down with the little, pointed ears shifting. The aroma of the land was good but the silence worried the dogs as it did me. If there was a sound or a smell in the air it was not sufficiently definite to be exciting to the canines.

To me there was a distant rumble—the grinding, cracking ice of the polar sea against some rocky point. This noise, coming in muffled tones at long intervals, made the silence of the icy wilderness more impressive and more disheartening. I had heard the frozen thunder from so many angles for so long a time that it was a message of gloom, a reminder of the battle for life against hunger and despair of regions farther north.

The potential power of the expanding circumpolar ice pack against the surrounding lands on a point of which we were camped would probably turn all the wheels of our machine age. But how could we harness this wasteful expenditure of energy? To the present it had harnessed us to a fate which might end in death. And yet, as I sat there trying to mend and devise means to enable us to survive, I wondered whether Nature wastes anything. The polar regions deliver the power which by elemental contrast circulates air and water. Without this aid life on earth would not be possible. Furthermore, to life in the aggregate even death supplies fertilizer to enliven plants, while to surviving animals the body, the product of death, is not only fertilizer to land but food for other hungry animals who have an equal right with us to subsist; and thus ages of death revitalize other ages of life.

While thus mentally adrift between breathing spells of

trouble, the making and breaking of the polar pack which had so nearly destroyed us seemed worthy of further study. Such tremendous power must have some good in it for the benefit of mankind. It is hard to be at enmity with Nature, even when forced to meet it as a bitter foe. After all, bitterness is an important ingredient in most tonics.

Hours passed while waiting for my kindly savage companions. Occasionally I could see them wandering over far-off hills. Their interest now was my interest. Their pleasure was my pleasure. I had placed no limit on the time they were to stay or upon the character of their activities. I knew them well enough to understand that whatever they did was for our common good. Like the dogs, with eye, ear, and nose, I felt for something within the sense horizon that might be helpful.

The wind was from the south. It was a kindly wind, bringing harmony with what seemed like messages of peace and good will from homelands. In this wind, as it increasingly engaged my attention, there was a new noise, a blowing sound. When the recuperating dogs got this, one after the other rose and pointed their pointed noses and ears windward. The poor bony creatures became restless and began to howl in a wolf-like chorus. With voices increasing in vigor, they continued to howl. Then they jerked at their traces as if to face a turn with a polar bear.

Through my glasses I searched the channel ice. The tide was rising, permitting the ice to separate. Here and there were open spaces of blue water. Rising over one of these there came sprouts of spray. Was it walrrus, or narwhal or white whales? It surely was the breath of some marine monster, but I could detect no head, no motion, no living thing.

In about five minutes the noise again came from the same direction. Then I saw it was a whale, with two babies, the right or Greenland whale, the precious whalebone whale then scarce and valuable. This was a discovery of great importance, for the Greenland whale had almost vanished from its usual haunts in the North Atlantic. We were in the Pacific area of the Arctic sea. Had these valuable creatures sought security among the island channels of the American Archipelago? My anxiety was aroused. Thoughts came fast. What to do was the urgent problem. I could not venture out on the moving pack alone, could do nothing if I went to the scene of the monster mother with her babies. But how desperately I wanted to fly to get a better view!

The cracking push of the Arctic pack would, I thought, probably bring Etuq and Wela back. It did; for after all, this maddening stream with its upturned hummocks of over-sliding ice sheets was our only highway. Coming into camp along shore with smiling faces and each with a load of dry moss and willow roots and stems for a fire, the boys sat down on a rock with a grunt of gladness. For a long time they said nothing. They were tired and hungry, but expected me to give the order to move onto the moving ice. To me it seemed that food and rest, with the full benefit of the day's gladness, were now most important. We had fuel for a fire, meat to eat and big, dry rocks to sleep on. Such luxury might not be our good fortune for a long time on the wet ice as we drifted south. So I said, "Let's make a fire. Let's eat and sleep where the earth is good to us."

The hungry dogs were given a fill of bear meat until too heavy to stand. Over a nice blazing fire we placed a pot of meat to cook. Then, half reclining on broken stone, we ate by way of an appetizer some raw meat. We had found an oasis of delight in an Arctic desert. How good it seemed to live! With this wonder region before us and the prospect of other lands farther south richer in the life that might better feed us, why should we worry?

Etuq opened the conversation to record the day's doings. He had gone straight to a green depression, a dimple on the face of good Mother Earth, and there he had found the lemming nests. This discovery was first in the eye of his ambition for the day. He was led by tiny tracks in sand to a hole into a tuft of tall grass. With the steel-pointed handle of the ice ax, he began to dig into the burrow. The location was far enough above the bottom of the depression to escape flooding by the water of early summer thaw of snow. The burrow was upward, also to prevent being filled by water. As the channel was uncovered many ramifications appeared. All, in Etuq's judgment, had openings to the outside. At a fork of one of these side openings there was a roomy dome. In this there was a nest-like bed of dry grass and woolly fur. All was clean and neat and dry.

The lemming den with its nursery had been vacated lately. The babies were already large enough to be mothered outside, so Etuq took up the search for feeding grounds, knowing their taste for grass and willow roots. He next searched the drier upper slopes where these roots were most easily secured. There he found many tracks and among them the tiny toe imprints of babies in great numbers. His search was rewarded by a sight of many groups. As soon as he approached them, however, the little ones would gather about the adults and then all would disappear in a burrow. The lemming, it seems, is best and most easily fortified not only against the hard elements but also against its enemies, the foxes and the hawks. How well Mother Nature provides opportunities for even wild rats!

While digging about among little patches of bunch grass and dwarf willows he found resting places for the Arctic hare, but all were deserted. The habits of these creatures were not new to Etuq. He had sought them in Greenland ever since he was able to walk. He knew that the mother hare with its babies sought ever higher ground as the season advanced, to secure the tender young sprouts which come up within a few days after the snow melts. And, since snow melts first at the seashore and last on the upper slopes, there is a succession of gardens of delight provided by Nature for these hardy bunnies. So upward into the cold mist Etuq climbed and there he saw many happy hare families, the adults white, the babies straw-colored with rusty streaks, at school with their elders, learning the art of finding the tenderest green of all the scarce greens in a world predominantly white and gray and blue.

One hawk and several ravens followed Etuq wherever he went. Their nests and their babies he had seen before, and since their wings carried them far from their own nesting places, no attempt was made to locate their homes. But a few ptarmigan and some snow buntings had been feeding in the same areas chosen by the lemming and the hare. Though these in all their home habitats were known to him, he was eager to study their nests in this most desolate of Arctic lands.

He found, however, that their habits differed little from the life in Greenland. Having fewer enemies, they were less wild and less cautious about hiding the location of nests.

They ate grass, plant seeds and some lichens, built their nests among rocks not easily found by hawks or foxes. He found a snow bunting nest on the top of a high rock protected against foxes by perpendicular sides, hidden from hawks in a little cave along a crack with an overhanging roof of stone. The ptarmigan nested almost anywhere in rocks among grass. One ptarmigan nest was found built up among eroded rocks.

Wela, ever restless and excitable, became more so as Etuq calmly recited his experience. He was by nature a killer, a carnivorous animal to whom every living creature was a prospect for food. Etuq was a lover of animals and killed only when the urge of hunger forced action. On this day I wanted nothing killed. We had more meat than we could carry by our troublesome route. I had tried to make this clear to both. In starting, there had been some discussion about weapons of defense. Ordinarily the Eskimo feels safe with the bow and arrow or the harpoon and lance. We had no native implements. In launching out over the lifeless polar sea, the prospect of finding game was too indefinite to be encumbered with these. Furthermore, we figured that in an emergency we might make new weapons from the hickory and metal of our sleds.

Wela said, "We are in a strange land, where bears, wolves, and hostile humans might attack us."

Etuq was satisfied with the ice ax; Wela asked for the .22 rifle. I gave it to him with the understanding that it was only to be used if he were attacked.

Now Wela had a tale of woe and disappointment to tell. He had been following game trails all day, had seen lemming, snow bunting, ptarmigan, hawks, ravens, foxes and wolves. All in the air or on the ground had babies some-where. He saw the nests, the dens and the tracks which indi-cated that youngsters were about in great numbers.

The foxes and wolves excited Wela very much, so much so that in his account thoughts came faster than he could find words that I would understand. This made him stutter a little. The animals had no fear, were inquisitive, and came up to within shooting range. The adult foxes were yellow, still in a ragged winter coat. The babies were a light rusty brown. He saw no blue foxes. Several groups of foxes were seen but they did not bark like the blue variety of Green-land. One group of wolves followed at some distance all day. They howled at him when far off but were silent when they edged up around the rocks to look at him. In color the adult wolves were nearly white with some gray along the back. The young were darker. In size and behavior all were much like Eskimo dogs, but larger. There were two adults and seven youngsters. They made no attempt to attack but on one occasion came too close for his comfort.

Tracks of a small herd of musk oxen with babies were seen. Fresh dung indicated that the animals were not far away. Many old reindeer tracks were seen. The fresh track of a mother and calf were noted not far from camp. Some seagulls were observed at a distance over the shore ice. No bear and no bear tracks had been seen. Wela had not climbed into the high lands. The land as a whole was very rocky but there was found much grass, moss, and willow, for reindeer and musk ox to eat. This ample vegetation, coupled with the observation that hawks, ravens, foxes and wolves were in evidence, indicated that game was abundant, and that if we were eventually stranded in a worse place we might return to this land.

Wela had a dramatic sense, and usually held back something, the best of his story, as a climax. I said, "Yes, where animals have their babies, there the earth is good; but what else did you see? You have not yet told us all."

Wela turned as if ready to perform a magic trick, and then said, "Yes, I found this," handing me a stone arrow-point. Then, silent for a moment to let the surprise arouse Etuq's sluggish temperament, he said, "Yes, people have lived here. I found the place of an old Eskimo settlement. Three tent floors with the stones all in place. There were not many bones about. The people did not eat much."

This was indeed news of great moment to us, for it proved that we were back to where people had lived and where we could survive. The finding of a stone arrow-point at the ruins, however, indicated a very old abode. It might be a hundred or a thousand years old. Furthermore, Eskimo tent rings are found over much of the coast near the north-ernmost lands. We longed to stay longer and explore more of this wonderland, but the ice jam was now in motion and after a good rest we went with the ice to reach out for a place where living people now exist.

Perhaps my most important discovery here was gained by a better understanding of myself. The same is true of Wela and Etuq. When food out of the mental horizon is reduced, we must root in and spread out like the desert plant. Everything that the eye, the ear or the nose brings into the field of feeling perception becomes a study with keen interest and lasting profit. We left this seeming desolation with enraptured souls, because with little else to engage the brain we had sought and found the animal babies of the icy wilds who, with double animation under double motherly love, rapidly attain maturity and self-dependence in a short summer where snow and ice are never out of sight. To us, who for months had been in the abysmal depths of dire want, with the borderland of death just beyond, this study of the cradle life of wild creatures afforded a divine inspiration. Where animals can live and nest their young, there surely we should be able to travel and survive. And, if we survived, this experience would serve as important schooling useful ever after.

n

↑

7

A WEEK OF INDECISION

We now had struggles of a new kind. The land from which we had departed too rapidly had for us a strange lure. It is on the map as Grinnell Peninsula, but we called it Baby Land. And thus it proved to be after many other visits further along the south. The pack of the channel jam became less and less serviceable to us as a means to drift southward. Along the shore of Baby Land the coast became precipitous. The water there was deep. Here and there was to be seen a rocky isle, where eider ducks nested in great numbers. Now and then a narrow green valley appeared to divide the low line of sea rocks. The heavy fields of ice slipped out of the jam and drifted to the east against land of greatest interest to us. This was favorable for landing and debarking. The small crushed ice seemed to separate and drift toward the opposite shores, indicating the trend of a current too dangerous for us. So we edged as closely as we could along Baby Land, going ashore whenever the pack was not moving. For a week we lived a life of luxury with indecision as to our future. This week in its lack of progress decided our fate for a long year of hermit existence.

In leaving the land it was necessary to drive the dogs with two sleds heavily loaded with meat over wobbly pieces of field ice. Since with drifting ice we could not divide the loads and make several trips onto the pack and back again, we must carry the full load or leave it. We had underestimated the difficulties and dangers of crossing this small shore ice. There were good safe fields of big ice about a mile ahead. In efforts to get to these the dogs missed jumps, the men slipped much and often lost footing.

Dogs and men were thus in icy sea water so often that it was necessary to throw away most of our meat. This to us indicated a calamity, but if we were to move on and not be lost in the sea the sacrifice must be made. The sledges were quickly unlashed and lightened and then on we went over the icy mire. As we reached the big ice, we noted that it was drifting rapidly towards a point of land five miles ahead. To get to a safer riding position we moved southwesterly for the midstream of the drift. Traveling was not difficult on this ice with light sledges, but the crossings from one field to the other were dangerous because of the rapidity and smashing crushes and sudden tilting of small pieces which acted as buffers between the heavy fields. These crossings worried us very much. If we continued we might be separated and go adrift in different directions, for the ice had many counter-currents.

We were wet. The dogs were wet and though the temperature was only just below the freezing point—28.5° above zero—we shivered and felt colder than during the winter nights. There was no means of drying our clothing. The rapidity of ice action was such that we must keep ready and in motion. No fire, therefore, could be started. We must rest on sleds in ever-ready positions. How we longed to go back to Baby Land and sleep on the safe bosom of Mother Earth!

We were anxious to go south speedily but the rapidity with which these fields went to destructive disruption indicated for us a similar end. We held on for a while because at the time there was nothing else we could do. Beyond the rocky point the coast had a straight southeastward trend, but the shore was abrupt cliffs of low rocks, difficult to reach from the ice. There was some water along the shore in that direction. Rising to a hummock for a better point of observation, at a time when the ice jam was maddening in action, I saw that the ice stream was soon to fork. The active current, taking mainly the smaller ice, was going due south, into what is mapped as Queen's Channel. The bigger fields were going more slowly and edging the coast to the east. It did not take us long to decide what to do. The stream to the south was a hopeless mass of ice, where only animals with wings or flippers would be safe. We loved Baby Land and we were in urgent need of big ice for our means of travel. Our course was shaped accordingly to the east.

When next we were again able to breathe at ease, we were

on land, on the shores of Baby Land. Of all ice horrors the past twenty-four hours gave us the worst jam. So dangerous was this adventure in the smashing channel pack that for us the hope of getting through to Lancaster Sound, where we might find whaling ships and other Eskimos, was now about shattered. We must find some way of moving along land and must begin to think of some alternative in case we failed in the original plan towards the Magnetic Pole.

During the twenty-four-hour torture on the pack, we had little to eat but raw bear meat and only water enough from our emergency can to satisfy the most urgent thirst. The hard work of shifting quickly from one ice field to another left us so weary and tired that we fell down on the rocks for a few moments' recuperation before any plans could be made to camp. The dogs, as much exhausted as were we, did the same. In a half hour we woke up in the shivering chill of wet boots and soggy clothing. We must make a fire to dry things and prepare something to eat. There was fresh clear water near by. How good it seemed to get a fill even of ice water, and how the dogs enjoyed it! After that all the world seemed brighter, though the sky was dark with a cold mist.

But to make a fire was for us at this position even on land a difficult task. We had lost about all of our bear and seal fat on the troublesome pack. There was almost no vegetation, except rock lichens. Etuq said, "If we live we must have a fire. I will try to secure some fuel up among the rocks."

Wela said he was so cold and stiff that he could not walk. Would we let him strip off his wet clothing and wrap up in dry skins long enough to get a little fire in his frozen blood?

"Yes," I said, "make yourself comfortable as best you

can, while we try to find some fuel." I felt about the same as
Wela did, but for me to lie down was to prolong the icy torture to a dangerous degree. Putting on some half-dry boots,
I also climbed up among the rocks to find moss or willow
sprigs. The exercise, I felt, would at least start up a better
circulation. Even if I found no fuel, from a higher altitude I
could get a better view of our surroundings.

Without much difficulty I climbed to an altitude of about
500 feet. There were local banks of fog and a frosty haze
preventing a comprehensive view, but we had come ashore
on a point of land which was the most sterile and desolate of
the regions for miles about. To the east, but a few miles
away, there was a rich green valley, and beyond, some black
cliffs facing the sea. In the valley I felt sure we would find
game, and along the cliffs I thought there would be found
bird rookeries. Though I could gather no other positive information, the distant outlook at least was promising for
something good to eat. There was some open water along the
land, but there was too much fog over the channel ice to
permit a view of the drifting ice conditions. In coming back
I found a few dry and some green willow sprigs, a little
moss and a few small dry bones. Etuq came back with about
the same news as to the outlook over land and sea. He
proudly carried an armful of moss and willows but he also
brought some old musk-ox dung which he said would make
a hot fire.

As we thus returned to camp carrying packs of doubtful
fuel, the dogs greeted us with a wolfish howl of delight.
Wela, stripped naked, rose from his bed of half-dried bearskin and got into his damp clothing, smiling with happiness.
We spent some time in an effort to build the foundation of a

lasting fire. In the center we placed a tripod of bones; about this, some moss and bits of dry willow; over all, a few strips of blubber; and above, some green willow. In the lee of a big rock, with a firebox of small rock, we soon had a nice fire going. When the green willow burned and sank into the mass of burning stuff, the musk-ox dung was added. This gave us a successful fire to cook and dry our things. In the meantime we had gained an outlook of good cheer with better prospects and had by exercise become warm, comfortable and happy.

Now for a time at least there was no need for economy of food. We had little, but still too much to carry with an overland and oversea route in prospect. We could carry the load more easily in our stomachs than on our backs, or on sleds that must be carried at times. So the gladdening order was given to get ready for a big feed.

We boiled pot after pot, bear pots alternating with seal. How good it tasted! There was no bread, no seasoning, no salt. But carnivorous animals need no salt, and no palate agitators from plants. We had been carnivorous so long that only meat, and plenty of it, was in demand. The dogs like ourselves, filled up, took a few winks and then ate some more. We had only one meal, but that lasted all day, a day of twenty-four hours.

In the meantime our future activity was acutely analyzed. Would we try to continue our efforts for Lancaster Sound, along Wellington Channel, or would we cross over the neck of Grinnell Peninsula and try to back-trail along Bay Fjord to Cape Sabine and to Greenland, over part of our route to the Pole? Or would we cross overland into Jones Sound and endeavor to find a way from there back to Annoatok? Wela

favored the Bay Fjord route. Etuq was inclined toward the
Jones Sound way of return. I tried to argue in favor of continued efforts to Lancaster Sound and there to board some
Scottish whaler. It was agreed that all plans must be suspended for a few days to learn what there was before us
along the land partly in sight to the east.

At the end of twenty-four hours of eating and resting and
dreaming, we rose to some higher rocks to study our prospects. Though the sun occasionally burst through clouds
and mist, low fogs still obscured much of the channel and
some of the land. The temperature on land was steadily a
few degrees above the freezing point. The wind was very
light—a mere air—shifting in direction. There were birds
about, eider ducks and gulls and guillemots in great numbers.
We had seen fresh fox, wolf, and deer tracks, but we saw no
moving land creatures except birds. From our point of observation we could see the green valley about ten or fifteen
miles to the east. Though we could not move our dogs with
all equipment over land without making back packs for the
dogs with a complete change in our means of travel, we did
plan to have two men with back packs to advance to the
valley, establish camp, and hunt while one remained with
the dogs and the heavy sled equipment.

As we came down to the sea, the fog of the channel pack
lifted and partly exposed the land to the north. It was high
tide. The pack began to move and spread. This interested us
very much, for we were seeking a piece of ice large enough
to serve as a raft, and of a shape to enable us to paddle and
steer it near the coast where there was some free water. The
ice nearest was drifting northward in irregular eddies. The
mid-channel jam was crushing southward. All sea ice was

now beginning to rot. There were pools of water on the large fields. Along the edges, sea algae were climbing out of the sea and planting themselves in the ice as soil. This ice vegetation was spreading rapidly, presenting spots and long lines of a rusty color which looked like earth-soiled ice, due to landslides. With the ice thus spotted, many darker spots appeared. These looked like animals but were usually shadows of algae holes in the rotting ice. We noted three such spots for some time with some suspicion.

Etuq, whose distant sight was best, said, "They move."

Wela said, "They are seals turning."

Through the glasses I was able to distinguish three four-footed animals. Passing the glasses along, both agreed that the spots were reindeer.

The animals were apparently as much in doubt as to their best direction as we had been while out on the channel ice, and, like ourselves, they were adhering to large fields of solid old ice. We reasoned that since this was the migrating season, the deer were bound northward. For a time we found it most profitable to sit down and watch the creatures. When it became possible to shift from one floe to another, they sought the ice nearest our shore. This chase excited us very much, for here meat was coming to camp. How heartless the hungry human is! Like wolves we were planning the strategy to capture every living thing. We were about out of meat. We knew the pain of hunger. The prospect of tender *tooktoo* steaks was worth more to us now than a bag of gold, or the aesthetic admiration of the graceful deer.

Would they linger on the pack, or would they continue to make for the ice nearest the shore and then swim for the point of land on which we were camped? They were bound for the nearest land but the dogs and the odor of our camp would frighten them. There was open water to the east but the near land in that direction was not enticing. Did the deer know of the green valley to the east to which we were bound? Apparently they did, for they were not in a hurry to start for shore. The shore ice was drifting northward. Did they know that in an hour the ice would drift southeast with the change of tide? The deer seemingly knew all that we knew and a lot of things we did not know. We were ill at ease. The deer knew the country and were contentedly waiting for an opportunity. We thus spent two hours in trying to figure what was in the eye and nose of the deer. In the meantime the ice on which the animals were taking a ride broke out of the pack and into the free waters to the east. We followed behind a ridge of rocks, hiding like cats with eyes on the game but ever ready to make a sudden onslaught.

About four miles to the east of our camp and but a short distance from our position at this time, there was a little flat land with a sandy beach. This we reasoned would be their place to swim ashore from the drifting ice. Our guess proved correct. When they saw the sandy shore, the three plunged at once and pulled for land. We had ample time to arrange our strategy. Fortunately the sandy landing area was short. The valley to which it led was narrow. Our problem was easy. We had only to hide behind rocks and await the deer's coming. Either they swam slowly or the water distance was greater than we had estimated, for we had a long impatient wait. Finally, would we shoot while the animals were wading or await their landing?

Wela said, "Shoot when they get their footing while still far out. At that time they will be paralyzed from the cold water and must move slowly. If they get on land they will jump and run fast to get warm."

The two guns went off—two deer dropped. The third one took four cartridges, and still kept coming. He passed out on shore. The boys had their boots and coats off in a few seconds and with only the bearskin shorts they plunged into the icy sea after their plunder. In a few moments we had three deer placed safely on the beach. What a luxurious wealth for men who expected to go hungry for doubtful days to follow!

In rushing over the land to find a favorable position of attack upon the landing deer, we had noted that a half mile from shore the country had by no means the sterile aspect at first presented. There were miniature valleys, lined by leaping streams, fed by melting snow of the high lands, and above all, the earth dimples were here numerous. Here we could find fuel and a beautiful environment for camp, with plants in full blossom, while the next stage of progress was worked out. But how could we bring the dogs and all the cumbersome equipment over land? This was a grave question growing daily in importance.

The deer proved to be yearling bucks of the white variety. They were quickly skinned and dressed and cached under heavy stones. This was necessary even if we left our catch alone for only a few hours, for the wolves, foxes, and hawks would soon devour the precious prize.

In going back to camp we decided that somewhere we would stop long enough to make back-pack harness for the dogs. We saw that the time was at hand when the sled use was over for the summer. The dogs must be trained as pack animals. This would take some time and a lot of patience. At camp all was packed for a sea journey over drifting ice. To unpack and carry all over land would take several days. Furthermore we were not yet ready either to abandon the sea as a route, or to refit for land journeys.

While thus considering our traveling prospects, the channel pack jammed against the land. The sea beckoned. We were ready. The sleds were placed on the ice, the dogs hitched, and we were off. About a mile beyond, the ice again withdrew from shore and there we selected a small solid pan for a raft. This we pushed along by poles from other ice, by paddles when no ice gave us a brace. Unable to hold to land closely enough, we got the canvas boat ready to launch if necessary to go ashore from an adverse wind or current. Though we were excited and much worried, the ice raft carried us safely to a point of rocks only a few hundred feet beyond the sandy beach where our cache of deer meat had been placed.

In the excitement of pushing the square of ice which had served as a raft against the shore, and holding it there long enough to unload our precious store, containing all our earthly belongings, it became necessary to jump into the shallow shore waters. In the heat of action, this did not seem cold, but when we tried to sit on rocks for a few moments of rest, the salty ice water between skin and clothing became intolerable. The dogs shook off the dripping icy slime, jumped and howled and fought each other to keep from freezing. We jumped and ran like madmen to keep the chilled blood circulating, but we shivered more during every second of the torture.

Unable to withstand the freezing wetness longer, Wela stripped off all his clothing. As his naked skin dried, he said,

"Oona," meaning "I am warmer." We did the same and to our surprise all quickly felt a glowing skin.

In a little while the sun burst through a frozen mist and then the gladness of a summer day was briefly with us. The joy and the advantage of the nudist cult was never better demonstrated.

A good camp site was now an urgent necessity. There were bare rocks and sandy dunes near by, but we wanted a dry grassy bed. The dogs were fastened to rocks. Pieces of half-dry bearskin sandals were lashed to our feet and then in the pleasurable nakedness we sought a place where we could eat and sleep and dry our wet equipment. As we scattered and rose over a barren coastal line of rocks and hills, the sun went into a mist. The sky became gray and a little snow fell. The icy crystals falling on naked skin produced a tingling sensation not at all disagreeable, but we wondered how long this snowfall would last. As we had about decided to return to devise some kind of shelter under rocks or sand, we saw, beyond, a wide green depression and on it the sun was shining in all its summer glory.

The seeming valley had in it no center line with a visible stream, but there were miniature lakes and pools of water surrounded by a dense vegetation of green grass and brown mossy slopes. We quickly recognized the area as a region of earth dimples about which there was for us a paradise of pleasure in camp comforts.

Returning to the rocks where the dogs called for our companionship, we took the hungry creatures to the meat cache and fed them on our load of tasty deer meat. In the meantime we each tied a wet deerskin, fur inside, over our shivering shoulders and later returned the dogs to an anchorage among rocks on a hill high enough to watch for bears, who might destroy our belongings and attack us while asleep.

Then taking such camp equipment as we required and such meat and fat as was to be of immediate use, we moved over into one of our newly found earth dimples. Then on a warm mossy shelf we sat down to build a fire and to eat and rest in comfort.

After sleeping about twelve hours, we were awakened by the call of the dogs. The sun was pouring down a heavenly wealth of light and heat. Hawks and ravens were hovering over our camp. White bunnies bounced over the green slopes. Ptarmigan and ducks and geese were flying to and fro from rock to rock and from land to water. Bright flowers engaged the eye, while an aroma of green glory long absent from our senses of perception gladdened the heart. We were indeed in an Eden of animated delight. Both Wela and Etuq wanted the pleasure of a week's stay here. But to me there was the responsibility of devising a way to meet the gloomy uncertainty of being stranded in a world where only the short summer offers living conditions.

n

↑

8

AN ARCTIC EDEN

How quickly we went from havens of delight to periods of suffering and despair! Perhaps hunger billboards the destiny of all mankind, but to us the daily limit of subsistence forced peculiarly an outlook not for to-morrow but for the long winter and the long night soon to come over us. To live we must move daily until we could see a way out from our seemingly stranded destiny. Much as we would profit by a short stay here, we must go along the desolate seashore for some time. If we went over land we could not move our belongings, and so back to the pack-ice and back to an ice raft with all our equipment. And thus we went from heights of delight to depths of despair.

In the excitement of working further along shore, moving the ice-float with equipment and the dogs, again we became water-soaked. We had no time to feel cold; indeed, icy water after a time causes the skin to suspend the sense of feeling. Desperate action, sponsored by an urge to live, compelled quick thinking and quick, sure footing. The experience was not new to us, but there was more wetness and the moist shivers were more prolonged. After we had pushed and paddled and drifted about ten miles on our course, discomfort was such that a landing must be effected. Selecting a natural pier of rocks, we again went ashore.

Now as we stood on land, temporarily safe from the pack-ice damnation, with the sun shining, the aroma of land, and the sound of happy birds, we felt, as we often had in our tragic adventures, that it is good to live. But our elation was short-lived. Our leather clothing was pasted to our skins with icy brine. When salt water begins to evaporate under the influence of human heat, refrigeration begins. Action and quick exercise was necessary to keep from loosing teeth out of chattering jaws.

We took off our water-filled boots. It was good, even with the air at freezing point, to feel the dry rocks under our bare feet. Wela, blue with cold, said, "We must have fire." He had gotten entirely under water. Even his long hair was dripping icy water. But how were we to make a fire? There was no fuel. The deer which we had secured were thin, as all are at this season. Even the marrow was but a pasty jelly. Etuq, silent as he always was when suffering most, climbed up among the rocks for a few hundred yards and there he found an old musk-ox bed, with a goodly supply of dry dung which, like sheep droppings, hardens into

marble-like balls. Taking off his sealskin coat, he packed a
load of the precious find and brought it to camp for fuel. In
a little while we had a good fire going and a pot of meat simmering. In the meantime we had stripped off all our soggy
clothing and were sunning ourselves with the pleasure of
bathers in summer at Coney Island. Was it good to live? Life
was never sweeter to any mortals on earth. We again danced
the delight of an Arctic nudist cult.

Unwillingly we had received a full sea bath, not a mere
dip, the first in many long months. Now we examined each
other's bony bodies for signs of cleanliness, a social heritage
to us long forgotten.

Said Wela to Etuq, "Your ears are sooty."

Etuq replied, "Your feet are sooty."

There is no Eskimo word for dirt. "Powq" (with sar-
casm) is the expression of condemnation for dirt, but this
word really means soot, the pasty blackness from oil lamps;
and, as with the use of all Eskimo words, the meaning implied is not so much in the actual meaning of the word but
rather in the manner of expression behind it. The primitive
talks with his whole body.

After panning each other some more, eyes were turned
upon my bathed but unclean skin. Said Wela, "Our skin is
yellow; yours is less yellow. I thought your skin, like that
of white men, was white, but now you are yellow. In
another year it will be dark as ours."

I replied, "Yes, my skin is yellow. The skin of all white
men is yellow, less yellow than yours. Under the skin all
men are yellow, but the human heart is red in the people of
every race and color. All men are brothers. All women are
sisters. Humanity is, or should be, a family circle."

"Yes," said Etuq, "but why do men kill each other? Why do the Indians hate us and why do we hate the Indians?"

I had given a drift to the stream of conversation too far from our mental habits. There was silence for a time while we dressed for dinner by hanging over our shoulders whatever rags of fur skin were suitable. While we were naked and talking of nakedness, the sun went under dark clouds.

Wela said, "I am naked inside—when do we eat?"

The boiling kettle was giving voice to the call of his stomach. The dogs by this time were dry, and they also called for food. For a couple of hours all ate and became filled to capacity. There was plenty of good water near by for men and dogs to fill up. After all our troubles, the day had a good ending and was followed by a long restful sleep on cold, hard rocks that seemed soft and warm by comparison with our ice and icy water experience.

On the next day all the world was bright. It was still misty over the high lands and over the channel ice, but the sun was warm along the shore. The black cliffs and dark lichen-covered rocks took the heavenly heat like stones about a campfire. There was little wind. The barometer was steady, indicating settled weather. The thermometer along the shore was 33° but a few hundred yards inland, along the warm rocks, it was 40°. Summer, we felt, was not here to stay. We should have given more thought to the danger of becoming stranded, but with the favorable outlook our immediate prospects there were good. We found food and shelter whenever we found a suitable place to camp. The land looked promising and if traveling became impossible, we could winter here and return to Greenland at the end of the next winter night when the sea ice would carry us in any direction. However, with the warm weather of July, August, and September before us, we felt that in some way we could find a whaling ship or a native settlement. Or, better still, find a way back to Greenland, workable by a combination of sled travel and canoeing in the canvas boat. In this spirit we securely tied our dogs in friendly groups to rocks and went inland to explore the terrain.

Passing over the rocky shelf of the shore, we entered a region of earth dimples within a little valley which drained these depressions. Some of the concavities were still filled with snow. In others the snow had but recently melted. Still others were gardens of delight with vegetation in full bloom. There were flowers in white, yellow, pink, and purple, a profusion of color with every shade of brown and green as a local background. But the land as a whole was arrayed in cold gray and black with a liquid blue pouring from the hazy heavens.

Though we usually went in different directions in examining land about camp, on this day we kept together and talked about the future of our journey. A few miles away we noted a strip of rock with considerable elevation, which looked like an igneous intrusion. To this we aimed to go to get a general view of our situation. En route we picked up some lignite coal, samples of fossil rock with impressions of the bark and leaves of ancient trees, some garnets, and samples of copper, graphite, mica and iron ore. Though none of these finds was in place geologically, it was evident that a mineral belt was near.

We also passed an old raised beach, covered by a spread of miles of sea shells. This area was lifted out of the ancient sea about 500 feet. Land levels, from this and other evidence, it appeared, had changed here very much. We saw lemming tracks, fresh fox and wolf imprints, and also signs of reindeer and musk ox. In the air were gulls, ducks, guillemots, hawks, and some ravens. Now and then there were a few snow buntings and ptarmigan, but the surprise of the day was the sight of geese. Around a little lake at a distance too long to shoot, we saw a pair of blue geese and a pair of white geese. This sight was a rare thrill even to the Eskimos. Immediately the question arose: Do they nest here? The time at our command for this day's work was too limited to search for geese nests, but how we longed to do it! There was something about the grace and beauty and intelligence of wild geese which fascinated us at all times.

From a point somewhat above the top of the volcanic rock, we had a fairly good view to the north, northeast, and south. Though level banks of fog obscured the horizon in other directions, there was much open water to the north, making a return to Greenland along that way impossible. Looking toward Jones Sound there was still to be seen much snow on the land, but the crossing in that direction seemed low. This, then, was a possible route if we failed to go much farther south. The valley to the east which we had seen from other points was very small and so closely lined by low rocky bluffs that even on land we would there have difficulty traveling. The shore line from our camp southward was also not promising as a road to anywhere, for it was interrupted by low rocky elevations with rough stratas and cliffs. If we were to get anywhere, we must still follow the sea on drifting ice for some distance.

In going back to camp we saw that the channel pack was spreading landward. We prepared to take another ride with the ice drift. Without much difficulty we embarked on a heavy field which bumped the rocks just beyond a sandy beach and became grounded. The tide, however, was rising and this we knew would free the field to float somewhere. On this field we slowly drifted east, some distance from land, for about twelve hours. Then all the pack was again crowded up on shore and there we got off to study the land and the condition of the jam of ice in the channel.

Navigating as we must on ice floats, the landing was usually effected on projecting capes, mostly rocky points of land. To find land, game, and a camping ground covered with grass and moss such as we longed for, with running streams, it was necessary to enter bays and valleys. Thus, to live and find subsistence, progress on our chosen route was much interrupted. We were near the end of the easterly trend of the land with its favorable exposure to the south. This land was dark in color; the darkness, though gloomy, better facilitated the absorption of heat from the summer sun, and chiefly because of this negroid face southward, it is the place of birth for hardy Arctic creatures and plants.

Ahead, the outlook was not good. We were near the head of Pioneer Bay, a huge indentation where only small bays within the big bay had streams and valleys and vegetation. Beyond, on the distant horizon toward the south could be seen Mount Providence, a weather-beaten peak, perhaps not more than 3,000 feet high, but it stood in bold relief because the other land about it in most places was only about 1,000 feet in altitude. The coast here turned southward, cold gray in color, with no indications of life. To the north of Mount Providence the winter snow still covered the land. I reasoned that if this was sufficiently extensive it might offer a

sled route east to Jones Sound. We were now at the parting of two possible ways. Should we go east or should we
continue along the coast of North Devon, south to Lancaster Sound? Our future existence might depend upon decisions which must be made here.

My Eskimo companions, even after but a casual examination of the prospects of going further south, were opposed
to further movement in that direction. There might be no
whale ship. There might be no Eskimo camps within reach.
The gray, forbidding land before us had in its sterile aspect
the look of death. They were also opposed to an overland
journey into Jones Sound at this time of the year. To them
the coast of Jones Sound was infested with demons. Many
Eskimos, according to native legends, had been killed there.
They were still fascinated by the living prospects in Baby
Land and suggested wintering somewhere near. Though the
land had for me a similar fascination, I was not sure that
we could survive there with our lack of equipment, as isolated as we were from all other human life. To me there
was before us the advantage of midsummer. In favorable
weather, we should go somewhere from which escape during the current season would be possible. But on the whole
I agreed about the doubtful prospects southward. In this
spirit and with these ideas of doubt as to our future movement, we now determined to explore the land.

It has not often fallen to the lot of explorers to find the
sea bottom lifted above water and there left for examination, little changed except by weather erosion. Such a submarine landscape was here before us. How we longed to
linger to further study the handiwork of nature over passing
ages of topographic change! We are inclined to regard land

as the most permanent example of solidity, but land levels are less stable than sea levels. Though our visits had been too short, we had seen in part how this fascinating land of mystery rises along successive shore lines, exposing the uplift of older sea levels. A great mountain mass had here settled slowly into the sea and was again rising, exposing for our observation the tops of eroded peaks. About these ancient subsea mountains were fossils, minerals, coal, sands, and shells of the seashore and massive rock-embedded materials indicating life and conditions of remote geologic times.

And here under our eyes was the recent favor of a new creation, supplying a place for alpine vegetation to survive. Here migrating creatures found an Eden of delight to bring forth and nurse their young. One would hardly expect such a discovery within an oasis of the icy desert so near the end, so near the northward limits of lands of desolation. We wanted to know more of this wonder area, but our strained eyes closed to a needed sleep, while anxious premonitions of an uncertain future continued to trouble three stranded mortals nearing the grim test of a right to live.

n

↑

9

ENTRAPPED WITHIN OURSELVES

On a bed of rock and turf, I turned
from side to side, trying to read in the sleeping faces of my
companions the prospect of eventual endurance. Though
well fed, the possibility of physical failure worried me
greatly at this time. The immediate whither of lands that
could better offer a safe highway homeward would require
a long continued drain on our energy. New strength must
be generated and conserved, but conservation of bodily
force was not easy for us under the excitement of our situation.

After a worried sleep of eight hours, we rose to make

such investigations as would decide our fate. Etuq was to follow the coast westward and then go inland to the north. Wela chose a route inland to the east. I was to follow the coast south and then push inland. By this division of routes we believed we could in one day sufficiently examine the region to start on a new route for somewhere the next day.

We were in good health but still very thin. The weather was settled but somewhat hazy at times. The temperature was 37° but as we walked we were easily overheated. Carrying our sealskin *netshas* (coats) in arms, with torn boots and ragged bearskin pants and woolen shirts but bareheaded, we climbed over the near-by rocks and were soon lost to each other.

To me the rough coastline, though more barren, became intensely fascinating. Along the first few miles, I discovered many signs of ancient Eskimo wanderings. There were ruins not only of winter igloos but also summer camps, represented by tent stones left in the familiar oblong lines. These indications were old, very old; so old that few bones could be found about the remains. Looking about these old home sites, I saw several man-made domes of stone. These were graves, but the sacred resting places had been robbed, perhaps soon after the burial took place. The thieves were perhaps both human and wild animals. With a passing Eskimo, some of his favorite implements are buried. Since parts of these are stone, or ivory or iron or, as in the case of children, toys of ivory or bone, such hand work endures for ages. There was little or no soil to floor the grave, and though I dug in and searched, nothing tangible was found. The absence of such remains indicates human pilfering. None of the skeletons was complete and all graves were open. This would seem to indicate that the dead were robbed of parts of the body by foxes, wolves, or bears.

The graves were too numerous for the number of camp sites indicated. This would seem to imply that all had died, not a good prospect as a stopping place for us. I went on with mental blues and cold shivers down the spine.

A mile or two beyond, I found the beach strewn with whale bones. A wounded whale or one whose end came without warning had here beached its remains. The bones were white and eroded like old rocks, indicating the life of a monster that had long passed. It was the skeleton of a right or Greenland whale, the only variety with whalebone in his mouth. But most of the head was missing. Was this whalebone stolen or gathered by humans, or was it sent adrift in the sea?

Going over a neck of land, I found the antlers of a half dozen reindeer bucks and a little farther along the skulls and parts of the skeletons of two musk oxen. The horns and bones were old, bleached, and splintered. There were no fresh signs of recent movement of deer or musk ox or bear, but numerous tracks of lemming, foxes and wolves. There were very few birds about. Surely my route along shore had little of the cheer of living to offer. It had on every side the evidence of life long dead, as the Eskimo had said in the first outlook. But I continued further along and there I found large pieces of wood that had drifted ashore on some very high tide, and had been pushed farther inland by ice—a piece of spar of a vessel, a hatch door, and several planks. Some ship had gone to the sea bottom. Did it carry its crew to a watery grave or were they left to freeze and starve on land as did Franklin and his crew? Death—nothing but signs of death all along the coast to the south. And the entire reach of Wellington Channel was jammed with a backwash of small ice—too small for sled travel, too dangerous to risk for drift progress—and it was jamming northward. There was nowhere enough water to risk a canoe journey by the canvas boat.

There was no hope for subsistence or for progress by any means at our command along the land or over the sea. I next went inland.

In going overland I found myself close to a belt from which the huge winter drifts of snow were only partly melted. On the rocky ridges all was dry and gray. Only a few lichens rooted in rock cracks on the south face indicated life. These, however, were beautiful. Even Nature in its worst manifestations devises color to delight the eye. These Arctic rock lichens represent a form of living death. It would require the use of a microscope to determine in the substance of the plant where life ends and where death begins. To the eye and to the sense of feeling all the tissue seems cold and withered and devoid of life, but underneath, near the rock roots, there was some cold pasty substance in which future generations germinated. In color and form the lichens decorate the rocks with sublime magnificence. Here the rocks as a background were a dull, ashy gray—the lichen in black, blue, and straw-color so light that it often seemed white. In the endless profusion of these simple blends I was fascinated. If life and death in the human realm could thus be so beautifully portrayed, the grave would be a garden of glory.

Between these dry, rocky uplands were the ever-glorious earth dimples, depressions veiled with snow for ten months of each year. The depressions were small, visible mostly at close range. The withered uplands were extensive. This gave the entire country, when seen at a distance, the aspect of a forbidding desert. And in effect all the land was a cold Sahara, for the green dimples were mere disks, plant dots serving as oases in a frozen no man's land. But how I had learned to love those spots! On this day's travel a little snow still hung on the sides or rested in the lowest levels. Along the edge of this melting snow, grass and moss and a profusion of alpine plants began to sprout at once as the snow melted. Often green shoots would push through the snow. A few yards further from the banks of icy crystal some plants were already in full blossom. In those places I found the Arctic hare and the ptarmigan seeking tender morsels of food. Not far away were lemming and from the distant hills came the call of the wolf and the fox. In the air were a few birds: some talkative ravens, and an occasional hawk. To those accustomed as we were to an abode on the landless, lifeless ice of the polar sea, here was the Garden of Eden for little living things.

How my heart thrilled as I next went in search overland for a route which had sufficient continuous snow to offer a highway—the very object of my local search also proved that even snow had a use, warmly to blanket and water the soil.

I came back disappointed and glad. When sadness and gladness get mixed, existence becomes doubly interesting. From my day's observation, it seemed impossible to go further south during this season but it was possible for us to go east into Jones Sound, and perhaps southward later, where a better food supply would be found.

Returning to camp, I found that both of my companions had returned. They had fed the dogs, had made a fire, and had a pot of meat boiling. They too were glad. Against the dangers of our position, they had seen a land which pleased them very much. I related my experiences while drinking broth and eating a stew of hot meat.

Wela first reported his days' exploration. He had gone far east where, from a high point, he could see that progress southward was hopeless; but to the east we could go by an all-land route, and also southeast over old banks of continuous snow. He had seen many old reindeer horns and musk-ox heads but no fresh tracks. The land generally was dry and ridged with low rocky ranges, but there were some narrow green valleys and many of our favorite earth dimples. There were many foxes and wolves. The foxes were all white. They followed him and barked like dogs, but the wolves kept off on the hills. He thought the wolves were mainly mothers with young ones. Wela had seen many Arctic hare and brought back six. The country as a whole enraptured him.

Etuq had seen much more and made more detailed studies. He had seen signs of old native habitations—places where people lived during winter and summer. But the ruins were old. There were many graves but also stone mounds where meat had been cached. Along shore he had seen many parts of whale skeletons, and also parts of wood and some glass and iron from white men's ships. From this he concluded that the whalers had been active near here, and while killing whales had themselves been wrecked. Inland the country pleased him very much. In a lake he saw some large fish, and near there a considerable number of geese, both blue and white; lemming, snow bunting, ptarmigan, hawks, and ravens were everywhere numerous. The interior was rough and rocky but green grass and flowers covered about all valleys and low lands. We could go overland but it must be afoot. There was no snow of sufficient extent for sleds. In coming back along shore, he saw several seals, many gulls, and a great number of eider and long-tailed ducks. He brought back eight eiders. Etuq was delighted with the land and would prefer to stay here for the next winter and then return to Greenland by way of Eureka Sound and Bay Fjord.

Since we were all fascinated by Baby Land, and since this day's doings were really a pleasurable adventure on the neck of Baby Land, it now became necessary to examine carefully into our prospects and longings and hopes for the immediate future.

After a good rest, I said to the men, "We will examine further into the direction of the next stage of our journey."

That night I slept like a seal. It was a snug sleep on cold rocks. Turning every four or five minutes as the seal does to examine the horizon for friendship or enmity, I did a lot of thinking in efforts to devise means to relieve us in our desperate straits. Further south was from here impossible. Further delay was imprudent. Our meat supply was about all used. We could survive on birds but this would quickly exhaust our limited ammunition. We could not secure enough game to feed the dogs. We had, including the canines, thirteen mouths to feed, and each tongue called for about three pounds daily. We might overcome this, as my companions had suggested, by devising new implements of chase. However, a delay of a few days more meant a delay for a year and possibly death for all in the unknown of our isolation.

But we had discovered mystery and promise in a new wonderland. To each of us there was the urge to stay and build a new home in a new world. The exploring incentive to us was about as strong as the desire to live. We had lived so long under the whip of famine that hunger was really a pleasant passion. But this hunger was from all the senses and all the bodily tissue. We were hungry to see, to hear and smell and touch things. When we came out of the long battle against famine and frost in the midpolar basin, we were physically so thin and reduced in body capacity that only the tissue vital to further existence remained under our shriveled skins. Our animal status was like that of the reindeer at the end of a long hard winter night. All was atrophied. All substance that could be spared in the animal economy was absorbed and burned to keep the embers of life aglow for action. Like hibernating animals when the season for renewed life opens, we were eager to exercise every function of the system as, under fresh meat, our bodies now gained something like normal expanse of cellular substance. Rejuvenated tissue has a voice which calls for functional exercise. Within us there was this desire of new interest, and in many respects it was irresistible.

It is hard to convey this subhuman—or perhaps it is a superhuman—strain to those who have not long been denied the wants of a normal existence. We were nervously excited, almost hysterical to do things, locally, when our only thought should have been to plan for the escape from our trapped position.

All the world was open to us but we were entrapped within ourselves.

Grinnell Peninsula we must leave behind if we were to get back alive to our home environments. We had seen enough of it to understand that it was a favorite garden of life for animals. It is an Arctic Eden for the creation and recreation of animal migrants. It is swept by destructive winds but on all sides the polar ice jam is so active that open water must exist somewhere at all times of the year. The damnation of storm and milling ice currents, death-dealing to humans, here becomes an asset to modify the climate so that hardy creatures of the sea migrate at will. The air and waterborne life does not go much further north. Its haven is in the south. But the four-footed animals and perhaps humans go north to stay. Perhaps the barren-ground caribou is an exception, but even some of these have reconditioned themselves to stay as the white reindeer does. The hare, the fox, the wolf, and the bear do not return south. These animals have put on better coats of fur and developed a kind of intelligence which enables them to stay and enjoy the vigor of the ice world. The musk ox and the lemming are ever headed for the Ultima Thule, the end of land, the shores of the circumpolar sea. And they keep going, generation after generation, to be lost in the night or sterile sea of the farthest north. Here is a tragic trend in animal life for which at present there is no adequate explanation.

With my sense of reasoning adrift along serious problems of nature of this kind, I rose from my couch of granite after a sleepless rest for twelve hours. In talking to my companions, I found them so entranced with the local environment that they again and again expressed a desire to stay in Baby Land for a winter. Their first interest in life was the art of the chase, and they had new ideas to put into execution here. I could understand this lure, for the Eskimo is by habit an explorer with the capacity for invention and imagination. He gets as much pleasure from the shaping of a new device to secure animals as a poet or a painter does from creative work. With new problems to be worked out bearing upon our future, and to be put into execution, we could not stay. I could not afford to offend my primitive helpers. It therefore became necessary to offer a theory of travel which would suit their present ideas. To fit this situation I proposed that we should move all our belongings to some point in the middle of the neck of Baby Land. This would be near enough to the all-snow route into Jones Sound, and equally advantageous for a stay. The plan was promptly approved. In a short time a plan of action was agreed upon. A few hours were spent in explaining a route, and then all was ready to move over and into a new land of hope.

n

↑

10

BURIED IN MIDSUMMER SNOWS

We had learned that the only system
of successful travel over these Arctic lands in summer was
with an equipment so light that all could be carried on the
backs of men. Even dogs trained as pack animals are of little
use inland, for their food capacity is greater in weight than
their capacity to carry. Where big game is scarce, dogs as
pack animals are not satisfactory. We had often discussed
this, and in our desperate straits to make progress the thought
of throwing all but back packs away was daily considered.
With the kind of land before us we could sleep on rocks,
find shelter in caves, and secure meat enough to survive for

ourselves but not for the dogs during the current season. We were a long distance from human help if stranded before the long night. To winter without a reserve of fur, fuel, or meat was ever a challenge. During the summer, so close to the sea, we needed a boat; during the winter we must have a sled. If we were to live and continue to survive in the atmosphere of our present and future uncertainty, equipment for land and sea travel must be carried. From this urgency there was no escape.

What we were now undertaking was a very dangerous departure from our experience, where indeed life was seldom secure. We had, however, weathered hardship over sea and along land with such success that in looking backward that kind of life to us now seemed natural. But actually our exasperating troubles had only just begun. The first day overland to the interior with our complete equipment was hard. Nevertheless, there were thrills with every mile of progress. The land was beautiful and useful. Routing our line of march in zigzags from mossy slopes to grassy plains, over rocky portages, we left behind small lakes fed and drained by leaping streams of clear ice water. We left behind narrow strips of green in the valleys, and left behind the glory of the mossy, grassy earth dimples and the peculiar splendor of our beloved Baby Land. Ahead, all this became less and less apparent. We were to be submerged under obscuring mists. As we rose higher, all spread of plant life became less and less to mere patches of verdure, but here old snowbanks bridged the stony depths. With the load so packed that we could quickly load and unload the greatest weight from the sleds to our backs, permitting the dogs to drag the lightened sleds over grass or over snow-free ground and stones, we moved slowly but encouragingly toward the regions of permanent snows.

We camped for a midday rest beside a small clear lake. In this we saw some salmon trout. With spears and snares quickly devised, we secured in the course of an hour seven fish, each of good size. Not far away there was a patch of willows, the largest we had seen. Some of the stems were a half-inch thick and a yard high. To us this was a real forest of timber wood for a fire. We broiled some fish and ate without salt or flavoring. No full-course dinner was ever more complete. How good it felt to tap and pinch and rub the belly with a full stomach of fresh fish! The dogs received all that was left and their joy was at least equal to ours. With stomachs so full they were too logy to roll; they expressed their fun in fights. How they enjoyed the new vigor of healthful scraps!

En route we had seen geese, ptarmigan, hare, foxes, and wolves. The wolves greatly excited the dogs, but like all wolves seen here, they were respectful and friendly to our intrusion. We saw them either in mated pairs or in mother herds with young frisky cubs. No wolves ever attacked us. Extremely cautious, they seldom came within shooting range, but all followed wherever we went for long periods, giving us the howl-music of the wilds.

We were now 500 feet above sea level and in the route before us this altitude was steadily rising to the permanent snow line for this season at about 2,000 feet. We reasoned from the force of the draft of the winds that there would be found a lower pass which served as an air trough from the east. Progress after dinner was slow but steady over a rather even rise on a surface of grass, moss or snow. There were bare rocky ridges and many big loose rocks, but by keeping one man ahead as a trail scout, it was possible to drag the sledges without unloading to back service. The wind increased as we rose. The temperature fell. We were entering a cloudy haze which gave poor visibility, but the route in which we worked was lined with game trails. There were a few fresh tracks of deer, musk ox, and wolves; also many old footprints. Bones of creatures long dead were strewn all along. We even found the skeleton remains of bears, wolves, and foxes, the first evidence of death of these fast-moving creatures. Etuq said we could live where these land prowlers found food and, in my own confidence in our capacity to survive, I often said, "Yes, if man had the intelligence with which he is credited, he should be able to live where foxes die."

When too tired and exhausted to continue longer, we sought a camp spot on some dry wind-swept rocks. We were now far along in the pass and from points at times we could see the sea: east and west Jones Sound and Wellington Channel. Here we spent the Fourth of July in desperate efforts to keep from freezing in midsummer snows.

Sitting down on the cold rocks for a breathing spell before the camp arrangements were begun, we noted that the surrounding region of rock and snow was wind-rasped. Pasty snow filled the rock crevices and earth irregularities like wet concrete on a new road. This was ample evidence that we were in a storm trough but for us there was no alternative. We must push through here or go back to winter in Baby Land. We should have continued while the weather permitted, but human energy and dog power for the time had reached limits.

Our position on a saddle of dry rocks was not bad for camp under the weather conditions at the time. By moving a few big rocks and piling up some small stone, we could and did provide an open cave-like den as shelter for a fire, and in an emergency it might serve as housing against storm. We preferred this to tent shelter at this time. The kind of fire which would result from our peculiar makeshift for fuel was too smoky and dirty for the silk tent.

With us fire-making became an art. In the most hopeless desolation we usually found something to serve as fuel and a place to serve as a stove or a fireplace. We had an Eskimo lamp, a half-moon-shaped dish which we hammered out of copper to take the place of a native stone lamp. But here we could not get a position suitably sheltered for such a device. There were no willows and no musk-ox or deer droppings for fuel. Wela packed some old thighbones found by the wayside. These he broke and split and said, "Here is wood for fire." This to me was a new suggestion but I wondered how old weathered bones with no fat could serve as fuel. In a short time I was taught an important lesson in fire-making.

Piling up the bones in a tripod arrangement, he placed over the fractured bones some strips of fat. Then taking from his fire bag a little block of dry moss which we at all times carried as an emergency base for a fire starter, he lighted the moss and placed over this a small strip of blubber. As fire rose along the strips of bone, the fat from above came slowly down and filled the bone. The most important problem in this fire technique was to feed fat slowly from above. This fire, if you except smoke, soot, and fish aroma, was much like an Indian wood fire. It was small but gave off an immense amount of heat with very little consumption of oil. Over the fire we now set a pot of hare meat for a stew. In the meantime, by way of relishes, we ate first some fish leavings from lunch, then some raw fish, some raw duck, and giblets. Then a real delight—Arctic hare stewed with the plant greens of the stomach. It was only parboiled, but this was the usual limit to our system of cooking. A Paris chef could not have given us a more satisfactory meal.

To me this day of trouble had been the opening of a new school of life. We were living from and moving over land where Franklin and other explorers, bleached and blued in scurvy, had died with shiploads of supplies and equipment to aid them. We had almost nothing except native adaptability, but we lived in the thrill of native luxury.[10]

We had put the fire of life into dead bones; had put the products of the soil of a desert to such use as to extend our own lives. Surely we could live where foxes died.

We needed sleep very much, but about us was a condition which delayed bedtime: there was no sky. It was not dark, though it was the time of the twenty-four-hour day which by habit we called night. The sun was lost somewhere in a high mist, so thick that we could not determine its position. Now the low heavens were a dull gray blue, with a cold steel blue on that part of the land visible. Then it was gray with some pearl luster in the mist, again it was black, a blanket of gloom of the Arctic night on everything. We could see, but the objects seen were illusive. A little rock now seemed like a mountain, and again it was a mere dot on the surface under rapid transformation. When we thought we saw a little ridge across our path, we lifted legs to step up only to find it was a ditch. The angles of all slopes were distorted. What looked like an upward trend of the land surface was often a downward slope. We were mentally and optically deluded by the aspect of all about. All of this was not particularly new for us during the hallucinatory twilight of winter, but in our usual experience it was not a danger to be considered among our other troubles during midsummer.

Altogether we felt gravely ill at ease now, with uncomfortable premonitions for the future. We went to sleep in the open on wet rocks. The dogs howled and whined almost continuously. After trying unsuccessfully to go to sleep for an hour, I was not only uncomfortable but much worried with dark problems to be solved by such gray matter as I could put to work. I rolled over from one rock shelf to another to find a soft place. Sleep for me was impossible, but I could rest and think if the noisy canines could be reduced to silence. I went over to them and chatted in dog lore for a while, but their noses were in the air and all looked in one direction. I could see nothing and hear nothing, and to me there was no smell to the air but the pasty, freezing humidity. Going about a half mile in the direction of their pointing noses, I found a dead fox. It was not long dead, for the body was still pliable. I picked it up, heading for camp, and then I heard a fox bark at some distance.

A few hundred paces toward camp, I saw a suspicious object, partly covered with sand and snow. This on examination proved to be a dead wolf. The carcass of the fox and that of the wolf both were very thin and shaggy. I threw the fox carcass by the side of that of the wolf, and then returned to camp resolved not to tell of the discovery. My companions were too low in spirit for me to describe to them the sight of famished animals. The dogs, however, were not satisfied. Their shrill voices enlivened the dead world about for many hours, but the Eskimos slept soundly as I went back to my hard bed.

A few hours later, when I awoke from a momentary slumber, the dogs were silent. The air had become less pasty. There was no wind. All was still. I lifted the face cover from my furs and then discovered that it was snowing. It was a real wintry snowfall, not the scattered flakes seen in Arctic summers, occasionally like hail in temperate zones. "Now the weather will be better," was the glad thought, for the snow would take the icy taste out of the air. A windless snowfall in a region of icy storms such as our world had been, can be and was to us on this memorable day a restful joy. In this spirit we bedecked ourselves with the canvas sled covers and slept in peace for many hours.

We all woke up at once—men and dogs—and out of surprised eyes we gazed on a world anew, arrayed with a soft blanket of feathery crystal. The dogs arose, shook off the snow, stretched themselves, kicked like horses to free the fur-adhering snowballs, and then began to growl and fight. After this there was a reunion, for all sat with tails curled and gave voice in a chorus of wolf howls. In spirit we did much the same, except that we did not fight. All animal life has a way of expressing its appreciation of the goodness of Nature. Man, gifted with language and a recording system, can perhaps give a better mental picture in such a way that others may grasp his vent of gladness. But it is really doubtful if we have any pleasurable sensations not reached to some extent by all animation. So we were glad, men and dogs were glad, and gladness gives strong, refreshing heartbeats.

The sun was shining. The sky was blue and clear. The air was cold but freshening. It felt good to take a full free breath and not feel the gluey pastiness of the days previous. The snowfall was seven inches. How beautifully it gave a velvety softness and roundness to the weather-beaten rocky slopes! All was white in the glory of crystal splendor, but snow is seldom really white, being a crystal aggregation with no color to the individual crystal. Snow absorbs, reflects, refracts, and polarizes the color of the light over it. The color now changed with the change of the direction of the eye in its relation to the sun, and the trend of earth slopes. In one direction it was gold; in another it was orange; but over all, if carefully noted, there was a mass liquid from the heavens, which gave expression in a million variations of blue and gold.

How sweet it is to live in an array of splendor of this kind! This thought was in the feeling of each as we dressed for the day. We started out to examine the route to travel with fairly dry clothing, though our boots were as usual still wet and frozen stiff. There was no time for a camp-fire or for breakfast. We must move to get through the pass while the weather permitted, for a wind trough, a storm canal, an ocean air chimney between two great oceans like the gorge into which fate now forced us, can be an Arctic Inferno. We knew the dangers. To live, we must keep going.

We were thirsty, and like camels, must have water before the long hike over the snowy desert. After we had made a few miles through deep soft snow with the sleds cutting down to rocks over old icy surfaces, where snow, sand and gravel had mixed and frozen to form a conglomerate rock-like surface hard on steel shoes of the sleds, we became overheated. Beads of perspiration streamed along the lines of our sooty wrinkled faces.

Since we worked as the dogs did to aid in pushing and pulling sleds, we followed somewhat the habits of the dogs. Lapping snow to cool the tongue and quench the thirst, every few hundred yards the dogs sat down for a rest. We did the same. During these breathing spells, while exhausted and trying to rest, I was looking ahead to determine the trend of our route. Etuq sought water. Wela readjusted the loads and got the dog harness untangled. We could see very little from any position thus far. It was even impossible to determine if we had crossed the watershed of the divide. With a route winding about snow-covered hills, land visibility was limited to a mile or two ahead or behind. There was no wind, and the sun was shining. Even if the footing was bad, the weather outlook was good. In looking backward, I noted that at times our sled tracks looked blue when moving over a perfectly level surface.

I said to Etuq, "Perhaps under those blue lines of sled track there is a lake or a pool of water, and if so, at this time of the year the ice should be thin."

Etuq took the ice ax, went back and cut in. Much to his surprise, the ax went through with the first blow. Though he was famished for water, the danger of falling through thin ice to an unseen lake of unknown depth was such that he hastened back without a drink to tell of the imminent danger to all.

Further examination indicated that the sleds were on thin ice over the same water. We did not stop to drink or measure the depth of the water. If the ice went down, even a few feet of the icy water would so mire us that death for all was a certainty. With the spiked sounding pole I went ahead to explore a safe route to the unseen shores. The distance to the rising land slopes was not far, perhaps only a half mile, but the thought of a watery grave made that short distance very long. We spread out to divide the weight on the thin ice, winged apart like butterflies to find a safe resting place.

I went ahead on snowshoes, listening for and expecting creaking ice. Wela and Etuq, each behind or beside a sled, were even more anxious. If I went through I could throw the long sounding pole over the ice and thus remain afloat for a time. If the drivers went through, they could grab a sled. But if we had really broken through, the struggle in the mire of thin ice and snow would probably have prevented any attempt at rescue. Roping like mountaineers at this time and under these conditions was impracticable, but a coil of rope was ready on each sled. One was also across my shoulder. A rope to throw as a life line was thus ever at hand. For many other reasons these ready coils of line were always easy of access. But even with a line, we would be lost if much of the lake ice went down as it frequently does on pools where the water seeps off, leaving a lower level.

I had seen similar accidents before. One of my boyhood friends slipped through thin snow-covered ice into the Delaware River. Kynna, a friend of the boys, went into the Unknown off the Greenland coast. Thin ice covered by new snow is the most dangerous of all possible Arctic entrapment. We were in such a trap and knew it.

When eventually we reached solid rocks of the unseen lake shore safely, we breathed long breaths of relief, in a new lease of life. The thought so common after each calamity, "It is good to live," came now to each of us with a double thrill. My inner feeling now, as many times before and in the future, was "Yes, in our experience as it runs between the tortures of famine and frost, we have little to live for, but we have less to expect in death."

In considering the next move, a blind alley of indecision offered confusion in long minutes of hard thinking.

Locally the weather was clear, but to the east and west low clouds of mist brushed all the land in sight. We sat down on our sleds, ate some half-frozen meat and pressed some snowballs in our mitts to warm and take in bits as a drink. We were wet from a cold sweat, the reaction of a passing fear of imminent death, and now that our excitement was over, our clothing hung like wet blankets on our shivering skins. We could not go back. Forward was our only way. But what was there before us?

We knew we were not far from the sea of the opposite side. The shore of Jones Sound could not be more than ten to fifteen miles away. But could we find a gradual descent or were we to find precipitous cliffs ahead? While we were trying to plan a new route, the weather made decisions for us.

In a pass, weather can change suddenly without warning. Along lower levels on both sides it may be calm and clear or the reverse. But the floor of the pass for us was now a trough for the flow of almost liquid air to equalize conditions at sea levels.

Moving cautiously to the east, we found that our forced choice for a route offered a bad flooring for sleds. The deep soft snow so evenly blanketed all surfaces that we were unable to pick a smooth bottom. The sleds cut through, dragged on rocks and got jammed often in a mixture of sand, snow and rocks. Wet and half frozen, their feet and legs pasted with the freezing snow, the dogs frequently refused to go further. However, we made progress for a few miles. There was little change in the topography. At a breathing spell, while untangling dog harness and cleaning dog feet and legs of fur-adhering frozen stuff, we saw between the snowy domes ahead a little patch of blue sky. This was a gladdening sight. Were we breaking through the pass?

Wela said, "Yes, in that blue is the sky of the other side."

With the renewed vigor of a fresh urge, another start was made. A little later this bit of clear sky did not look so well. Smoky fragments of clouds were rising into and tumbling out of it. A storm was brewing. What could we do for shelter? A storm with the amount of loose snow on the surface could give us an awful experience.

To safeguard ourselves and the equipment from the danger of a storm where there was no means of erecting shelter or digging into the earth like ground rats, with the serious risk of being buried under mountains of drifting or avalanching snow, it seemed best to seek a lower level quickly. To push through somehow as rapidly as possible was clearly our first and best line of defense. The bottom of the air trough would have been the shortest route through, but we had sufficient warning of the danger of small lakes or moving pools of water-soaked snow. This entrapment must now be avoided, so we sought a safe route, winding as we had been doing before along rock-strewn slopes. How we hurried, worked and sweated with the arduous problem of finding footing among rocks in deep snow!

The storm blast struck us like a hurricane. At once the

air was thick with flying snow. The wind was warm. Soon the snow became more wet and pasty. There was snow from above, snow from below, snow sliding down the mountain slopes, snow from everywhere. We could do nothing but get between some rocks, where the wind would not tear us to pieces. Men and dogs huddled together like cattle in a storm. Thus beset we awaited our fate. The agony endured beggars description.

Only in our position can it be realized that 32°, the freezing point of fresh water, can become the hardest temperature to endure. Most life is destroyed by frost at or near 32°. A degree or two above and all about us is snowy slime; a degree or two below and frost begins to kill. The great worldwide danger to plant life by frost is of this nature. On the frozen sea we had withstood changes of forty degrees in a few hours without any great discomfort, but here in midsummer and on land not far from green plants in full blossom, we suffered discomfort and imminent dangers by a one-degree rise or fall of the thermometer from 32°.

We were hours in this position. Men, dogs, sleds, all our belongings in a heap, and all buried under drifting snows. Now it was thawing; again it was freezing. Soaked with ice water to the skin and then coated by a freezing sheet of sleet, could this discomfort be measured by the slide of the thermometer up or down only a degree or two? It was dark —not a night blackness, but worse. When we could open our eyes at all the air was so thick that we could not see each other a yard away. Feeling was now the only usable sense. Had we been submerged in ice water there would have been less suffering.

We were familiar with the gunshot wads of wind which

often mark the end of an Arctic storm, and waited for the interrupted rushes. But we had long to wait. When the teeth chatter and the skin shivers with but little internal heat in reserve, minutes can seem like hours.

At last, however, the wind eased. It became suddenly much colder. The pasty humidity fell, and then a few double blasts of passing air and the storm was over.

We pulled ourselves together, untangled the dogs, cleared the sleds of snow and ice, and prepared to move. There was as yet no sky and only a limited horizon. When we moved we must still move in a blind alley, but move we must to shake the frozen crystals from our clothing and equipment. When we had worked for an hour and again got into a sweat and out of breath, to our surprise, the air began to come from the Pacific side. At first the wind came in mild drafts, rather jerkily. This we knew to be a bad omen. A storm from the opposite direction was soon likely to follow. We must get ready to meet it if preparedness was possible in our position.

There was an overhanging ledge of rocks to the north. This seemed to offer a lee shoulder to the changing wind and it was in a position not likely to be swept by avalanches. Could we plant a camp there and weather the storm? The distance was less than a mile, but we must climb a few hundred feet. I went ahead on snowshoes to explore a route. The temperature was 2° below freezing and I hoped it would remain there or get colder until we could get some protection against a thaw. In about twenty minutes I was in a position to suggest a possible route and accordingly gave signals to advance, while with the footprints of snowshoes, I packed down a trail in deep snow for the dogs. In the meantime, the storm was following in a steady blow. As we started, the drift was a mere surface float of snow over a thin crust, but by the time we got near the cliff the air was so completely charged with flying snow that we had some difficulty in finding the cliff. When at last we were under and behind the protective rocks, we found that they did give shelter against the noisy blasts of wind, but the eddying air currents brought an excess drift of snow, so finely powdered that its frozen dust so pasted our eyes and noses that work or breathing became exceedingly difficult. We had, however, selected this as our nesting place and must somehow arrange protection as best we could.

The dogs settled down between projecting rocks to keep from being blown away, closed their eyes, wrapped a coil of furry tail about the nose to enable breathing through the fur as a sieve screening the snow out of the air, and went to sleep. If men had a fur-covered skin and a bushy tail, how much better they might endure the Arctic elements!

The slopes all about were such that any water from the melting snow would drain to lower levels. This was of first importance. By digging under the snow, we found some loose rocks, to wall off a little shelter. The loose snow was wet enough to pack like cement. In a short time we had a hole in the cliff, reinforced by stones, where three men could sit up. But there was neither room to stand nor place to lie down. Part of the silk tent served as a window. At last we had a nesting place. It was a rock-bound mountain den which in other weather might have been snug and picturesque, but in a snow-charged storm was stuffy and gave off a damp chill that pierced the body with a sickening effectiveness. However, we could open our eyes and could breathe without getting noses filled with wads of snow-powder. Here we were forced to stay for forty-one hours; eating only raw meat and squeezing snowballs for water, we gained some nourishment. At any rate, we kept alive to experience other and worse troubles—other and greater pleasures. Yes, men can live where foxes starve and freeze, but not often.

n

↑

11

DOWN FROM FROZEN HEAVENS

The storm broke suddenly, and as suddenly we were on our way to get out of the pass down from the frozen heavens. Etuq believed the spirit of demons ruled there. I was not yet converted to Eskimo religion, but in this I agreed with him. Since earth demons are supposed to feed on human trouble, surely there was food for devils in the sewage of weather in this highland trough of storms.

We had withstood the hardship of midsummer snow damnation without much damage to courage or physical power. Suffering from cold, lack of water, and insufficient food was now a normal part of our existence. As we again sought a safe footing through deep snow crusted by storm, we were forced to follow a circuitous route in moving downward. Slowly our spirits rose with the descent. The snow crust in places carried us; in other places we went down eight to ten inches to a hard bottom of rock or ice. After we made a few turns in the winding pass, a clear sky and the clear waters of Jones Sound became visible. We had no way to gauge the distance to the end of snow-covered land, or to the shores of the sea. All visible lowlands in the distance were free of snow. Sweat again dripped from our faces, but a kindly sun dispelled the chill of icy perspiration. The weather remained steadily good with a light wind on our backs, and a temperature about two degrees below the freezing point. Some favor of frost was with us.

At the end of about eight hours of hard sledding, we could see the end of the highland snow line. Though exhausted to that degree where leg-lifting became difficult, we determined to get to dry snow-free land before camp ground was selected. At the end of another two hours, traveling over a rock-studded surface of melting snow, we picked a camp site beside a tumbling stream of clear ice water. We were still a day's journey from sea-level rocks. Here about, all the surface was in slabs of stratified layers of shifted stone. There was very little soil, except along the little creeks, and of these there were many with a narrow belt of hardy vegetation. The advantage which had determined the choice of our resting place was a series of rock ledges level enough for a bed with vertical walls for a shelter against wind. This rock bed was open to the sun at all hours. We were particular as to the kind of rocks to sleep on and we preferred at this time sunny rocks rather than tent life, for we expected to sleep twenty-four hours or longer to make up for the suspended rests and sleeps of the cloud world in the pass. And what a joyland this new domain of big rocks proved to be for a limited period!

As we now reclined in peace and contentment on dry rocks, hunger was the most urgent passion. Hunger not so much for meat but for sunshine, for water, and for undisturbed rest. We ate the warm glow of the sun, drank water, and kept on drinking sleep. No palatial luxury could have satisfied us better than the bed on these ice-free rocks—with a new dreamland ahead in good view for fifty miles.

Our preferred bedtime or rising time was, if possible, at midnight. At this hour it was coldest. The sun was in the north and lowest. Strangely too, at this time near the sea the sky was most often clear, over all of the heavens. The midnight sun at all times gave the greatest profusion of color. At this hour the silence and glory of all nature seemed at its best.

After twenty-four hours of dreamy comfort on rock that seemed like a soft bed, the urge to move and to find food was again upon us. Wela was awake first. He was fully dressed and had a fire started when I awoke to turn a cold side to the sun. Almost all our possessions had gotten damp and soggy from the pasty wetness in coming through the pass. We delayed longer to dry our belongings more thoroughly and repack them for the change in means of travel suggested by the aspect of the new way ahead. In the meantime we wanted more food, more sun, more fire—and more fire. I wonder if men were ever in a position where they needed heat as badly as we did. To us Heaven should be a place of eternal fire.

But with all our shortcomings we were at last on the waters of the Atlantic slope with twin channels to the north and west, leading back to the troubled area of the Pacific in which we enjoyed the peace, but mostly the worst tortures, of the Arctic. Now a new world was before us. What had this to offer? There was ice-free water as far as the eye would carry us in the center of the broad expanse of Jones Sound. The coast was studded with picturesque but dangerous cliffs of angular rocks. There were also wide stretches of lowland, free of snow, but all was too far off to study in detail for its productive capacity to serve our dire needs. The shores on both sides were jammed with pack-ice of a kind which did not look good for sled travel. There was least ice along the north shore. Since we realized that we must soon put aside sleds and risk our future in a canvas boat in order to make progress, I believed it prudent to seek a water way out to Baffin Bay and northward, keeping the land in sight. This route was agreeable to my companions, for by it we should be able to return to Greenland before the end of the long day of the current year.

We had reached the sea at the head of a fjord. The old winter ice was there, still adhering to the shore, but the ice foot was cut by land streams and so much destroyed by the hot summer sun that this shore shelf of ice could not be used as a highway. The sea ice along shore was rotted. Pools lined by sea algae were rapidly spreading, leaving rusty cavernous spots. The ice surface was thus beset by miniature lakes, over which some thin ice bridged dangerous holes and weak spots and crevasses. Over this, surface travel would be extremely difficult. The distance, however, to better ice and open water as we saw it through the glasses, was not many miles. Under any consideration, over this rotten ice was our only avenue of escape. Plans were now made accordingly.

There was much work in repairs and readjustment of equipment before we could risk a start. Boots and clothing required mending. The sleds required relashing; the overland trip had about wrecked them. Long continued wet conditions such as those of our recent experience were disastrous to Eskimo equipment. The leather-stretched lashings on the sleds and all joints were loose. The sinew threads in boots and fur clothes had become elastic and left open seams. To make these extensive repairs we decided to rest a day or two to mend, and also to augment our depleted food supply.

We located in an area where the conditions were favorable for the kind of camp best suited to our desires. There were many large flat rocks to serve as a bed or a table or a work-bench. The weather, though somewhat windy, was warm. The sun was pouring down heat in bright sunbeams. In the sun the temperature was 40°, but in the shade it was still close to the freezing point. Small patches of dry, grassy slopes were near by. There were also small patches of swampy tundra covered by deep velvety moss. Much of this was in full blossom. In other places were patches of poppies flowering in gold and white, and more long lines of saxifrage in purple.

Here and there we found patches of sorrel. We ate the flowers and leaves of the sorrel with a pleasing relish. There were many bones and horns scattered about—wolf bones and parts of skeletons of musk ox and reindeer. Along shore many whale bones were seen. Slowly we gathered or located raw local resources which might prove of great value to us, for in the absence of wood or coal, bones and horn became to us material of great value for new implements.

In the air there were many birds hastily going to and fro, and we reasoned their activity represented trips from feeding grounds to breeding places. We were tempted to use the rifles often, but shooting birds with rifle shot we had learned was not very profitable. Our supply of ammunition was now low. In the future we must conserve cartridges for big game and find some other way of securing birds and small game. Eider ducks and blue geese were extremely abundant. There were tracks of Arctic hare and lemming, but no fresh signs of musk oxen or deer.

On the sea ice and in the open water we were sure we would find seal, walrus, and white whale, but we were not yet ready with an equipment to risk this kind of hunting.

Wela set for himself the task of finding fuel to keep up a campfire. There was plenty of moss and small bones about, but this material required drying before it could be used for fire. He was not long in placing a pile of wet bones and moss in the sun on the rocks to dry. Then he explored the surroundings for meat and fat. He came back with ten eider duck eggs, an Arctic hare, and a duck. This success surprised me for he had not taken a rifle along in his wanderings. Laying his plunder on the rocks with pride, he expressed regret that he had been unable to get meat for the dogs or fat for the fire. I complimented him, and then asked, "How did you do it?"

An Eskimo detests boastful individuals. To afford time to discount this tendency, with due modesty he remained silent for a few moments, and then said he must use some of our small supply of bear fat to make a fire. I was most eager to hear how he had secured a hare without a gun. The Arctic hare is of all creatures the most inquisitive and for short distances the most speedy. What art of the chase had he invoked to capture the animal? The explanation was long delayed and, though I was anxious for the story, it did not seem good policy to press for information too hastily. After a while, when the hare was in the pot and cooking, I again pressed for information. "You have become a master craftsman in hunting. Now tell us about it. Tell us about the capture of the hare first."

We were sitting close together mending boots, with appetites fired by aroma of the boiling pot. Wela pulled out a leather strip of the length and thickness of a shoestring and said, "With this I trapped the hare," and then he proceeded to tell about eider ducks, but I was still ignorant of his method of capturing a hare with a string.

I asked specifically, "How did you string the hare?"

It developed that he used the animal's curiosity and its tendency to follow beaten paths to entice the hare to hang itself. The method was very simple. He hung a looped shoestring across a fresh hare trail, trusting that the creature by its intense curiosity would nose about the loop and become entangled. It did just that and was waiting for him when he returned from the quest of eider ducks.

"Now, about the ducks. Are the eggs fresh, and how did you secure the duck?"

"The eggs," he said, "were red-centered," by which he meant that the embryo ducks were beginning to form in the yolk. This was not good news to me, but to the natives duck eggs at this time have a flavor as delicious as ripe cheese is to us.

"The duck," said Wela, "I secured with another string."

He had suspended a looped line over the nest. The duck slipped its head into the loop and then struggled to free itself, but with each effort the slip loop tightened.

Here was the beginning of a new art of the chase which was to save our lives later when in greater distress for food.

We did not complete the mending. With no dog food it was felt that we must move onward and again establish a mending camp in a position where meat for dogs could be secured. Though the local bird supply was ample for our needs, each dog required a duck for a meal, and to secure ducks enough it would be necessary to use precious ammunition which might later be required to avert starvation. So, with repairs but partly completed, we ventured out on the rotten sea ice.

The snow had melted. The ice surface, where we could walk on it, was hard and rough. The temperature was 30°, not low enough to freeze the salt water but low enough to freeze the fresh-water pools, which were under thin slabs of glass-like ice which would not bear our weight. The going was hard on the sleds and hard on the dogs' feet, which were cut by little icy prongs and sharp edges of freshly broken ice. We figured that if these conditions continued at our next camp it would be necessary to cut up one of our sealskin coats and make leather pads for the dogs' feet. To get around the big pools of water in the algae-rotted spaces it was necessary to make frequent detours. Progress was thus delayed. As we came out of the fjord and rounded a cape of rocky cliffs, the temperature rose to 34°. Here all was wet and melting, but we must somehow keep going to find a safe route to the north shore of Jones Sound.

The ice now was in motion. To get anywhere it was

necessary to put prudence aside and take dangerous risks—risk in being carried adrift and also some risk in falling into the icy sea through weak ice. Most of the dogs had already broken through, but they swam and scrambled out. If they failed we could haul them out by the traces. But men in the ice water could not be rescued so easily. The ice became worse, so much so that we could not keep near the land, where the heat reflection disrupted the ice surface most. We now saw an occasional seal, and heard the bull call of the walrus. The dogs became so eager to hunt that sufficient control for a safe course became impossible. In this exciting scramble, the drivers one after another got an unexpected bath—the first bath in a month. The sun was shining with a good deal of warmth. We wore little clothing. When we climbed out, we shook the ice water from the skins, dumped the briny water from the boots, and kept going with sufficient vigor to get warm.

Neither the dogs nor the men could, however, keep up this kind of travel long. We saw some big ice bumping along shore in the direction we desired to go. The ice outside was drifting in the opposite direction. In the hope of finding a resting place on land and from there better studying the impossible condition of the ice under our feet, we took desperate chances by steering for an overland course. We were in water quite as much as we were on ice, but to live we must keep going. There was open water along shore. To cross this we must find a loose ice block to serve as a raft. This dangerous experiment was not new to us.

At last we were able to go on shore, but not where we wanted to go. It was a cape with precipitous cliffs and almost no low shore land. But our ice raft had gone aground and the tide was falling. For the time being we must stay where fate had put us. We were wet, and the cliffs left us in cold freezing shadows. The sun for a time would be denied us. There was no suitable rock bed, and no place for a camp in the sun. But we had been in worse places, so we jumped about on the narrow rocky shore with gloomy overlying cliffs about us. These cliffs worried us, for a fractured cliff might tumble on us. We tied the dogs and then discussed the possibility of comfort while our wet clothes became a little dry on the inside but icy on the outside. Effects of summer and of winter are never far apart here. In crossing overland we had winter torture of the worst kind in midsummer. Now at the sea level, full sunshine and the blue shadows of the north face of cliffs again presented winter and summer on the same day, with disastrous results.

We could climb out of these freezing shadow temperatures, but could not take the dogs nor the equipment with us. Furthermore, there was the chance that a piece of ice to serve as a raft might come along and we could not afford to miss such an opportunity.

Great numbers of gulls hovered about us, also many eiders, blue geese, and long-tail ducks. Did they nest in these cold cliffs? A few we thought might, though a well-grounded bird instinct leads them to warm cliffs with a southward exposure to the sun. A diligent search among the rocky shelves and crevices gave no prospect for food. No birds nested there. We were eager for more eggs; even eggs with embryo transformation were now highly prized in our search for food. But even rotten eggs were absent. We did find some dry moss and piles of dry excreta from birds.

"This," said Wela, "will give us a fire," and over it he soon had a pot boiling of odds and ends, mainly duck heads and feet and hare legs from our last catch. It was a good tasty meal.

In the meantime the sun was passing northward and would soon give us the benefit of its cheering glow, while the tide was at a period when ice floats should soon come along to enable us to go. We spent six hours in this shadow land in cold shivers—it seemed like twenty-four hours—but we got some rest, made some repairs, and ate some food. The dogs, though getting nothing to eat for forty-eight hours, recuperated rather better than we did. They had only to shake themselves to become dry. With us, drying is a long, suffering job.

Ahead, just barely visible, was a low island. To each side of this island there was a channel jammed with big ice. Both channels led to a narrow gorge of huge rocky cliffs out into the desperate north waters of the Pacific over which we had come in passing along Baby Land into Wellington Channel. We were on the eastward neck of Baby Land, but from here it is not enticing. There is no soil visible; all was a cold dead display of hard rocks. Even lichens were scarce.

In our plans we were to try to reach the island and there await an opportunity to cross the east channel which had been designated Hell Gate because of the speed of the ice jam passing through. In due time a suitable float came along. This enabled us to leave the land and cross the narrow band of ice-free water between the land and the polar pack of big ice passing the island. We had become experts in taking advantage of currents and countercurrents in pack-ice jams. The ice surface was here much better for travel than that of the rotten land-adhering ice of the day before. Since the west channel was blocked, we reached the island and the damnation of Hell Gate without any great hardship. Though we saw many gulls, ducks, and geese, many seals and walrus, we did not dare interrupt our progress for hunting. We must go with all possible speed to the island while the west channel was blocked.

The island proved to be a beautiful haven of peace in a region where the storms of the Atlantic and the Pacific meet to exchange blows. For twenty-four hours we watched this battle line of the great oceans. The wind and the drift ice seldom traveled in the same direction. The pack jammed mostly from the north and west. It also changed suddenly and came for brief periods from the east. The milling ice changed in force and direction, mostly at high tide, and it ran with what seemed like the speed of war vessels. However, all this wasted power of destruction did not worry us very much. We had seen and felt its power during the anxious months previously.

On the island, king eider ducks were in charge. It was their domain, undisturbed by foxes or wolves; not even lemmings rooted the grassy humps in which their nests were placed. The nests were lined with dry silk down. There were thousands of these ducks. What a cheering sight! They are the most beautiful and most prudent of all the ducks of the ice world. Their nests were filled with eggs, always covered and guarded by one of the well-mated creatures. The ducks seemed to know that our dogs were not loose to prowl wolf-like over the rocks. Also, the ingenious creatures sensed that we were not using guns. Strange how quickly these European creatures are able to estimate the human intent of visitors. We were hungry, but two or three ducks and a few eggs satisfied our wants. This supply we got with ease, but to feed the dogs would require a slaughter that we had not the heart to inflict. Furthermore there were seals and walrus and white whales in the offing. These would make staple dog food, and we must invent some new art of the chase to secure such animals.

While we were discussing this problem, a seal asleep on a piece of ice passed by so rapidly that we condemned ourselves for inattention. This must not happen again, but we could not risk the danger of an attack on freely moving ice with much open water about. We had a harpoon point but no shaft, and little suitable line. Etuq quickly affixed the harpoon to a line and tied it to a piece of sled hickory to serve as a shaft. With this equipment and an ice ax, he scoured the shore for another opportunity to get a seal. In an hour he came back and said he had a seal beached just across a neck of land—would we take the dogs over there and feed them? We did this, and also built a campfire near by for a happy feed for men and dogs.

Then a sleep on dry rocks under bright warm sunshine—with full stomachs. How could Trouble trouble us in this glory of dreamland! And for once the elements favored us. When we awakened, the blocked jam to the west was free and that to the east over Hell Gate was blocked with heavy polar ice. Without breakfast we embarked on the jammed ice. In a few hours we were safely on the north shore of Jones Sound, along which we must find a way back to Greenland.

n

↑

12

PARTING WITH DOG COMPANIONS

We were camped with comfort, as we understood comfort, beside a clear-water stream, coming out of a small rock-ribbed valley. The rocks were warm. The weather was good. In cozy, granite-blocked places we were sheltered from the cold blasts of rushing winds through Hell Gate. The temperature was 42° in the sun, 33° in the shade. The land about was thrown-up perpendicular cliffs with granite spires that pierced the cold blue of the heavens. There was in near-by regions little vegetation and few signs of animal life. What a quiet haven of rest! But Hell Gate was all agitation, with rushing jams of polar ice and exploding icebergs just beyond.

We had reached the stage in a diverse adventure which forced a change in our fight for life against famine and frost. Land travel was now hopelessly impossible. Progress over sea ice was equally impossible. We must prepare the folded canvas canoe with its accessory equipment to meet the hardship and dangers of navigating open waters. This forced the thought, sad to us, that we must part with our loyal dog friends. The hope of meeting whale ships or of finding Eskimo settlements must now be abandoned.

Reason too often fathers the wishbone of desire. We still entertained the hope of a pleasing escape from trouble for months to come. Many mistakes had been made. Among these was the mistake of not remaining in Baby Land for the winter, as the Eskimos had urged. Had we done this we might have saved our dogs and on the whole perhaps would have fared better. We now made the same mistake in not sitting down and preparing to winter where we were camped. With our dogs and a new equipment to hunt, we could have caught here, from the open water and disrupted ice of Hell Gate, seals and walrus enough to keep us in an ample supply of meat and fat for the winter. At sunrise the sea ice would offer us a secure highway eastward out of Jones Sound, and back to Greenland along the shores of Baffin Bay, or northward into Bay Fjord and back by the route covered in the journey to the North Pole.

Wela and Etuq were willing to stay, but to me delay was impossible. We had thus far overcome all difficulties. We could risk further dangers and return to Greeland during the current season. This decision caused suffering and brought us often to death's door.

My companions were loyal and reasonable in every conference, and since every prospect was but an opinion based upon inexperience, they at all times yielded to my judgment even if it differed from their sense of reasoning, as it often did. Whatever we did now would require a week of exploration with a readjustment of all our clothing and equipment. The temporary absence of game favored my plans, though we agreed that at this point sea game would be plentiful later.

The boat problem was the first to be solved. To hunt, and to transport ourselves with a heavy equipment over water and back to land on pack-ice quickly in a frail collapsible boat, involved a system of mechanical aids not yet worked out. This required much study and experiment, to perfect a technique never before tried. Thus far the boat had served mainly as a floor for the sleds or as a floor for the snow camps. It could not be used to cross open water in low temperatures. At these times, if it was not cut by the rapidly forming glassy sheets, it was so quickly pasted up by accumulating snow and ice that it became dangerous and useless. All this we knew from the use of skin boats like the kayak and umiak. The boat fabric of canvas was not yet waterproofed. For material in use at low temperatures waterproofing is disastrous, because when it hardens under cold the fabric becomes brittle and breaks. For this reason we carried no waterproofed clothing and had delayed the waterproofing of the boat canvas until now.

We also found that the take-down or collapsing devices were not suitable for our use, for the waterproofed canvas would not withstand folding without cracking even in the cold weather of summer.

The remaking and adjustment in the construction of the

folding canvas boat to the needs in prospect was, therefore, our first duty. The frame was made much more rigid, but still left in such form that it could be taken down. Much of the spreading wood had been used in the sleds. Therefore, it was necessary to take the sleds apart to set up the boat. The hickory slats forming the sled flooring were set into the boat sides to better spread the canoe. This plan also conserved the precious hickory for later use. We had secured waterproofing for the canvas without oil because we figured seal oil would better serve our purpose, and thus we would be relieved from carrying the processing oil. By the end of the first day we gave the canvas a coat of the new mixture. Two days later another coat was given. Two days later we put the boat in water and thereafter made little change either in construction or waterproofing. It served its purpose admirably.

Both sleds were still in good condition except that most of the lashings were loose. We divided one near the middle and made it collapsible, so we could take it down and place it in the boat. Our repair tools were ample for this work. Experiments proved that it would be necessary often to carry the boat over ice on a sled, and at times it was necessary to keep a sled lashed to the bottom of the boat while crossing narrow expanses of water. This arrangement was modified and readjusted many times to suit changing conditions. On the whole it proved a valuable make-fit, for with the combination it was necessary later to zigzag to and fro over Jones Sound for about a thousand miles.

While these experiments and repairs and plans of reconstruction were in progress, we explored the near-by environment. The weather continued fair on land but for the sea, and particularly Hell Gate, there was a different ruling by the weather creator. There the winds and tides and ice jams formed a focal center for strong air and sea currents. This did not look good, for we did not know how far out this disturbance extended. There were few geese or eiders here, but many guillemots and gulls were in evidence. We sought for but found no bird rookeries near enough to be reached. We heard the distant call of wolves. Two of our dogs cut their lines and deserted. We believed they had joined the wolves. The Eskimo dog is but a half-tamed wolf, and easily takes to the wilds with wolves when he can. Foxes barked from distant rocks. Fresh signs of hare, caribou and musk ox were seen, but the most diligent search failed to reveal to us any big game. It was a game country seemingly abandoned at this season of the year.

Now it was necessary to make the most momentous decision of our weird existence. Henceforth we must go by boat. Our little canvas canoe was only twelve feet long. After we had reduced our load to the utmost, packed our precious cargo in the boat and taken our positions, the boat was so low in the water that there was great danger. Our gunwales were only six or seven inches above water. Even one dog in such a position could dangerously disturb our equilibrium in quiet water. What would we do in a running sea? It was thus necessary to leave not only the dogs behind but much important equipment.

To leave the dogs! How could we live without our faithful companions? When all had been dull and dark and blue, when death by cold and starvation was near, the dogs had howled the coming of the moon and the cheer of better days. When our strength failed, their more enduring energy pulled us over dangerous places. Loneliness could never be painful with these wolf companions. But now we must part. Tears rolled down our cheeks. How would we part? The dogs looked at us appealingly. They seemingly knew what we had in mind. Their tails were down. They howled not in the usual chorus but one at a time in a tone that brought condemnation with sadness and more tears.

Should we kill them and end their future misery? We had not the ammunition to spare. To use a knife or an ax—no, it would be the murder of friends if undertaken by any kind of a weapon.

Etuq said, "Let us reverse the status. If we were in the dogs' places would we want to be killed?"

Of course we answered, "No. Where there is life there is a chance. Death is too permanent for thought to grasp it—it is the end. No, let the dogs live. They will seek wolf companions and mate to the joys of a new domain. They deserve all that the cold earth can give. Let the dogs live. Where wolves and foxes live, our dogs with greater intelligence will not starve."

But figure the tragedy as we would, the parting was that at the graveyard of loved ones. We stepped into the boat and pulled east. We heard their parting howls for an hour, and in our dreams for months and years. And how lonely life was to us in the months of famine, cold, and darkness to follow! We had yet to learn that heart-hungers for dog companions can open the door to the doom of suicide.

Jones Sound is perhaps roughly 190 miles long, with an average breadth of say forty miles. It is a large body of water, a mighty ocean of trouble for three men in a frail canvas boat only twelve feet long. There was here no possible human aid, nor in regions further south for hundreds of miles. Our destiny must be worked out by our own hands, with equipment that must later be invented or reconstructed from the scant material of our old camps, where nothingness had been the chief asset. For two weeks we paddled desperately in such waters as we could risk, making about thirty miles daily, two-thirds of which was lost by circuitous courses. We averaged about ten miles daily in a straight line towards Baffin Bay.

Though we had encountered and weathered, as we thought, about all kinds of ice conditions, this experience in a canvas boat was a new adventure. It proved we still had much to learn. It was interesting and it was exciting not only because of its novelty but because we were daily and almost hourly in such danger that life at no time was more certain than a prize with the toss of dice. We gambled with fate, with the privilege of living ever at stake.

For the first few days our progress was not good. We had traveled by leg use but now we must move by arm energy. We were not yet mentally or physically fitted to wing and fin sea distances in the crude makeshift of canvas boat life. Afraid to risk being smashed or upset far from land or drifting ice in a running sea, we tried to hold a course close to the north shore. But this shore, to our sorrow, proved to be a succession of big indentations of fjords and bays, into which and out of which ran dangerous air and sea currents. The headlands of precipitous cliffs offered few safe landing places. In our course all along there were few places where we could get ashore with safety for a camp, to rest and eat. The most dangerous aspect of this new land was the capacity for sudden local disturbances. The mad air and sea currents coming out or going into the bays threatened navigation at every cape. Occasionally without any apparent cause a narrow stream would start far out in the waters of Jones Sound and, with railroad speed, rush floats of ice. Some icebergs and sea ice went with the same speed. At other times the icebergs would take a lateral or an opposite course to the current. Our chief business was either to dodge these currents and take advantage of eddies, or to steer with desperation into the rush and go with the jam.

We tried to cross the first bay from cape to cape by a straight line, but never again was such a crossing attempted. As we passed the nearest headland, the air was still, the sea was flat and glistening like a mirror. The distance across was perhaps not more than six miles, but it took us all day to get out of the later millrushes of troubled waters over which mountain air was funneled from every gully. Thereafter we either pulled up along the bays and crossed at some narrows or went deliberately further out to sea and pulled along under the protection of a tongue of drifting ice.

The selection of places and means of camping, the acquisition of and preparation of food became very difficult with the new method of travel. It was dangerous to go landward, it was dangerous in the limited areas of pack-ice near which our best progress was being made. Often we continued paddling for twenty-four or forty-eight hours with one dozing at a time in the boat. The usual camp, however, was on a heavy jam of ice fairly well jammed in a local area where all was adrift. Here we pulled out the canvas boat, dumped out the bilge water, dried the floor as best we could, and then on the boat floor made a bed. It was damp and shivery, but we were out of the wind and the camp arrangements were so simple that no time was lost. One was at all times on watch for bears or dangerous splits or drifts in the ice. The one on watch set up a little copper apparatus shaped in half-moon form like the Eskimo lamp. In this a blubber flame was kept up and over it a tripod was placed holding a kettle to melt ice for water or to cook an occasional gull or some eggs. We snared the gulls with looped lines; the eggs were a part of our eider-nest plunder. Those old eggs now became staple food. We preferred them cooked and cold. The mess within the shell was cheesy to the nose, fishy to the palate, and meaty to the eye, but it was highly nutritious food in condensed form. The fresh birds we usually ate raw.

During this part of our voyage we saw only an occasional seal or walrus or bear. The game apprehended was at no time in a position where we could risk the danger of an attack, but we lived somehow on old eggs and gulls and ducks.

Our manner of living, though strange and weird and unsatisfactory in its outlook, was by contrast to previous experience pleasing and inspiring. Though we were often worried by local wind gusts and water rushes, the general weather was fair. How we enjoyed the warm sun on our backs and faces and hands! The temperature was usually about 35°, coming down to freezing occasionally when a cold blast descended from glaciers at altitudes. We rapidly gained strength and courage. In our progress we went nearly the full length of Jones Sound, but troublesome pack-ice forced us further and further out in the midway channel and eventually to a position near the south shore. Beyond were a few islands and beyond them, the open Atlantic of Baffin Bay. In a few days we hoped we would turn northward, and in a few weeks be home among our friends in Greenland.

But an unexpected storm struck us with the suddenness of an avalanche. Our hopes, our temperament, our manner of living, our world, quickly changed.

Soon we had before us another conquest to make, another scheme of life, another foretaste of death. The worst series in our long run of battles for life against starvation and freezing was before us—another battle against the easy Arctic death, to be followed by the long night of the end. Fear of death troubled us very little, but hunger and suffering enforced a desire to live. A happy return to friends and relatives was still to be a far-off dream.

n

↑

13

ADRIFT

It was midnight. The sun was north. The sky was steel-blue and fairly clear. The air was still, suspiciously still. A few torn bits of clouds were being rushed now upward, now downward, and then east or west. The distant pack groaned, but nearly all was silent and motionless. It was our preferred camping time. We were tired and hungry after a long pull over water and ice, but there were premonitions of danger which we had not yet correctly appraised.

A storm was imminent, but was it to be local or general? Was it to come from the east, from the west, or out of one of the glacial fjords? The barometer for us had not been a good indicator of weather in this district, but it was low enough to excite attention.

We had weathered storms so often that the prospect of another disturbance did not greatly worry us, but our location differed from that of any previous experience. This alone should have been ample cause for quick preparations. However, there seemed little that we could do but each eat a raw gull and tank up on ice water, since it might be a long time before we could again eat or drink in comfort. On the whole we seemed to be well located to take the jam of a storm from any direction but due east. Storms from north to south across the sound were of short duration and usually local. The effect of these, if we were sufficiently centered in a turning aggregation of pack-ice, as we had learned by repeated experience, was to drive us either to the shores or to become a part of a larger pack aggregation in mid-waters. The most likely direction of enduring storms was from the west. Up to the present, westerly storms scattered the pack and left us in dangerous open water with rough seas. But now we could receive the air dooms and booms from the Pacific with the confidence that we would be packed against the islands ahead, which would act as gateposts to prevent us from being swept out into the open Atlantic waters of stormy Baffin Bay.

While thus the problems of self-defense were hastily analyzed, we firmly lashed the sled to the bottom of the boat so that we might quickly go from water to ice and keep going as new dangers made quick movement necessary. Suddenly the sky darkened, the sea blackened, the land on all sides disappeared. We were perhaps thirty miles from the

islands to the east, forty miles from the rough highland coast
to the north, and twenty miles from the ice-capped east end
of North Devon. There, over shallow submarine banks
which anchored icebergs, we decided to hold a position.
Later we would make for a glacier bay to the south as open
water and suitable ice presented a workable way.

The wind first came in gunshot gusts, followed by a few
seconds of thick still air and silence. This we knew to be the
voice of a dangerous storm. The ice about us quickly crum-
bled like a piecrust. We had selected an old blue field as our
floating anchorage. This we reasoned would not easily break,
but it turned and tilted and twisted about too much for our
sense of safety. After about a half hour of semi-darkness and
mysterious agitation in air and water, the storm came with a
steady blast from an angle west by north. We could not see
far enough in any direction to make intelligent decisions for
a change of position. Some snow was falling and the spray
of ice water froze on our skins. In silence we shivered; the
noise of the rushing wind was too great to hear voices.
Temporarily we were secure and knew it, but what was to
be the danger and damage of the drift?

In this uncertainty of action, moments seemed like hours.
Little by little we saw that the other ice was leaving us, and
we were left to hold on to an acre of blue crystal awash
with the force of increasing waves. At last it became necessary to move—but where to go? In storm-driven waters our
canvas boat would topple over in a few moments. We must
watch for the protection of coming ice and move along lee
slants, landward.

It was dangerous to move from the watery surface of
the ice under our feet. It was dangerous to stay. Though the

wind was from the west, we knew that the course of the drift might not be east but in some other direction. So the location of our position and the movement of the drift became a paradox. The points of the compass meant nothing to us now. Our life would depend upon our relation to the nearest stable patch of ice. We knew other ice was not far away, because the sea came in short swells with a push instead of a roll, but we saw none in the dark through the snowy smear which served as air.

While thus about resigned to a grave in stormy depths, Wela said, "I smell land." How he could smell land when my nose was so full of snow paste that it was hard to breathe, I did not stop to inquire. I looked to Etuq for confirmation.

He said, "I do not smell, but I feel land straight ahead."

My feeling was that we were adrift, in countercurrents, for the open sea westward. I cleaned my ears, my eyes, and nose of frosty paste and soon I heard what I took to be a land wash, but in a few minutes this proved to be the wash of the sea against an iceberg. The berg was aground and going to pieces under the blows of the storm. It got a little colder. The snow ceased, a wider horizon gladdened our eyes. The Eskimos were right! There was land straight ahead and plenty of pack-ice loosely strung out in long tongues along shore. The land was ten or fifteen miles to the southwest. For once in our lives we were as glad to see ice as we were to recognize land, for without the wind and sea protection of the ice we could never reach the land.

We were left no alternative but to seek the shelter of the disrupted pack, and press landward as best we could. We had hardly stepped out on the ice, and drawn our boat after us, when the wind struck us with such force that we could hardly stand it. The ice immediately started in a westward direction, veering off from the land a little and leaving open leads. These leads, we now saw, were the only possible places of safety. For, in them, the waters were easy, and the wind was slightly shut off by the walls of pressure lines and hummocks. Furthermore, they offered slants now and then by which we could approach the land.

The sledge was again set under the boat and lashed. All our things were lashed to the wooden frame of the canoe to prevent the wind and the sea from carrying them away. We crossed several small floes and jumped the lines of water separating them, pulling sledge and canoe after us. The pressure lines offered severe barriers. To cross them we were compelled to separate the canoe from its sledge and remove the baggage. All of this required considerable time. A sense of hopelessness filled my heart. In the meantime, the wind veered to the east and came with a rush that left us helpless. We sought the lee of a hummock, and hoped the violence of the storm would soon spend itself, but there were no easy spells in this storm, nor did it show signs of early cessation. The ice about us moved rapidly westward and slowly seaward.

It was no longer possible to press toward the land, for the leads of water were too wide and were lined with small whitecaps, while the tossing seas hurled mountains of ice and foaming water over the pack's edge.

The entire pack was rising and falling under swells, and gradually wearing to little fragments. The floe on which we stood was strong. I knew it would hold out longer than most of the ice about, but it was not high enough above water to give us a dry footing as the seas advanced.

From a distance to the windward we noted a low iceberg slowly gaining on our floe. It was a welcome sight. For it alone could raise us high enough above the soul-despairing rush of the icy water.

Its rich ultramarine blue promised ice of a sufficient strength to withstand the battling of the storm. Never were men on a sinking ship more anxious to reach a rock than we were to reach this blue stage of ice. It offered several little shelves upon which we could rise out of the water. We watched with anxious eyes as the berg revolved and forced the other ice aside.

It aimed almost directly for us, and would probably cut our floe. We prepared for a quick leap upon the deck of our prospective "craft."

Bearing down upon us, the berg touched a neighboring piece and pushed us away. We quickly pulled to the other pan and then found, to our dismay, a wide band of mushy slush, as impossible to us for a footing as quicksand would have been. As the berg passed, however, it left a line of water behind it. We quickly threw boat and sledge into this, paddled after the berg, and, reaching it, leaped to its security. What a relief to be raised above the crumbling pack-ice, and to watch from safety the thundering of the elements!

The berg which we had boarded was square, with rounded corners. Its highest points were about twenty feet above water; the general level was about ten feet. The ice was about eighty feet thick, and its width was about a hundred feet. These dimensions assured stability, for if the thing had turned over, as bergs frequently do, we should be left to seek breath among the whales.

It was an old remnant of a much larger berg which had

stood the Arctic tempest for many years. This we figured
out from the hard blue of the ice and its many caverns and
pinnacles. We were, therefore, on a secure mass of crystal
which was not likely to suffer severely from a single storm.
Its upper configuration, however, though beautiful in its
countless shades of blue, did not offer a comfortable berth.
There were three pinnacles too slippery and too steep to
climb, with a slope leading by a gradual incline on each side.
Along these the seas had worn grooves leading to a central
concavity filled with water. The only space which we could
occupy was the crater-like rim around this lake. At this time
we had to endure only the nauseating pitch of the sea and
the cutting blast of the storm.

The small ice near by kept the seas from boarding. To
prevent our being thrown about on the slippery surface, we
cut holes into the pinnacles and spread lines about them to
which we clung. The boat was securely fastened in a similar way by cutting a makeshift for a ringbolt in the floor of
ice. Then we pushed from side to side along the lines, to encourage our hearts and to force our circulation. Although
the temperature was only at the freezing point, it was bit-
terly cold, and we were in a bad way to weather a storm.

As the position changed, the small ice acting as oil to
water drenched us from head to foot. Only our shirts were
dry. With hands tightly gripped to the line and to crevasses,
we received the spray of the breaking icy seas while the
berg plowed the scattered pack and plunged seaward. The
cold, though only at the freezing point, pierced our snow-
pasted furs and brought shivers worse than those of zero's
lowest. Thus the hours of physical torture and mental anguish passed, while the berg moved toward the gloomy

black cliff of Hell Gate. Here the eastern sky bleached and the south blued, but the falling temperature froze our garments to coats of mail.

We were still dressed in part of our winter clothing. The coat was of sealskin, with hood attached; the shirt of camel's-hair blanket, also with a hood; the trousers of bear fur; boots of seal, with hair removed; and stockings of hare fur. The mittens were of seal, and there were pads of grass for the palms. Our garments, though not waterproof, shed water and excluded the winds, but there is a cold that comes with wet garments and strong winds that sets the teeth to chattering and the skin to quivering.

As all was snug and secure on the berg, we began to take a greater interest in our wind- and sea-propelled "craft." Its exposed surface was swept by the winds, while its submarine surface was pushed by tides and undercurrents, giving it a complex movement at variance with the pack-ice. It plowed up miles of sea ice, crushing and throwing it aside.

After several hours of this kind of navigation—which was easy for us, because the movement of the swell and the breaking of the sea did not inflict a hardship—the berg suddenly, without any apparent reason, took a course at right angles to the wind and deliberately pushed out of the pack into the seething seas. This rapid shift from comfort to the wild agitation of the bleak waters made us gasp. The seas, with boulders of ice, rolled up over our crest and into the concavity of the berg, leaving no part safe. Seizing our axes, we cut many other anchor holes in the ice, doubly secured our life lines, and shifted with our boat to the edge of the berg turned to the wind. The hours of suspense and torment thus spent seemed as long as the winters of the Eskimo. The pack soon became a mere pearly glow against a dirty sky. We were rushing through a seething blackness, made more impressive by the pearl and blue of the berg and the white, ice-lined crests.

What could we do to keep the springs of life from snapping in such a world of despair? Fortunately, we were kept too busy dodging the storm-driven missiles of water and ice to ponder much over our fate. Otherwise the mind could not have stood the infernal strain.

Our bronze skins were adapted to cold and winds, but the torture of the cold, drenching water was new. For five months we had been battered by winds and cut by frosts, but water was secured only by melting ice with precious fuel which we had carried thousands of miles. If we could get enough of the costly liquid to wash our cold meals down, we were satisfied. The luxury of a face wash or a bath, except by the wind-driven snows, or by accident, was never indulged in. Now, in stress of danger, we were getting it from every direction. Torments of frost about the Pole were nothing compared to this boiling blackness.

Twenty-four hours elapsed before there was any change. Such calls of nature as hunger or thirst or sleep were left unanswered. We maintained a terrible struggle to keep from being washed into the sea. At last the east paled, the south became blue, and the land on both sides rose in sight. The wind came steadily, but reduced in force with a frosty edge that hardened our garments to sheets of ice.

We were not far from the twin channels, Cardigan Strait and Hell Gate, where the waters of the Pacific and the Atlantic meet. We were driving for Cardigan Strait, past the fjords into which we had descended from the western seas two weeks before. We had, therefore, lost an advance of two weeks in one day, and we had probably lost our race with time to reach the life-saving haunts of the Eskimo.

Still, this line of thought was foreign to us. Not far away were bold cliffs from which birds descended to the rushing waters. At the sight, my heart rose. Here we saw the satisfying prospect of an easy breakfast if only the waves would cease to fold in white crests. Long trains of heavy ice were rushing with railroad speed out of the straits. As we watched, the temperature continued to fall. Soon the north blackened with swirling clouds of smoke. The wind came with the sound of exploding guns from Hell Gate. What, I asked myself, was to be our fate now?

The berg, animated by a mysterious push, took a southwest course. Freezing seas washed over the berg and froze our numbed feet to the ice, upon which a footing otherwise would have been very difficult. Adrift in a vast, ice-driven, storm-thundering ocean, I stood silent, paralyzed with terror. After a few hours, sentinel floes of the pack slowly shoved toward us, and unresistingly, we were ushered into the harboring influence of the heavy polar ice.

The berg lost its erratic movement, and soon settled in a fixed position. The wind continued to tear along in a mad rage, but we found shelter in our canoe, two of us dozing away for a few moments while one paced the ice as a sentinel. Slowly a lane of quiet water appeared to widen among the floes. We heard a strangely familiar sound which set our hearts throbbing. The walrus and the seal, one by one, came up to the surface to blow. Here, right before us, was big game, with plenty of meat and fat. We were starving, but we gazed almost helplessly on plenty, for its capture would be difficult.

We had only a few cartridges and four cans of pemmican in our baggage. These were reserved for use to satisfy the last pangs of famine. That time had not yet arrived. Made desperate by hunger, after a brief rest we began to seek food. Birds flying from the land became our game at this time. We could secure these with the slingshot made by the Eskimos, and later, by entangling loops in lines, and in various other ways which hunger taught us.

A gull lighted on a pinnacle of our berg. Quietly but quickly we placed a bait and set a looped line. We watched with bated breath. The bird peered about, espied the luring bait, descended with a flutter of wings, pecked the pemmican. There was a snapping sound—the bird was ours. Leaping upon it, we rapidly cut it into bits and ravenously devoured it raw. Few things I have ever eaten tasted so delicious as this meat—which had the flavor of cod-liver oil.

The ice soon jammed in a grinding pack against the land, and the wind spent its force in vain. We held our position and two of us, after eating the bird, slept until the sentinel called us. At midnight the wind eased and the ice started its usual rebound, seaward and eastward, with the tide.

This was our moment for escape. We were about ten miles off the shore of Cape Vera. If we could push our canvas canoe through the channels of water as they opened, we might reach land. We quickly prepared the boat. With trepidation we pushed it into the black, frigid waters. We hesitated to leave the sheltering berg which had saved our lives. Still, it had served its purpose. To remain might mean our being carried out to sea. The ultimate time had come to seek a more secure refuge on terra firma.

Leaping into the frail, rocking canoe, we pushed along desperately through a few long channels to reach a wide, open space of water landward. Paddling frantically, we made a twisting course through opening lanes of water, ice on both sides of us, visible bergs bearing down at times on us, invisible bergs with spear-points of ice beneath the water in which our course lay. We sped forward at times with quick darts. Suddenly, and to our horror, an invisible piece of ice jagged a hole in the port quarter. Water gushed into the frail craft. In a few minutes it would be filled. Fortunately, I saw a floe was near, and while the canoe rapidly filled we pushed for the floe, reaching it not a moment too soon.

A boot was sacrificed to mend the canoe. Patching the cut, we put again into the sea and proceeded.

The middle pack of ice was separated from the land pack, leaving much free water. But now a land breeze sprang up and gave us new troubles. We could not face the wind and sea, so we took a slant and sought the lee of the pans coming from the land.

Our little overloaded canoe weathered the seas very well, and we had nothing to gain and everything to lose by turning back. Again we were drenched with spray, and the canoe was sheeted with ice above water. The sun was passing over Hell Gate. Long blue shadows stretched over the pearl-gray sea. By these, without resort to the compass, we knew it was about midnight.

As we neared the land ice, birds became numerous. The waters rose in easy swells. Still nearer, we noted that the entire body of land ice was drifting away. A convenient channel opened and gave us a chance to slip behind. We pointed for Cape Vera, dashed over the water and soon, to our joy, landed on a ledge of lower rocks. I cannot describe the relief I felt in reaching land after the spells of anguish through which we had passed. Although these barren rocks offered neither food nor shelter, still we were as happy as if a sentence of death had been remitted.

Not far away were pools of ice water. These we sought first, to quench our thirst. Then we scattered about, our eyes eagerly scrutinizing the land for breakfast. Soon we saw a hare bounding over the rocks. As it paused, cocking its ears, one of my boys secured it with a slingshot. It was succulent; we cut it with our knives. Some moss was found among the rocks. I returned to prepare it. With the moss as fuel, we made a fire, put the dripping meat in a pot and, with gloating eyes, watched it simmering. I thrilled with the joy of sheer living, with hunger about to be satisfied by cooked food. This was a breakfast for a king.

Before the hare was ready, the boys came along with two eider ducks, which they had secured by looped lines. We therefore had now an advance dinner, with a refreshing drink and a stomach full, and solid rocks to place our heads upon for a long sleep. The world had indeed a new aspect for us. In reality, however, our ultimate prospect of escape from famine was darker than ever.

n

↑

14

FORCED RETREAT

No time was lost in our onward course. Endeavoring at once to regain the distance lost by the drifting berg, we sought a way along the shores. Here, over ice with pools of water and slush, we dragged our sledge with the canvas boat ever ready to launch. Frequent spaces of water necessitated constant ferrying. We found, however, that most open places could be crossed with sledge attached to the boat. This saved much time.

We advanced from ten to fifteen miles daily, pitching the tent on land or sleeping in the boat in pools of ice water, as the conditions warranted. The land rose with vertical cliffs two thousand feet high, and offered no life except a few gulls and guillemots. By gathering these as we went along, a scant hand-to-mouth subsistence daily was obtained.

Early in August we reached the end of the land pack, about twenty-five miles east of Cape Sparbo. Beyond was a water sky, and to the north the sea was entirely free of ice. The weather was clear, and our ambitions for the freedom of the deep rose again.

At the end of the last day of sledge travel, a camp was made on a small island. Here we saw the first signs of Eskimo habitation. Old tent circles, also stone and fox traps in abundance, indicated an ancient village of considerable size. On the mainland we discovered abundant grass and moss, with signs of musk ox, ptarmigan, and hare, but no living thing was detected. After a careful search, we took the sledge apart to serve as a floor for the boat. All our things were snugly packed. For breakfast, we had but one gull, which was divided without the tedious process of cooking.

As we were packing the things on to the edge of the ice, we espied an oogzuk seal.[11] Here was a creature which could satisfy our many needs for a while. Upon it one of our last cartridges was expended. The seal fell. The huge carcass was dragged ashore. All of its skin was jealously taken; for this would make harpoon lines which would enable the shaping of Eskimo implements to take the place of the rifles, which, with ammunition exhausted, would be useless. Our boots could also be patched with bits of the skin, and new soles could be made. Of the immense amount of oogzuk meat and blubber we were able to take only a small part; for, with three men and our baggage and sledge in the little canvas boat, it was already overloaded.

The meat was cached, so that if ultimate want forced our retreat we might here prolong our existence a few weeks longer. There was little wind, and the night was beautifully clear. The sun at night was very close to the horizon, but the sparkle of the shimmering waters gave our dreary lives a bright side. On the great unpolished rocks of the point east of Cape Sparbo a suitable camping spot was found, a prolonged feed of seal was indulged in, and with a warm sun and full stomachs, we did not need the tent. Under one of the rocks we found shelter, and slept with savage delight for nine hours.

Another search of the accessible land offered no game except ducks and gulls far from shore. Here the tides and currents were very strong, so our start had to be timed with the outgoing tide.

Starting late one afternoon, we advanced rapidly beyond Cape Sparbo, in a sea with an uncomfortable swell. But beyond the cape, the land ice still offered an edge for a long distance. While we were making a cut across a small bay to reach ice, a walrus suddenly came up behind the canoe and drove a tusk through the canvas. Etuq quickly covered the cut, while we pulled with full force for a pan of drift ice only a few yards away. The boat, with its load, was quickly jerked on the ice. Already there were three inches of water in the floor. A chilly disaster was narrowly averted. Part of a boot was sacrificed to mend the boat.

While we were at work with the needle, a strong tidal current carried us out to sea. An increasing wind brought breaking waves over the edge of the ice. The wind fortunately gave a landward push to the ice. A sledge-cover, used as a sail, retarded our seaward drift. The leak securely patched, we pushed off for the land ice. With our eyes strained for breaking seas, the boat was paddled along with considerable anxiety. Much water was shipped in these dashes; constant bailing was necessary. Pulling continuously along the ice for eight miles, and when the leads closed at times, jumping on cakes and pulling the boat after us, we were finally forced to seek a shelter on the ice field.

With a strong wind and a wet fall of snow, the ice camp was far from comfortable. As the tide changed, the wind came from the west with a heavy, choppy sea. Further advance was impossible. Sleeping but a few minutes at a time, and then rising to note coming dangers, as does the seal, I perceived, to my growing dismay, a separation between the land and the sea ice. We were going rapidly adrift, with only interrupted spots of sea ice on the horizon!

There were a good many reefs about, which quickly broke the ice, and new leads formed on every side. The boat was pushed landward. We pulled the boat on the ice when the leads closed, lowering it again as the cracks opened. By carrying the boat and its load from crack to crack, we at last reached the land waters, in which we were able to advance about five miles further, camping on the gravel of the first river which we had seen. Here we were stormbound for two days.

There were several pools near by. Within a short distance from these were many ducks. With the slingshot a few of these were secured. In the midst of our trouble, with good appetites, we were feeding up for future contests of strength.

With a shore clear of ice, we could afford to take some chance with heavy seas, so before the swell subsided, we pushed off. As we came out of Braebugten Bay, with its discharging glaciers and many reefs, the water dashed against the perpendicular walls of ice, and presented a disheartening prospect. These reefs could be passed over only when the sea was calm.

As we neared our objective point, on the fast ice inside of a reef, we were greeted with the glad sight of what we supposed to be a herd of musk ox. About three miles of the winter ice was still fast to the land. Upon this we camped, cleared the canvas boat, and prepared to camp in it. I remained to guard our few belongings, while the two Eskimo boys rushed over the ice to try to secure the musk ox with the lance. It was a critical time in our career, for we were putting to test new methods of hunting, which we had partly devised after many hungry days of preparation.

I followed the boys with the glasses as they jumped the icy crevasses and moved over the mainland with the stealth and ease of hungry wolves. It was a beautiful day. The sun was low in the northwest, throwing beams of golden light that made the ice a scene of joy. The great cliffs of North Devon, fifteen miles away, seemed very near through the clear air. Although enjoying the scene, I noted in the shadow of an iceberg a suspicious blue spot, which moved in my direction. As it advanced in the sunlight, it changed from blue to a cream color. Then I made it out to be a polar bear which we had attacked forty-eight hours previously.

The sight aroused a feeling of elation. Gradually, as Bruin advanced and I began to think of some method of defense, a cold shiver ran up my spine. The dog and rifle, with which we had met bears before, were absent. To run, and leave our last bit of food and fuel, would have been as dangerous as to

stay. A polar bear will always attack a retreating creature,
while it approaches very cautiously one that holds its position. Furthermore, for some reason, the bears always bore a
grudge against the boat. None ever passed it without testing
the material with its teeth or giving it a slap with its paw. At
this critical stage of our adventure, the boat was linked more
closely to our destiny than the clothes we wore. I therefore
decided to stay and play the role of the aggressor, although
I had nothing—not even a lance—with which to fight.

Then an idea flashed through my mind. I lashed a knife
to the steering paddle, and placed the boat on a slight elevation of ice, so as to make it and myself appear as formidable
as possible. Then I gathered about me all the bits of wood,
pieces of ice, and everything which I could throw at the
creature before it came to a close contest, reserving the
knife and the ice-ax as my last resort. When all was ready, I
took my position beside the boat and displayed a sledge-
runner moving rapidly to and fro.

The bear was then about 200 yards away. It approached
stealthily behind a line of hummocks, with only its head occasionally visible. As it came to within 300 feet it rose frequently on its hind feet, dropped its forepaws, stretched its
neck, and pushed its head up, remaining motionless for several seconds. It then appeared huge and beautiful.

As it came still nearer, its pace quickened. I began to hurl
my missiles. Every time the bear was hit, it stopped, turned
about, and examined the object. But none of them proving
palatable, it advanced to the opposite side of the boat, and
for a moment stood and eyed me. Its nose caught the odor
of a piece of oogzuk blubber a few feet beyond. I raised the

sledge-runner and brought it down with desperate force on the brute's nose. It grunted, but quickly turned to retreat. I followed until it was well on the run.

Every time it turned to review the situation, I made a show of chasing it. This always had the desired effect of hastening its departure. It moved off, however, only a short distance and then sat down, sniffed the air and watched my movements. As I turned to observe the boys' doings, I saw them only a short distance away, edging up to the bear. Their group of musk oxen had proved to be rocks, and they had early noted my troubles and were hastening to enter the battle, creeping up behind hummocks and pressure ridges. They got to within a few yards of the brute, and then delivered their two lances at once, with lines attached. The bear dropped but quickly recovered and ran for the land. We had lost our game. But he died of the wounds, for a month later we found his carcass on land, near that camp.

For two days, with a continuation of bad luck, we advanced slowly. Belcher Point was passed at midnight of August 7, just as the sun sank under the horizon for the first time. Beyond was a nameless bay, in which numerous icebergs were stranded. The bend of the bay was walled with great discharging glaciers. A heavy sea pitched our boat like a leaf in a gale. However, by seeking the shelter of bergs and passing inside of the drift, we managed to push to an island for camp.

With moving glaciers on the land, and the sea storming and thundering, sleep was impossible. Icebergs in great numbers followed us into the bay, and later the storm-ground sea ice filled the bay. On August 8th, following a line of water along shore, we started eastward.

A strong wind on our backs, with quiet waters, sent the little boat along at a swift pace. After we had made a run of ten miles, a great quantity of ice, coming from the east, filled the bay with small fragments and ensnared us.

Now the bay was jammed with a pack as difficult to travel over as quicksand. We were hopelessly beset. The land was sought, but it offered no shelter, no life, and no place flat enough to lie upon. We expected that the ice would break. It did not; instead, new winter ice rapidly formed.

The setting sun brought the winter storms and premonitions of a long, bitter night. Meanwhile we eked out a meagre living by catching occasional birds, which we devoured raw.

Toward the end of August we pushed out on the ensnaring pack to a small but solid floe. I counted on this to drift somewhere—any place beyond the prison bars of the glaciers. Then we might move east or west to seek food. Our last meal was used, and we maintained life only by an occasional gull or guillemot. This floe drifted to and fro, and slowly took us to Belcher Point, where we landed to determine our fate. To the east, the entire horizon was lined with ice. Belcher Point was barren of game and shelter. Further efforts for Baffin Bay were hopeless. The falling temperature, the rapidly forming young ice, and the setting sun showed us that we had already gone too long without finding a winter refuge.

Our only possible chance to escape death from famine and frost was to go back to Cape Sparbo and compel the walrus that ripped our boat to give up his blubber, and then seek our fortunes in the neighborhood. This was the only reachable place that had looked like game country. With empty stomachs, and on a heavy sea, we pushed westward to seek our fate. The outlook was discouraging.

We were near to the land where Franklin and his men had starved. They had had ammunition. We had none. A similar fate loomed before us. We had seen nothing to promise subsistence for the winter, but this cheerless prospect did not interfere with such preparations as we could make for the ultimate struggle. In our desperate straits we even planned to attack bears, should we find any, without a gun. Life is never so sweet as when its days seem numbered. By an oversight, most of our Eskimo implements had been left on the returning sledges from Svartevoeg.

We were thus not only without ammunition, but also without harpoons and lances. We fortunately had the material of which these could be made, and the boys possessed the savage genius to shape a new set of weapons. The slingshot and the looped line, which had served such a useful purpose in securing birds, continued to be of prime importance. In the sledge was excellent hickory, which was utilized in various ways. Of this, bows and arrows could be made. The combination of slingshot and looped line snares would make our warfare upon the feathered creatures more effective. We counted upon a similar efficiency with the same weapons in our hoped-for future attack upon land animals.

The wood of the sledge was further divided to make shafts for harpoons and lances. Realizing that our ultimate return to Greenland, and to friends, depended on the life of the sledge, we used the wood sparingly. Furthermore, hickory lends itself to great economy. It bends and twists, but seldom breaks in such a manner that it can not be repaired.

We had not much of this precious fibre, but enough to serve our purpose for the time. Along shore we had found musk-ox horns and fragments of whalebone. Out of these the points of both harpoon and lance were made. A part of the sledge shoe was sacrificed to make metal points for the weapons. The nails of the cooking-hook served as rivets. The sealskin, which we had secured a month earlier, was now carefully divided and cut into suitable harpoon and lasso lines. We hoped to use this line to capture the bear and the musk ox. Our folding canvas boat was somewhat strengthened by the leather from our old boots, and additional bracing by the ever-useful hickory of the sledge. Ready to engage in battle with the smallest and the largest creatures that might come within reach, we started west for Cape Sparbo. Death, on our journey, never seemed so near.

n

↑

15

NEAR THE BRINK

In the hopeful start to find a retreat from our gloomy destiny, we were forced by storm to climb again out of the dangerous ice-strewn sea to an island, a small, partly submerged glacial moraine with a few big rocks above shallow water. Here we were delayed for several days. Unable to move, we crept under skins and sought some rest on cold sands between ice-transported boulders. I was comfortable enough to think and dream in this storm-swept camp during several days of watchful waiting. Though the icy world about us was as bright and light as it could be with torn clouds of winter snow drifting over us landward, to me the future was getting darker every day. Misery and more misery was again to follow us.

Up to the present all had been done which in our desperate situations could be done to enable us to survive. If now the curtain of night should come over us to end all, we were resigned. In the passion of self-preservation we had waged a long war. Now our position was beyond rescue in the open field of icy gun blasts. Annihilation, it seemed, would be our fate.

The afterglow of life which precedes the twilight of the end was now for me to be a study in wakefulness for some long days. I had often been in a similar mental state during the passing six months and therefore had become familiar with the gruesome subject. Such a status perhaps appears in the beclouded brains of all men who die in a lingering prolongation of life. So long as the agitation of fear and the uncertainty of how we are to enter the darkness of the beyond rule, clear thinking is difficult, but when calm resignation fits an adaptation to the expectancy of death, then the brain is cleared for action; then that part of life which remains has a new motive and a new meaning.

If the thrills, the joys, the pains and sorrows of the end of passing existence could be put on record, how much better we might understand this good old world and the new of the next!

Because these passing flashes of thought usually pass into the grave, I have reasoned that every phase of our long struggle with death should here get some attention. Unlike other unfortunates who, as they near the end, pass into the cloudy gloom of disease, we, though half-starved, bodily withered, and under the strain of extreme exhaustion, were still in some healthful vigor, with a capacity for clear thinking which is a premonitory advantage to starving men in our position.

To me the end was now near. I knew it, and felt the chill of death coming from within and distantly approaching from without. Our lips were blue with that gray blueness which bespeaks the failing blood supply and the weakened heart action before the eyes finally close. "Now what has life to offer?" These questions came in the blast of the winds.

The time for mental telegraphy, of heartaches, had passed. There was, of course, the last dying urge to touch the hands and hear the voices of loved ones. In this respect we differed from millions of others in the silent moments when resignation to death comes. The oft-repeated anticipation of this thrill was now relegated to the subconscious. We were condemned to die; only a miracle could enable us to survive, and such a miracle would offer something like rising after death. We were past any thought of a parallel resurrection.

And yet there was something almost pleasing in our abject resignation. It was not gladness nor happiness. Something like a divine wine of action drove our feeble hearts. "So this is the end," came to me often while the motor vehicles of the brain slowed down.

How divine is this reign of peace near the end—the satisfaction which comes from this bodily ease! If this could be put into understandable words, what glory it might convey! But the shadowy domain between the past and the future deals with form-carriers of thought to which only angels could apply the superhuman gift of knowledge.

As a physician I had closed many eyes in that tragic spell of minutes when rigor mortis begins to ascend from cooling hands and feet. Now there came the question as applied to myself when life was slipping—what is it that leaves the body when the chill of death arrives? What dies at death and what lives in the beyond?

Not all dies at death; for the finger and toenails, also the hair, also the flora and fauna of the intestinal tract continue to grow after death. These surviving cells are a part of life. The same, still growing, are a part of death. What then is life? What is death? Where can we divide the past from the future?

Since what we ascribe as discernible life is a functional manifestation of active bodily cells, how can life rise from the dead body and persist in a future world? Without a body with organs to give an expression of life, what is the system which can prolong life in the future? Such questions must remain unanswered in the present state of all scientific knowledge. But the earth-living soul wants this knowledge.

That there is life after death on earth must be in reason conceded. Like all animals and plants, humans give to their offspring part of the living substance. Part of this is again passed along to our children's children, and thus onward indefinitely our lives continue in succeeding generations of the future. This is a very definite system of the prolongation of our lives into the remote future, and its branching ramifications can be easily envisioned.

In races and perhaps in all forms of civilization there is an enzyme, a transferred ferment, which is conserved and passed along by progenitors. Because this is so, human nature is old and fairly uniform through long, passing ages. Perhaps all intelligence begins and ends in the mental format of the savage.[12] The culture of civilization is but the midriver current; the shore line is ever a neglected wilderness. Our education is only a refreshing drink out of this midstream, but to get to it we go from shore to shore, out of and into the primitive schooling of wild life. A few leave the main river of life and gather about special watering places. There they dig wells. There they dream dreams, and create stuff for future dreamers, but their method and their products are also old.

Philosophy, art, literature, and religion all come out of old oaken buckets, out of buckets which dipped deep and long in the well of time to bring up liquid to quench the thirst for knowledge. Here is a phase of enduring heritage which gives color and force to all human existence. It is the essence of life which survives on earth after individual death. How little do we think of this pulsating stream of power as it passes onward to us through forgotten progenitors. When all goes well, the divinity of earthly advantages is lost in self-made darkness. When, however, the mind sees through owl eyes, as with us, in the resigned expectancy of death there is gratefulness for this long-lived goodness in the passing humanity to which we have contributed our share.

The thought now came over me as this fleeting appraisal of the capacity of life assumed dreamy ramifications, that the power of the brain was to man his only real wealth, and yet in the vigor and passion of existence we seldom think of this. We should treat the brain as we do the farm. It is our garden of life. The mental sphere must be fertilized, must be cultivated, must be planted, must be given time for seasonal germination and sprouting growth, before a brain harvest can be reaped. And all must be often repeated to farm the life we humans live.

Life after death—what dies at the end? Again and again
this thought seeks an answer in the twilight of our death
wake. I have previously referred to specific examples to
prove that not all dies at death. Part of every human body
still lives when it is buried, if not injected with chemical
poison or cremated. When a seal is killed it is often buried
under a mound of rocks without being stripped of its ab-
dominal organs. The living ferment of the intestinal con-
tents begins double activity at once after death. The fauna
and flora thus continuing to function were a part of the living body, and in double vigor this life now begins to devour
the tissue of the dead body. So much heat is generated by
this bio-chemical reaction that even in low zero weather the
interior remains warm. In from one to three years the entire
carcass becomes a cheesy mass of steaming fermentation.
This rotted meat and fat and other tissue to the Eskimo
palate becomes a delicacy to give vitality to their own anemic
bodies during the long night. In other words, the life of a
dead body supplants the lack of vigor in the winter food
and sunless air for the living.

Perhaps we can better grasp this capacity for life after
death if we seek for examples in the death realm of plants.
An old tree, in the passing years of its slow ending, becomes
the nesting place of a new universe of life. The tree has for
ages served as house and grave for fungus plants, for bugs
and worms and birds. Now the rodents, the foxes, and other
four-pawed creatures dig in to winter. The center begins to
rot. The heart of the old tree becomes the generating soil
for ages of life to come. As the live sap slowly recedes from
the woody mass, the chemical transformation of death already in progress generates more heat. After the tree dies,

the life on and within its body increases. Now rain, snow, and sunshine continue to give the dead body of the tree the quality of active soil to continue the living life of the tree in its colonies for years beyond its death.

On earth in some plants, in some animals, and in all humans there is life within the body for limited periods after death. As we now seek the Beyond for a status of living existence without body or form or tangible material quality in what we call the spiritual world, the brain refuses to forecast a future.

For this the Bible and other religious works and the religious folklore in unwritten history give the only outlook. The research of science here aids us very little. Many conflicting views of ancient and modern thought confuse and prevent a vision of this quite generally conceded life of the future. But as I now sought to see into this unknown over the great divide, I felt confident that life in the future is possible. To me and to my Eskimo companions the life beyond bodily death was a conception which implied the light of life, the afterglow of a fire which must in some way be given fuel to continue in the next world.

When, with this thought uppermost, I now sought to envision the beyond, the eternity above the blue of the sky became a fascinating study. It was worth the cost of having been at the doors of death to feel the peace and inspiration of this new thought. The light-beam of life like the sunbeam lives forever, but full expression of this hypothesis must be delayed for another time.

While thus happy in new thoughts and new visions, I turned from side to side with eyes closed to our adverse environment. Sleep was easy now. After an hour or two I woke up, feeling much better. The shivers and the darkness of coming death were now dispelled. I pulled the furs from my face. All was bright. Some snow had fallen. The temperature was a few degrees below the freezing point. Our camp was icy but dry. The sun for a few moments appeared in a split between parting clouds. A little cheerful warmth was in the big bars of sunlight. Both Etuq and Wela were awake. Etuq was resigned and sad. Wela was alive and agitated, with sparkling eyes. There was no conversation, no wind; not a sound echoed among the icy cliffs. To my eyes a new world of icy splendor appeared.

But in the face of Etuq, as I glanced sideways out of one eye, there was a look of utter despair. The cold smear of death oozed from the edge of his half-closed eyes. Icy, pasty, oily tears rolled down emotionless cheeks. Further down in his matted long black hair globules of half-frozen tears became enmeshed. A more desperate picture of sadness for the end of life's trail could not have been composed.

In our misfortunes we had never all been discouraged at the same time, which was to us a fortunate division of opinion. It would have been easier to die than to live in many of our entrapped positions, if we had been of one mind to quit life's claims and resign in unison to closed eyes. But when cheer was absent in one there was the outlook of gladness in two. It was so on this memorable day. I had passed the stage of doom in our most recent gloom.

Wela was up to something I had yet to learn about. I got up to dress and do something to put Etuq in a more cheerful mood. As I rose, Wela said, "Aureti" (keep quiet). I responded by lying down without further orders. Some gulls were active beyond near-by rocks. Then I noted Wela had there set a looped-line trap. He gave a sudden jerk to a line and then pulled in two fat gulls. The net of looped lines was set again, and in a few moments another gull was captured. Now we had three gulls—one for each. A good meal was in prospect.

Then we all arose, shook the snow from our furs, and entered a discussion on the manner of eating our new catch. We had some seal blubber, a few dry bones, and some moss. Soon a fire was aglow in an improvised fireplace among the rocks. The gulls were skinned, dressed and placed in a pot. In an hour we had a fill of tasty gull broth and meat. And then the shivers of death were for a time dispelled.

New resolutions were made, including new plans better to fit ourselves to a new life of action. The urge to survive had received a new impulse in the foresight of death. All was stored and securely lashed in the boat, and again we were off to find ourselves a new Promised Land westward, with sunshine and quiet waters for a fresh start.

As we now paddled among separating lanes of sea, among the parting fields of ice, each had in mind some serious thought to engage attention. To me it seemed that death must be looked for in the background of every picture of life and must therefore be rated as a guiding force to extract the best out of existence before the sorrows of the end. But, above all, that resigned expectancy of death in which I had lived with profit for days now offered a new dominion of life, a reawakening, a regeneration almost in the nature of a resurrection.

n

↑

16

TUG OF WAR WITH A WALRUS

The stormy sea rose with heavy swells. Oceanward, the waves leaped against the horizon tumultuously. Pursuing our vain search for food along the southern side of Jones Sound, early in September, we had been obliged to skirt rocky coves and shelves of land on which we might seek shelter should harm come to the fragile craft in which we braved the ocean storms and the spears of unseen ice beneath water.

We had shaped crude weapons. We were prepared to attack game. We were starving; yet land and sea had been barren of any living thing.

Our situation was desperate. In our course it was often necessary, as now, to paddle from the near refuge of low-lying shores, and to pass precipitous cliffs and leaping glaciers which stepped threateningly into the sea. Along these were no projecting surfaces, and we passed them always with anxiety. A sudden storm or a mishap at such a time would have meant death in the frigid sea. And now, grim and suffering with hunger, we clung madly to life.

Passing a glacier which rose hundreds of feet out of the green sea, we encountered heavy waves that rolled furiously from the distant ocean. Huge bergs rose and fell against the far-away horizon like Titan ships hurled to destruction. The waves dashed against the emerald walls of the smooth icy Gibraltar with a thunderous noise. We rose and fell in the frail canvas boat, butting the waves, our hearts each time sinking.

Suddenly something white and glittering pierced the bottom of the boat! It was the tusk of a walrus, gleaming and dangerous. Before we could grasp the situation he had disappeared, and water gushed into our craft. It was the first walrus we had seen for several weeks. An impulse, made under the circumstances, rose in our hearts to give him chase. It was the instinctive call of the hungering body for food. But each second the water rose higher; each minute was imminent with danger. Instinctively Wela pressed to the floor of the boat and jammed his knee into the hole, thus partly shutting off the jetting, leaping inrush. He looked mutely at me for orders. The glacier offered no stopping place. Looking about with mad eagerness, I saw, seaward, only a few hundred yards away, a small pan of drift ice. With the desire for life in our arms, we pushed toward it with all our might.

Before the boat was pulled to its slippery landing, several
inches of water flooded the bottom. Once upon the drift ice,
leaping in the waves, we breathed with panting relief. With
a piece of boot the hole was patched. Although we should
have preferred to wait to give the walrus a wide berth, the
increasing swell of the stormy sea and a seaward drift forced
us away from the dangerous ice cliffs.

Launching the boat into the rough waters, we pulled for
land. A triangle of four miles had to be made before our
fears could be set at rest. A school of walrus followed us in
the rocking waters for at least half of the distance. Finally,
upon the crest of a white-capped wave, we were lifted to
firm land. Drawing the boat after us, we ran out of reach
of the hungry waves, and sank to the grass, desperate, de-
spairing, utterly fatigued but safe.

Now followed a long run of famine luck. We searched
land and sea for a bird or a fish. In the boat we skirted a barren coast, sleeping on rocks without shelter and quenching
our thirst by glacial liquid till the stomach collapsed. The
indifferent stage of starvation was at hand when we pulled
into a nameless bay, carried the boat onto a grassy bench,
and packed ourselves into it for a sleep that might be our last.

We were awakened by the glad sound of the distant walrus calls. Through the glasses, we located a group far off
shore, on the middle pack. No famished wolf ever responded
to a call more rapidly than we did. Quickly we dropped the
boat into the water with the implements, and pushed from
the famine shores with teeth set for red meat.

The day was beautiful, and the sun from the west poured
out a wealth of golden light. Only an occasional ripple disturbed the glassy blue through which the boat crept. The

pack was about five miles northward. In our eagerness to reach it, the distance seemed to spread to leagues. There was not a square of ice for miles about which could have been sought for refuge in case of an attack. But this did not disturb us now. We were blinded to everything except the dictates of our palates.

As we advanced, our tactics were definitely arranged. The animals were on a low pan, which seemed to be loosely run into the main pack. We aimed for a little cut of ice open to the leeward, where we hoped to land and creep up behind hummocks. The splash of our paddles was lost in the noise of the grinding ice and the bellowing of walrus calls.

So excited were the Eskimos that they could hardly pull an oar. It was the first shout of the wilderness which we had heard in many months. We were lean enough to appreciate its import. The boat finally shot upon the ice, and we scattered among the ice blocks for favorable positions. Everything was in our favor. We did not for a moment entertain a thought of failure, although in reality, with the implements at hand, our project was tantamount to attacking an elephant with pocket knives.

We came together behind an unusually high icy spire only a few hundred yards from the herd. Ten huge animals were lazily stretched out in the warm sun. A few lively babies tormented their sleeping mothers. There was a splendid line of hummocks, behind which we could advance under cover. With a firm grip on harpoon and line, we started.

Suddenly Etuq shouted, "Nannook!" (bear). We halted. Our implements were no match for a bear. But we were too hungry to retreat. The bear paid no attention to us. His nose was set for something more to his liking. Slowly but deliberately he crept up to the snoring herd while we watched with a mad, envious anger welling up within us. Our position was helpless. His long neck reached out, the glistening fangs closed, and a young walrus struggled in the air. All of the creatures woke, but too late to give battle. With dismay and rage, the walruses sank into the water, and the bear slunk off to a safe distance, where he sat down to a comfortable meal. We were not of sufficient importance to interest either the bear or the disturbed herd of giants.

Our limbs were limp when we returned to the boat. The sunny glitter of the waters was now darkened by the gloom of danger from enraged animals. We crossed to the barren shores in a circuitous route, where pieces of ice for refuge were always within reach.

On land, the night was cheerless and cold. We were not in a mood for sleep. In a lagoon we discovered moving things. A little study of their vague darts proved them to be fish. A diligent search under stones brought out a few handfuls of tiny finny creatures. With gratitude I saw that here was an evening meal. Seizing them, we ate the wriggling things raw. Cooking was impossible, for we had neither oil nor wood.

On the next day the sun at noon burned with a real fire— not the sham light without heat which had kept day and night in perpetual glitter for several weeks. Not a breath of air disturbed the blue shine of the sea. Ice was scattered everywhere. The central pack was farther away, but on it rested several suspicious black marks. Through the glasses we made these out to be groups of walruses. They were evidently sound asleep, for we heard no calls. They were also so distributed that there was a hunt both for bear and man without interference.

We ventured out with a savage desire sharpened by a taste of raw fish. As we advanced, several other groups were noted in the water. They gave us most trouble. They did not seem ill-tempered, but dangerously inquisitive. Our boat was dark in color and not much larger than the body of a full-sized bull. To them, I presume, it resembled a companion in distress or sleep. A sight of the boat challenged their curiosity, and they neared us with the playful intention of testing with their tusks the hardness of the canvas. We had experienced such love-taps before, however, with but a narrow escape from drowning, and we had no desire for further walrus courtship.

Fortunately, we could maintain a speed almost equal to theirs, and we also found scattered ice pans, about which we could linger while their curiosity was being satisfied by the splash of an occasional stone.

From an iceberg we studied the various groups of walruses for the one best situated for our primitive methods of attack. We also searched for meddlesome bears. None was detected. Altogether we counted more than a hundred grunting, snorting creatures arranged in black hills along a line of low ice. There were no hummocks or pressure lifts, under cover of which we might advance to within the short range required for our harpoons. All of the walrus-encumbered pans were adrift and disconnected from the main pack. Conflicting currents gave each group a slightly different motion. We studied this movement for a little while.

We hoped, if possible, to make our attack from the ice. With the security of a solid footing there was no danger and there was a greater certainty of success. But the speed of the ice on this day did not permit such an advantage. We must risk a water attack. This is not an unusual method of the Eskimo, though he follows it with a kayak, a harpoon and line fitted with a float, and a drag for the end of this line. Our equipment was only a makeshift, and could not be handled in the same way.

Here was food in massive heaps. We had had no breakfast and no full meal for many weeks. Something must be done. The general drift was eastward, but the walrus pans drifted slightly faster than the main pack. Along the pack were several high points, projecting a considerable distance seaward. We took our position in the canvas boat behind one of these floating capes, and awaited the drift of the sleeping monsters.

Their movement was slow enough to give us plenty of time to arrange our battle tactics. The most vital part of the equipment was the line. If the line were lost, we could not hope to survive the winter. It could not be replaced, and without it we could not hope to cope with the life of the sea, or even that of the land. The line was a new, strong sealskin rawhide of ample length, which had been reserved for just such an emergency. Attached to the harpoon, with the float properly adjusted, it is seldom lost, for the float moves and permits no sudden strain.

To safeguard the line, a pan was selected only a few yards in diameter. This was arranged to do the duty of a float and a drag. With the knife two holes were cut, and into these the line was fastened near its center. The harpoon end was taken into the boat; the other end was coiled and left in a position where it could be easily picked from the boat later. Important purposes were secured by this arrangement—the line was relieved of a sudden strain; if it broke, only half would be lost; and the unused end would serve as a binder to other ice when the chase neared its end.

Now the harpoon was set to the shaft, and the bow of our little twelve-foot boat cleared for action. Peeping over the wall of ice, we saw the black-littered pans slowly coming toward us. Our excitement rose to a shouting point. But our nerves were under the discipline of famine. The pan, it was evident, would go by us at a distance of about fifty feet.

The first group of walruses were allowed to pass. They proved to be a herd of twenty-one mammoth creatures, and entirely aside from the danger of attack, their unanimous plunge would have raised a sea that must have swamped us.

On the next pan were only three spots. At a distance we persuaded ourselves that they were small—for we had no ambition for formidable attacks. One thousand pounds of meat would have been sufficient for us. They proved, however, to be the largest bulls of the lot. As they neared the point, the hickory oars of the boat were gripped—and out we shot. They all rose to meet us, displaying the glitter of ivory tusks from little heads against huge wrinkled necks. They grunted and snorted viciously—but the speed of the boat did not slacken.

Etuq rose. With a savage thrust he sank the harpoon into a yielding neck. The walruses tumbled over themselves and sank into the water on the opposite side of the pan.

We pushed upon the vacated floe without leaving the boat, taking the risk of ice puncture rather than walrus thumps. The short line came up with a snap. The ice pan began to plow the sea. It moved landward. What luck! I wondered if the walrus would tow us and its own carcass ashore. We longed to encourage the homing movement, but we dared not venture out. Other animals had awakened to the battle call, and now the sea began to seethe and boil with enraged, leaping red-eyed monsters.

The float took a zigzag course in the offing. We watched the movement with a good deal of anxiety. Our next meal and our last grip on life were at stake. For the time being nothing could be done.

The three animals remained together, two pushing the wounded one along and holding it up during breathing spells. In their excitement they either lost their bearings or deliberately determined to attack. Now three ugly snouts pointed at us. This was greatly to our advantage, for on ice we were masters of the situation.

Taking inconspicuous positions, we awaited the assault. The Eskimos had lances; I, an Alpine ax. The walruses dove and came on like torpedo boats, rising almost under our noses, with a noise that made us dodge. In a second, two lances sank into the harpooned strugglers. The water was thrashed. Down again went the three. The lances jerked back by return lines, and in another moment we were ready for another assault from the other side. But they dashed on, and pulled the float-ice, on which we had been, against the one on which we stood, with a crushing blow.

Here was our first chance to secure the unused end of the line, fastened on the other floe. Wela jumped to the floe and tossed me the line. The spiked shaft of the ice ax was driven in the ice and the line fixed to it, so now the two floes were held together. Our stage of action was enlarged, and we had the advantage of being towed by the animals we fought.

Here was the quiet sport of the fisherman and the savage

excitement of the battlefield run together in a new chase. The struggle was prolonged in successive stages. Time passed swiftly. In six hours, during which the sun had swept a quarter of the circle, the twin floes were jerked through the water with the rush of a gunboat. The jerking line attached to our enraged pilots sent a thrill of life which made our hearts jump. The lances were thrown, the line was shortened, a cannonade of ice blocks was kept up, but the animals gave no sign of weakening. Seeing that we could not inflict dangerous wounds, our tactics were changed to a kind of siege, and we aimed not to permit the animals their breathing spells.

The line did not begin to slacken until midnight. The battle had been on for almost twelve hours. But we did not feel the strain of action, nor did our chronic hunger seriously disturb us. Bits of ice quenched our thirst and the chill of night kept us from sweating. With each rise of the beasts for breath now, the lines slackened. Gently they were hauled in and secured. Then a rain of ice blocks, hurled in rapid succession, drove the spouting animals down. Soon the line was short enough to deliver the lance in the one walrus at close range. This wounded animal was now less troublesome, but the others tore under us like submarine boats, and at the most unexpected moments would shoot up with a wild rush.

We did not attempt to attack them, however. All our attention was directed to the end of the line. The lance was driven with every opportunity. It seldom missed, but the action was more like spurs to a horse, changing an intended attack upon us to a desperate plunge into the deep, and depriving the walrus of oxygen.

Finally—after a battle of spasmodic encounters which had

lasted fifteen hours—the enraged snout turned blue, the fiery eyes blackened, and victory was ours, not as the result of the knife alone, not in a square fight of brute force, but by the superior cunning of the human animal under the stimulus of hunger.

During all this time we had been drifting. Now, as the battle ended, we were not far from a point about three miles south of our camp. Plenty of safe pack-ice was near. A primitive pulley was arranged by passing the line through slits in the walrus's nose and holes in the ice. The great carcass, weighing perhaps 3,000 pounds, was drawn onto the ice and divided into portable pieces. Before the sun poured its morning beams over the ice, all had been securely taken ashore.

With ample blubber, we now made a camp fire between two rocks by using moss to serve as wick. Soon pot after pot of savory meat was voraciously consumed. We ate with a mad, vulgar, insatiable hunger. We spoke little. Between gulps, the huge heap of meat and blubber was cached under heavy rocks, and secured—so we thought—from bears, wolves, and foxes.

When eating was no longer possible, sleeping dens were arranged in the little boat, and in it, like other gluttonous animals after an engorgement, we closed our eyes to a digestive sleep. For the time, at least, we had fathomed the depths of gastronomic content, and were at ease with ourselves and with a bitter world of inhuman strife.

At the end of about fifteen hours, a stir about our camp suddenly awakened us. We saw a huge bear nosing about our fireplace. We had left there a walrus joint, weighing about one hundred pounds, for our next meal. We jumped up, all of us, at once, shouting and making a pretended rush. The bear took up the meat in his forepaws and walked off, man-like, on two legs, with a threatening grunt. His movement was slow and cautious, and his grip on the meat was secure. Occasionally he veered about, with a beckoning turn of the head, and a challenging call. But we did not accept the challenge. After moving away about 300 yards on the sea ice, he calmly sat down and devoured our prospective meal.

With lances, bows, arrows, and stones in hand, we next crossed a low hill, beyond which was located our previous cache of meat. Here, to our chagrin, we saw two other bears, with heads down and paws busily digging about the cache. We were not fitted for a hand-to-hand encounter. Still, our lives were equally at stake, whether we attacked or failed to attack. Some defense must be made. With a shout and a fiendish rush, we attracted the busy brutes' attention. They raised their heads, turned, and to our delight and relief, grudgingly walked off seaward on the moving ice. Each had a big piece of meat with him.

Advancing to the cache, we found it absolutely depleted. Many other bears had been there. The snow and the sand was tramped down with innumerable bear tracks. Our splendid cache of the day previous was entirely lost. We could have wept with rage and disappointment. One thing we were made to realize, and that was that life here was now to be a struggle with the bears for supremacy. With little ammunition we were not at all able to engage in bear fights. So, baffled, and unable to resent our robbery, starvation again confronted us. We packed our few belongings and moved westward over Braebugten Bay to Cape Sparbo.

n

$\uparrow$

17

CONQUERING THE MUSK OX

As we crossed the big bay to the east of Cape Sparbo, our eyes were fixed on the two huge Archean rocks which made remarkable landmarks, rising suddenly to an altitude of about 1,800 feet. They appear like two mountainous islands lifted out of the water. On closer approach, however, we found the islands connected with the mainland by low grassy plains, forming a peninsula. The grassy lands seemed like promising grounds for caribou and musk ox. The off-lying sea, we also found, was shallow. In this, I calculated, would be food to attract the seal and walrus.

In our slow movement over the land-swell of the crystal waters, it did not take long to discover that our conjecture was correct. Pulling up to a great herd of walrus, we prepared for battle. But the sea suddenly rose, the wind increased, and we were forced to abandon the chase and seek shelter on the nearest land.

We reached Cape Sparbo, on the shores of Jones Sound, early in September. Our dogs were gone. Our ammunition, except for four cartridges which I had secreted for use in a last emergency, was gone. Our equipment consisted of a half sledge, a canvas boat, a torn silk tent, a few camp kettles, tin plates, knives, and matches. Our clothing was splitting to shreds.

Cape Sparbo, with its huge walls of granite, was to the leeward. A little bay was noted where we might gain the rocks in quiet water. Above the rocks was a small green patch where we hoped to find a soft resting place for the boat, so that we might place our furs in it and secure shelter from the bitter wind.

When we landed we found to our surprise that it was the site of an old Eskimo village. There was a line of old igloos partly below water, indicating a very ancient time of settlement, for since the departure of the builders of these igloos the coast must have settled at least fifteen feet. Above were a few other ruins.

Shortly after arriving we sought an auspicious place, protected from the wind and cold, where later we might build a winter shelter. Our search disclosed a cave-like hole, part of which was dug from the earth, and over which, with stones and bones, had been constructed a roof which now was fallen in.

The long winter was approaching. We were over 300 miles from Annoatok, and the coming of the long night made it necessary for us to halt here. We must have food and clothing. We now came upon musk oxen and tried to fell them with boulders, and bows and arrows made of the hickory of our sledge. Day after day the pursuit was vainly followed. Had it not been for occasional ducks caught with looped lines and slingshot, we should have been absolutely without any food.

By the middle of September, snow and frost came with such frequency that we omitted hunting for a day to dig out the ruins in the cave and cut sod before permanent frost made such work impossible. Bone implements were shaped from skeletons found on shore for the digging. Blown drifts of sand and gravel, with some moss and grass, were slowly removed from the pit. We found under this, to our great joy, just the underground arrangement which we desired; a raised platform, about six feet long and eight feet wide with suitable wings for the lamp, and foot space, lay ready for us. The pit had evidently been designed for a small family. The walls, which were about two feet high, required little alteration. Another foot was added, which leveled the structure with the ground. A good deal of sod was cut and allowed to dry in the sun for use as a roof.

While engaged in taking out the stones and cleaning the dungeon-like excavation, I suddenly experienced a heart-depressing chill when, lifting some debris, I saw staring at me from the black earth a hollow-eyed human skull. The message of death which the weird thing leeringly conveyed was singularly unpleasant; the omen was not good. Yet the fact that at this forsaken spot human hands had once built shelter, or for this thing had constructed a grave, gave me a certain companionable thrill.

On the shore not far away we secured additional whale ribs and with these made a framework for a roof. This was later constructed of moss and blocks of sod. We built a rock wall about the shelter to protect ourselves from storms and bears. Then our winter home was ready. Food was now an immediate necessity. Game was found around us in abundance. Most of it was large. On land there were bear and musk ox, in the sea the walrus and the whale. But what could we do without either dogs or rifles?

The first weapon that we now devised was the bow and arrow, for with this we could at least secure some small game. We had in our sledge available hickory wood of the best quality, than which no wood could be better; we had sinews and seal lashings for strings, but there was no metal for tips. We tried bone, horn, and ivory, but all proved ineffective.

One day, however, Etuq examined his pocket knife and suggested taking the side blades for arrow tips. This was done, and the blade with its spring was set in a bone handle. Two arrows were thus tipped. The weapons complete, the Eskimo boys went out on the chase. They returned in the course of a few hours with a hare and an eider duck. Joy reigned in camp as we divided the meat and disposed of it without the process of cooking.

A day later, two musk oxen were seen grazing along the moraine of a wasting glacier. Now the musk ox is a peace-loving animal and avoids strife, but when forced into fight it is one of the most desperate and dangerous of all the fighters of the wilderness. It can and does give the most fatal thrust of all the horned animals. No Spanish bull of the pampas, no buffalo of the plains, has either the slant of horn or the intelligence to gore its enemies as has this inoffensive-looking bull of the ice world. Their intelligence, indeed, is an important factor; for after watching musk oxen for a time under varied conditions, one comes to admire their almost human intellect as well as their superhuman power of delivering self-made force.

Our only means of attack was the bow and the arrow. The boys crept up behind rocks until within a few yards of the unsuspecting creatures. They bent the bows, and the arrows sped with the force and accuracy that only a hungry savage can muster. But the beasts' pelts were too strong. The musk oxen jumped and faced their assailants. Each arrow, as it came, was broken into splints by the feet and the teeth.

When the arrows were all used, a still more primitive weapon was tried, for the slingshot was brought into use, with large stones. These missiles the musk oxen took good-naturedly, merely advancing a few steps to a granite boulder, upon which they sharpened their horn points and awaited further developments. No serious injury had been inflicted and they made no effort to escape.

Then came a change. When we started to give up the chase they turned upon us with a fierce rush. Fortunately, many big boulders were about, and we dodged around these with large stones in hand to deliver at close range. In a wild rush a musk ox cannot easily turn, and so can readily be dodged. Among the rocks two legs were better than four. The trick of evading the musk ox I had learned from the dogs. It saved our lives.

After a while the animals wearied, and we beat a hasty retreat, with new lessons in our book of hunting adventures. The bow and arrow was evidently not the weapon with which to secure musk oxen.

The musk ox of Jones Sound, unlike his brother farther north, is ever ready for battle. He is often compelled to meet the bear and the wolf in vicious contests, and his tactics are as thoroughly developed as his emergencies require. Seldom does he fall the victim of his enemies. We were a long time in learning completely his methods of warfare and if, in the meantime, we had not secured other game our fate would have been unfortunate.

Harpoons and lances were next finally completed, and with them we hastened to retrieve our honor in the "ahming-ma" (musk-ox) chase. For, after all, the musk ox alone could supply our wants. Winter storms were coming fast. We were not only without food and fuel, but without clothing. In our desperate effort to get out of the regions of famine to the Atlantic, we had left behind all our winter furs, including the sleeping bags; and our summer garments were worn out. We required the fuel and the sinew, the fat and the horn.

One day we saw a herd of twenty-one musk oxen quietly grazing on a misty meadow, like cattle on the western plains. It was a beautiful sight to watch them, divided as they were into families and in small groups. The males were in fur slightly brown, while the females and the young ones were arrayed in magnificent black pelts.

To get any of them seemed hopeless, but our appalling necessities forced us onward. There were no boulders near, but each of us gathered an armful of stones, the object being to make a sudden bombardment and compel them to retreat in disorder and scatter among the rocks.

We approached under cover of a small grassy hummock. When we were detected, a bull gave a loud snort and rushed toward his nearest companions, whereupon the entire herd gathered into a circle, with the young in the center.

We made our sham rush and hurled the stones. The oxen remained almost motionless, with their heads down, giving little snorts and stamping a little when hit, but quickly resuming their immobile position of watchfulness. After our stones were exhausted, the animals began to shift positions slightly. We interpreted this as a move for action. So we gave up the effort and withdrew.

The days were long and the nights still light enough to continue operations as long as we could keep our eyes open. The whip of hunger made rest impossible. So we determined to seek a less formidable group of oxen in a position more favorable. The search was continued until the sinking glimmer of the sun in the north marked the time of midnight—for with us at that time the compass was the timepiece.[13]

When Etuq secured a hare with the bow and arrow, we ascended a rocky eminence and sat down to appease the calling stomach without a campfire. From here we detected a family of four musk oxen asleep not far from another group of rocks.

This was a call to battle. We were not long in planning our tactics. The wind was in our favor, permitting an attack from the side opposite the rocks to which we aimed to force a retreat. We also found small stones in abundance, these being now a necessary part of our armament. Our first effort was based on the supposition of their remaining asleep.

They were simply chewing their cud, however, and rose to form a ring of defense as we advanced. We stormed them with stones and they took to the shelter of the rocks. We continued to advance slowly upon them, throwing stones occasionally to obviate a possible assault from them before we could also seek the shelter of the rocks.

Besides the bow and arrow and the stones, we now had lances and these we threw as they rushed to attack us. Two lances were crushed to small fragments before they could be withdrawn by the light line attached. They inflicted wounds, but not severe ones.

Noting the immense strength of the animals, we at first thought it imprudent to risk the harpoon with its precious line, for if we lost it we could not replace it. But the destruction of the two lances left us no alternative.

Wela threw the harpoon. It hit a rib, glanced to a rock, and was damaged. Fortunately we had a duplicate point, which was quickly fastened. Then we moved about to encourage another onslaught.

Two came at once, an old bull and a young one. Etuq threw the harpoon at the young one, and it entered. The line had previously been fastened to a rock, and the animal ran back to its associates, apparently not severely hurt, leaving the line slack. One of the others immediately attacked the line with horns, hoofs, and teeth, but did not succeed in breaking it.

Our problem now was to get rid of the other three while we dealt with the one at the end of the line. Our only resource was a sudden fusillade of stones. This proved effective. The three scattered and ascended the boulder-strewn foreland of a cliff, where the oldest bull remained to watch

our movements. The young bull made violent efforts to
escape but the line of sealskin was strong and elastic. A
lucky throw of a lance at close range ended the strife. Then
we advanced on the old bull, who was alone in a good position for us.

We gathered stones and advanced, throwing them at the
creature's body. This, we found, did not enrage him, but it
prevented his making an attack. As we gained ground he
gradually backed up to the edge of the cliff, snorting viciously but making no effort whatever either to escape along
a lateral bench or to attack. Big brown eyes were upon us;
his sharp horns were pointed at us. He evidently was planning a desperate lunge and was backing to gain time and
room, but each of us kept within a few yards of a good-sized
rock.

Suddenly we made a combined rush into the open, hurling
stones, and keeping a long rock in a line for retreat. Our
storming of stones had the desired effect. The bull, annoyed
and losing his presence of mind, stepped impatiently one
step too far backwards and fell suddenly over the cliff, landing on a rocky ledge below. Looking over we saw he had
broken a foreleg. The cliff was not more than fifteen feet
high. From it the lance was used to put the poor creature
out of suffering. We were rich now and could afford to
spread out our stomachs, contracted by long spells of famine. The bull dressed about 300 pounds of meat and 100
pounds of tallow.

We took the tallow and as much meat as we could carry
on our backs, and started for the position of our prospective
winter camp, ten miles away. The meat left was carefully
covered with heavy stones to protect it from bears, wolves,

and foxes. On the following day we returned with the canvas boat, making a landing about four miles from the battlefield. As we neared the caches we found to our dismay numerous bear and fox tracks. The bears had opened the caches and removed our hard-earned game, while the foxes and the ravens had cleared up the very fragments and destroyed even the skins. Here was cause for vengeance on the bear and the fox. The fox paid with his skin later, but the bear outgeneraled us in nearly every maneuver.

We came prepared to continue the chase but had abandoned the use of the harpoon. Our main hope for fuel was the blubber of the walrus, and if the harpoon should be destroyed or lost we could not hope to attack so powerful a brute as a walrus with any other device. In landing we had seen a small herd of musk oxen at some distance to the east, but they got our wind and vanished. We decided to follow them. One day we found them among a series of rolling hills, where the receding glaciers had left many erratic boulders. They lined up in their ring of defense as usual when we were detected. There were seven of them; all large creatures with huge horns. A bitter wind was blowing, driving some snow, which made our task more difficult.

The opening of the fight with stones was now a regular feature which we never abandoned in our later development of the art, but the manner in which we delivered the stones depended upon the effect which we wished to produce. If we wished the musk oxen to retreat, we would make a combined rush, hurling the stones at the herd. If we wished them to remain in position and discourage their attack, we advanced slowly and threw stones desultorily, more or less at random. If we wanted to encourage attacks, one man advanced and delivered a large rock as best he could at the head. This was cheap ammunition and it was very effective.

In this case the game was in a good position for us and we advanced accordingly. They allowed us to take positions within about fifteen feet, but no nearer. The lances were repeatedly tried without effect, and after a while two of these were again broken.

Having tried bow and arrow, stones, the lance, and the harpoon, we now tried another weapon. We threw the lasso —but not successfully, owing to the bushy hair about the head and the roundness of the hump of the neck. Then we tried to entangle their feet with slip loops just as we trapped gulls. This also failed. We next extended the loop idea to the horns. The bull's habit of rushing at things hurled at him caused us to think of this plan.

A large slip loop was now made in the center of the line, and the two Eskimos took up positions on opposite sides of the animal. They threw the rope, with its loop, on the ground in front of the creature, while I encouraged an attack from the front. As the head was slightly elevated the loop was raised, and the bull put his horns in it, one after the other. The rope was now rapidly fastened to stones and the bull tightened the loop by his efforts to advance or retreat. With every opportunity the slack was taken up, until no play was allowed the animal. During this struggle all the other oxen retreated except one female, and she was inoffensive. A few stones at close range drove her off. Then we had the bull where we could reach him with the lance at arm's length, and plunge it into his vitals. He soon fell over, the first victim to our new art of musk-ox capture.

The others did not run very far away. Indeed, they were

too fat to run, and the two more were soon secured in the same way. This time we took all the meat we could with us to camp and left a man on guard. When all was removed to the bay we found the load too heavy for our boat, so, in two loads, we transported the meat and fat and skins to our camp, where we built caches which we believed impregnable to the bear, although the thieving creatures actually opened them later.

Our lances repaired, we started out for another adventure a few days later. It was a beautiful day. Our methods of attack were not efficient, but we wished to avoid the risk of the last plunge of the lance, for our lives were in the balance every time if the line should break, and with every lunge of the animal we expected it to snap. In such case, we knew, the assailant would surely be gored.

We were sufficiently independent now to proceed more cautiously. With the bull's willingness to put his head into the loop, I asked myself whether the line loop could not be slipped beyond the horns and about the neck, thus shutting off the air. So the line was lengthened with this effort in view.

Of the many groups of oxen which we saw we picked those in the positions most to our advantage, although rather distant. Our new plan was tried with success on a female. A bull horned her vigorously when she gasped for breath, and thus aided our efforts. A storming of stones scattered the others of the group, and we were left to deal with our catch with the knife.

Our art of musk-ox fighting was now completely developed. In the course of a few weeks we killed enough to secure comfort and ease during the long night. By our own efforts we were lifted suddenly from famine to luxury. But it had been the stomach with its chronic emptiness which had lashed the mind and body to desperate efforts with sufficient courage to face the danger. Hunger, as I have found, is more potent as a stimulant than barrels of whisky. Beginning with the bow and arrow we tried everything which we could devise, but now our most important acquisition was our intimate knowledge of the animal's own means of offense and defense.

We knew by a kind of instinct when an attack upon us was about to be made, because the animal made a forward move, and we never failed in our efforts to force a retreat. The rocks which the animals sought for an easy defense were equally useful to us, and later we forced them into deep waters and also deep snow with similar success. By the use of stones and utilizing the creatures' own tactics we placed them where we wished. And then again, by the animal's own efforts, we forced it to strangle itself, which, after all, was the most humane method of slaughter. Three human lives were thus saved by the invention of a new art of the chase. This gave us courage to attack those more vicious but less dangerous animals, the bear and the walrus.

The musk ox now supplied many wants in our "Robinson Crusoe" life. From the bone we made harpoon points, arrow pieces, knife handles, fox traps, and sledge repairs. The skin, with its remarkable fur, made our bed and roofed our igloo. Of it we made all kinds of garments, but its greatest use was for coats with hoods, stockings, and mittens. From the skin, with the fur removed, we made boots, patched punctures in our boat, and cut lashings. The hair and wool which were removed from the skins made pads for our palms in the mittens and cushions for the soles of our feet in lieu of the grass formerly used.

The meat became our staple food for seven months, without change. It was a delicious product. It has a flavor slightly sweet, like that of horseflesh, but still distinctly pleasing. It possesses an odor unlike musk but equally unlike anything that I know of. The live creatures exhale the scent of domestic cattle. Just why this odd creature is called "musk" ox is a mystery, for it is neither an ox, nor does it smell of musk. The Eskimo name of "ah-ming-ma" would fit it much better. The bones were used as fuel for outside fires, and the fat as both fuel and food.

At first our wealth of food came with surprise and delight to us; for, in the absence of sweet or starchy foods, man craves fat. Starch and sugar are most readily converted into fat by the animal laboratory, and fat is one of the prime factors in the development and maintenance of the human system. It is the confectionery of aboriginal man, and we had taken up the lot of the most primitive aborigines, living and thriving solely on the product of the chase without a morsel of civilized or vegetable food. Under these circumstances we especially delighted in the musk-ox tallow, and more especially in the marrow, which we sucked from the bone with the eagerness with which a child jubilantly manages a stick of candy.

n

↑

18

TECHNIQUES OF HUNTING

In two months, from the first of September to the end of October, we passed from a period of hunger, thirst, and abject misery into the realm of abundant game. The spell for inactivity had not yet come. Up to this time we were too busy with the serious business of life to realize thoroughly that we had really discovered a new natural wonderland. The luck of Robinson Crusoe was not more fortunate than ours, although he had not the cut of frost, or the long night, or the torment of bears to circumscribe his adventures. In successive stages of battle our eyes had opened to a new world.

In the Arctic, nature tries to cover its nakedness in places where the cruel winds do not cut its contour. The effort is interesting, not only because of the charm of the verdant dress, but because of the evidence of a motherly protection to the little life cells which struggle against awful odds to weave that fabric wherever a terrestrial dimple is exposed to the kisses of the southern sun. In these depressions, sheltered from the blasts of storms, a kindly hand spreads a beautiful mantle of colorful grass, moss lichens and flowery plants.

Here the lemming digs his home under the velvet cover, where he may enjoy the roots and material protection from the abysmal frost of the long night. Here in the protected folds of Mother Earth, blanketed by the warm white robe of winter, he sleeps the peace of death while the warring elements blast in fury outside.

Here the Arctic hare plays with its bunnies during summer, and as the winter comes the young grow to full maturity and dress in a silky down of white. Under the snow they burrow, making long tunnels, still eating and sleeping on their loved cushions of frozen plants, far under the snow-skirts of Mother Earth, while the life-stilling blasts without expend their wintry force.

Here the ptarmigan scratches for its food. The musk ox and the caribou browse, while the raven, with a kind word for all, collects food for its palate. The bear and the wolf occasionally visit to collect tribute, while the falcon and the fox with one eye open are ever on the alert for the exercise of their craft.

In these little, smiling indentations of nature, when the sun begins to caress the gentle slopes, while the snow melts and flows in leaping streams—the sea still locked by the iron grip of the winter embrace—the Arctic incubator works overtime to start the littles ones of the snow wilds. Thus in these dimples of nature rocks the cradle of boreal life.

Relieved of the all-absorbing care of providing food, I now was often held spellbound as I wandered over these spots of nature's wonders. Phases of life which never interested me before now riveted my attention. When I wandered from the softly cushioned gullies, the harsh ridge life came under my eyes. While the valleys and the gullies become garden spots of summer glory, the very protection from the winds which makes this life possible buries the vegetable luxuriousness in winter under unfathomable depths of snow. The musk ox and the caribou, dependent upon this plant life for food, therefore become deprived of the usual means of subsistence. But Mother Nature does not desert her children. The same winds which compel man and feebler animals to seek shelter from its death-dealing assault, afford food to the better-fitted musk ox and caribou. In summer, plants, like animals, climb to ridges, hummocks, and mountain slopes, to get air and light and warm sunbeams. But the battle here is hard, and only very strong plants survive the force of wind and frosts.

The plant fibers here become tenacious; with a body gnarled and knotty from long conflict the roots dig yards deep into the soil. This leaves the breathing part of the plant dwarfed to a few inches. Here the winter winds sweep off the snow and offer food to the musk ox and caribou. Thus the wind, which destroys, also gives means of life. The equalizing balance of nature is truly wonderful.

In small, circumscribed areas we thus found ourselves in a new Eden of primeval life.

The topography of North Devon, however, placed a

sharp limit to the animated wilderness. Only a narrow strip of coast about Cape Sparbo, extending about twenty-five miles to the east and about forty miles to the west, presented any signs of land life. All other parts of the south shore of Jones Sound are more barren than the shores of the polar sea.

Although our larder was now well stocked with meat for food and blubber for fuel, we were still in need of furs and skins to prepare a new equipment with which to return to the Greenland shores. The animals whose pelts we required were abundant everywhere. But they were too active to be caught by the art and weapons evolved earlier in the chase of the walrus, bear and musk ox.

A series of efforts, therefore, was directed to the fox, the hare, the ptarmigan and the seal. It was necessary to devise special methods and means of capture for each family of animals. The hare was perhaps the most important, not only because its delicately flavored meat furnished a pleasing change from the steady diet of musk ox, but also because its skin is not equalled by any other for stockings. In our quest of the musk ox we had started little groups of creatures from many centers. This winter fur was not prime until after the middle of October. Taking notes of their haunts and their habits, we had, therefore, reserved the hare hunt until the days just before sunset.

We had learned to admire this little aristocrat. It is the most beautiful, most delicate of northern creatures. Early in the summer we had found it grazing in the green meadows along the base of bird cliffs. The little gray bunnies then played with their mothers about crystal dens. Now the babes were full-grown and clothed in the same immaculate white of the parents. We could distinguish the young only by their greater activity and their ceaseless curiosity.

In the immediate vicinity of camp we found them first in gullies where the previous winter's snow had but recently disappeared. Here the grass was young and tender and of a flavor to suit their taste for delicacies. A little later they followed the musk ox to the shores of lagoons or to the windswept hills. Still later, as the winter snows blanketed the pastures and the bitter storms of night swept the cheerless drifts, they dug long tunnels under the snow for food, and when the storms were too severe remained housed in these feeding dugouts.

An animal of rare intelligence, the hare is quick to grasp an advantage, and therefore as winter advances we find it a constant companion of the musk ox. For in the diggings of the musk ox this little creature finds sufficient food uncovered for its needs.

With a skeleton as light as that of the bird and a skin as frail as paper, it is nevertheless as well prepared to withstand the rigors of the Arctic as the bear with its clumsy anatomy. The entire make-up of the hare is based upon the highest strain of animal economy. It expends the greatest possible amount of energy at the cost of the least consumption of food. Its snow is as white as the boreal snows and absorbs color somewhat more readily. In a stream of crimson light it appears red and white; in a shadow of ice or in the darkness of night it assumes the subdued blue of the polar world. Nature has bleached its fur seemingly to afford the best protection against the frigid chill, for a suitable white fur permits the escape of less bodily heat than any colored or shaded pelt.

The fox is its only real enemy, and the fox's chance of success is won only by superior cunning. Its protection against the fox lies in its lightning-like movement of the legs. When it scents danger it rises by a series of darts that could be followed only by birds. Its expenditure of muscular energy is so economical that it can continue its run for an almost indefinite time. Shooting along a few hundred paces, it then rises to rest in an erect posture. With its black-tipped ears in line with its back, it makes a fascinating little bit of nature's handiwork. Again, when asleep, it curls up its legs carefully in the long fur of its body, and its ever-active nose, with the divided lip, is then pushed into the long soft fur of the breast where the frost crystals are screened from the breath when storms carry drift snow. It is a fluffy ball of animation which provokes one's admiration.

Deprived as we were of most of the usual comforts of life, many things were taught us by the creatures about. From the hare, with its scrupulous attention to cleanliness, we learned how to cleanse our hands and faces. With no soap, no towels, and very little water, we had some difficulty in trying to keep respectable appearances. The hare has the same problem to deal with, but it is provided by nature with a cleansing apparatus. Its own choice is the forepaw, but with its need for snowshoes the hind legs serve a very useful purpose, and then, too, the surface is developed, a surface covered with tough fur which, we discovered, possessed the quality of a wet sponge, and did not require, for efficiency, either soap or water. With hare paws, therefore, we kept clean. These paws also served as napkins. To take the place of a basin and a towel we therefore gathered a supply of hare paws, enough to keep clean for at least six months.

The hare was a good mark for Etuq with the slingshot, and many fell victims to his primitive genius. Wela, never an expert at stone slinging, became an adept with the bow and arrow. Usually he returned with at least one hare from every day's chase. Our main success resulted from a still more primitive device. Counting on its inquisitiveness, we devised a chain of loop lines arranged across the hare's regular lines of travel. In playing and jumping through these loops, the animal tightened the lines and became our victim automatically.

The ptarmigan chase was possible only for Wela. The bird was not at all shy, for it often came close to our den and scattered the snow like a chicken. It was too small a mark for the slingshot and only Wela could give the arrow the precise direction for these feathered creatures. Altogether, fifteen were secured in our locality, and all served as dessert for my special benefit. According to Eskimo custom, a young married man or woman cannot eat the ptarmigan, or "ahr-rish-shah" as they call it. That pleasure is reserved for the older people, and I did not for a moment risk the sacrilege of trying to change the custom. It was greatly to my advantage, for it not only impressed with suitable force my dignity as a superior Eskimo, but it enabled me to enjoy an entire bird at a time instead of only a teasing mouthful.

To us the ptarmigan was at all times fascinating, but it proved ever a thing of mystery. Descending from the skies at unexpected times it embarks again for haunts unknown. At times we saw the birds in great numbers. At other times they were absent for months. In summer the bird has gray and brown feathers, mingled with white. It keeps close to the inland ice, making its course along the snowy coast of Noonataks, beyond the reach of man or fox. Late in September it seeks the lower ground along the sea level.

Like the hare and the musk ox, it delights in windy places where the snow has been driven away. There it finds bits of moss and withered plants which satisfy its needs. The summer plumage is at first sight like that of the partridge. On close examination one finds the feathers are only tipped with color; underneath, the plumage is white. In winter it retains only the black feathers of its tail; otherwise it is as white as the hare. Its legs often are covered with tough fur, like that of the hare's lower hind legs. The meat is delicate in flavor and tender. It is the most beautiful of the four birds that remain in the white world when all is bleak during the night.

We sought the fox more diligently than the ptarmigan. We had a more tangible way of securing it. Furthermore, we were in great need of its skin. Etuq and Wela regarded fox hams as quite a delicacy, a delicacy which I never willingly shared when there were musk tenderloins about. We had no steel traps, and with its usual craft the fox usually managed to evade our crude weapons by keeping out of sight. Bone traps were made with a good deal of care after the pattern of steel traps. We used a musk-ox horn as a spring. But with these we were only partially successful. As a last resort, little domes were arranged in imitation of the usual caches, with stone trap doors. In these we managed to secure fourteen white and two blue animals. After that they proved too wise for our craft.

The fox becomes shy only at the end of October, when its fur begins to be really worth while. Before that it followed us everywhere on the musk-ox quest, for it was not slow to learn the advantage of being near our battle scenes. We frequently left choice bits for its picking, a favor which it seemed to appreciate by a careful watchfulness of our camps. Although a much more cunning thief than the bear, we could afford its plunderings, for it had not so keen a taste for blubber and its capacity was limited. We thus got well acquainted.

Up to the present we had failed in the quest of the seal. During the open season of summer, without a kayak, we could not get near the animal. As the winter and the night advanced, we were too busy with the land animals to watch the blowholes in the new ice. When the sea is first spread with the thin sheet of colorless ice, which later thickens, the seal rises to the surface, makes a breathing hole, descends to its feeding grounds on the sea bottom for about ten minutes, then rises and makes another hole. This line of openings is arranged in a circle or a series of connecting oblong lines, marking that particular seal's favorite feeding ground. Before the young ice is covered with snow, these breathing holes are easily located by a ring of white frost crystals, which condense and fall as the seal blows. But now that the winter had sheeted the black ice evenly with a white cover, the seal holes, though open, could not be found. We were not in need of either fat or meat, but the sealskins were to fill an important want. We required for boots and sled-lashing the thin, tough seal hide. How could we get it?

From our underground den we daily watched the wanderings of the bears. They trailed along certain lines which we knew to be favorable feeding grounds for seals, but they did not seem to be successful. Could we not profit by their superb scenting instinct and find the blowholes? The bear had been our worst enemy, but unconsciously it also proved to be our best friend.

We started out to trail the bears' footprints. By these we were led to the blowholes, where we found the snow about had been circled with a regular trail. Most of these had been abandoned, for the seal has a scent as keen as the bear, but a few "live" holes were located. Sticks were placed to locate these, and after a few days' careful study and hard work we harpooned six seals. Taking only the skins and blubber, we left the carcasses for Bruin's share of the chase, to be consumed later. We did not hunt together with the bear—at least, not knowingly.

In these wanderings over game lands we were permitted a very close scrutiny of the animals about, and it was at this time that I came to certain definite conclusions as to prevailing laws of color and dress of our cohabitants of the polar wastes.

The animals of the Arctic assume a color in accordance with their needs for heat transmission. The prevailing influence is white, as light furs permit the least escape of heat. It is evidently more important to confine the heat of the body than to gather heat from the sun's feeble rays. The necessity for bleaching the furry raiment becomes most operative in winter when the temperature of the air is 150° below that of the body. In the summer, when the continued sunshine is made more heating by the piercing influence of snowfields' reflection, there is a tendency to absorb heat. Then nature darkens the skin, which absorbs heat accordingly.

The relative advantage of light and dark shades can be

easily demonstrated by placing pieces of white and black cloth on a surface of snow, with a slope at right angles to the sun's rays. If after a few hours the cloth is removed, the snow under the black cloth will be melted considerably, while that under the white cloth will show little effect.

Nature makes use of this law of physics to ease the hard lot of its creatures fighting the weather in the icy world. The laws of color protection as advocated in the rules of natural selection are not operative here, because of the vitally important demand of heat economy.[14] If we now seek the problem of nature's body-coloring dyes, with heat economy as the key, our calculations will become easy. The serwah, a species of guillemot, which is as black as the raven in summer, is white in winter. The ptarmigan is light as pearl in winter, but its feathers become tipped with amber in summer. The hare is slightly gray in summer, but in winter becomes white as the snow under which it finds food and shelter.

The white fox is gray in summer, the blue fox darkens as the sun advances, while its under-fur becomes lighter with increasing cold. The caribou is dark brown as it grazes the moss-colored fields, but becomes nearly white with the permanent snows. The polar bear, as white as nature can make it, with only blubber to mix its paints, basks in the midnight sun with a raiment suggestive of gold. The musk ox changes its dark under-fur for a lighter shade. The raven has a white undercoat in winter. The rat is gray in summer but bleaches to blue-gray in winter time. The laws of selection and heat economy are thus combined.

While we were thus preparing for the coming winter by seeking animals with furry pelts, the weather conditions made our task increasingly difficult. The storm of the descending sun whipped the seas into white fury and brushed the lands with icy clouds. With the descent of the sun, nature again set its seal of gloom on Arctic life. The cheer of a sunny heaven was blotted from the skies, and the coming of winter blackness was signaled by the beginning of a warfare of the elements. All hostile nature was now set loose to expend its restive battle energy.

For brief moments the weather was quiet, and then in awe-inspiring silence we steered for sequestered gullies in quest of little creatures. This death-like stillness was in harmony with our loneliness. As the sea was stilled by the iron bonds of frost, as life sought protection under the storm-driven snows of land, the winds, growing even wilder, beat a maddening onslaught over the dead, frozen world. The thunder of elements shook the very rocks under which we slept. Then again would fall a spell of that strange silence—all was dead, the sun glowed no more, the creatures of the wilds were hushed. We were all alone—alone in a vast, white, dead world.

19

THE UNDERGROUND DEN

The warm rays gradually merged in a perpetual blue frost. The air thickened. The land darkened. The day shortened. The night lengthened. The polar cold and darkness of winter came hand in hand. Late in September the nights had become too dark to sleep in the open, with inquisitive bears on every side. Storms, too, increased thereafter and deprived us of the cheer of colored skies. Thus we were now forced to seek a retreat in our underground den.

We took about as kindly to this as a wild animal does to a cage. For over seven months we had wandered over vast plains of ice, with a new camp site almost every day. We had grown accustomed to a wandering life like that of the bear, and we had not developed his hibernating instinct. We were anxious to continue our curious battle of life.

In October the bosom of the sea became blanketed, and the curve of the snow-covered earth was polarized in the eastern skies. The final period for the death of the day and earthly glory was advancing, but Nature in her last throes displayed some of her most alluring phases. The colored silhouette of the globe was perhaps the most remarkable display. In effect, this was a shadow of the earth thrown into space. By the reflected, refracted, and polarized light of the sun, the terrestrial shadows were outlined against the sky in glowing colors. Seen occasionally in other parts of the globe, it is only in the polar regions, with air of crystal and surface of mirrors, that the proper mediums are afforded for this gigantic spectral show.

We had an ideal location. A glittering sea, with a level horizon, lay along the east and west. The weather was good, the skies were clear, and, as the sun sank, the sky over it was flushed with orange or gold. This gradually paled, and over the horizon opposite there rose an arc in feeble prismatic colors with a dark zone of purple under it. The arc rose as the sun settled; the purple spread beyond the polarized bow; and gradually the heavens turned a deep purple blue to the zenith, while the halo of the globe was slowly lost in its own shadow.

The colored face of the earth painted on the screen of the heavens left the last impression of worldly charm on the retina. At the end of October the battle of the elements, storms attending the setting of the sun, began to blast the air

into a chronic fury. By this time we were glad to creep into
our den and await the vanishing weeks of ebbing day.

In the doom of night to follow, there would at least be
some quiet moments during which we could stretch our legs.
The bears, which had threatened our existence, were now
kept off by a new device which served the purpose for a
time. We had food and fuel enough for the winter. There
should have been nothing to disturb our tempers, but the
coming of the long blackness makes all polar life ill at ease.

Early in November the storms ceased long enough to give
us a last fiery vision. With a magnificent cardinal flame the
sun rose, gibbered in the sky, and sank behind the southern
cliffs on November 3. It was not to rise again until February 11 of the next year. We were, therefore, doomed to
hibernate in our underground den for at least 100 double
nights before the dawn of a new day opened our eyes.

The days now came and went in short order. For hygienic reasons we kept up the usual routine of life. The midday light soon darkened to twilight. The moon and stars
appeared at noon. The usual partition of time disappeared.
All was night, unrelieved darkness, midnight, midday, morning or evening.

We stood watches of six hours each to keep the fires going, to keep off the bears, and to force an interest in a blank
life. We knew that we were believed to be dead. Our friends
in Greenland would not ascribe to us the luck which came
after our run of abject misfortune. This thought inflicted
perhaps the greatest pain of the queer prolongation of life
which was permitted us. It was loneliness, frigid loneliness.
I wondered whether men ever felt so desolately alone.

We could not have been more thoroughly isolated if we

had been transported to the surface of the moon. I find myself utterly unable to outline the emptiness of our existence. In other surroundings we never grasp the full meaning of the word "alone." When it is possible to put a foot out of doors into the sunlight without the risk of a bear's paw on your neck, it is also possible to run off a spell of blues, but what were we to do with the torment of a satanic blackness to blind us?

With the cheer of day, a kindly nature, and a new friend, it is easy to get in touch with a sympathetic chord. The mere thought of another human heart within touch, even a hundred miles away, would have eased the suspense of the silent void. But we could entertain no such hopefulness. We were all alone in a world where every pleasant aspect of nature had deserted us. Although three in number, a bare necessity had compressed us into a single composite individuality.

There were no discussions, no differences of opinion. We had been too long together under bitter circumstances to arouse each other's interest. A single individual could not live long in our position. A selfish instinct tightened a fixed bond to preserve and protect one another. As a battle force we made a formidable unit, but there were no matches to start the fires of inspiration.

The half-darkness of midday and the moonlight still permitted us to creep from under the ground and seek a few hours in the open. The stone and bone fox-traps and the trap-caves for the bears which we had built during the last glimmer of day offered an occupation with some recreation. But we were soon deprived of this.

Bears headed us off at every turn. We were not permitted

to proceed beyond an enclosed hundred feet from the hole
of our den. Not an inch of ground or a morsel of food was
permitted us without a contest. It was a fight of nature
against nature. We either actually saw the little sooty nos-
trils with jets of vicious breath rising, and the huge outline
of a wild beast ready to spring on us, or imagined we saw it.
With no adequate means of defense we were driven to im-
prisonment within the walls of our own den.

From within, our position was even more tantalizing. The
bear thieves dug under the snows over our heads and snatched
blocks of blubber fuel from under our very eyes at the port.
Occasionally we ventured out to deliver a lance, but each
time the bear would make a leap for the door and would
have entered had the opening been large enough. In other
cases we shot arrows through the peep-hole. A bear head
again would burst through the silk-covered window near
the roof, where knives, at close range and in good light,
could be driven with sweet vengeance.

As a last resort we made a hole through the top of the
den. When a bear was heard near, a long torch was pushed
through. The snow for acres about was then suddenly
flashed with a ghostly whiteness which almost frightened us.
But the bear calmly took advantage of the light to pick a
larger piece of the blubber upon which our lives depended,
and then with an air of superiority he would move into the
brightest light, usually within a few feet of our peep-hole,
where we could almost touch his hateful skin.

Two weeks after sunset we heard the last cry of ravens.
After a silence of several days they suddenly descended with
a piercing shout which cut the frosty stillness. We crept out
of our den quickly to read the riddle of the sudden bluster.

There were five ravens on five different rocks, and the absence of the celestial color gave them quite an appropriate setting. They were restless; there was no food for them. A fox had preceded them with his usual craftiness, and had left no pickings for feathered creatures.

A family of five had gathered about in October, when the spoils of the chase were being cached, and we encouraged their stay by placing food for them regularly. Sometimes a sly fox, and at other times a thieving bear, got the little morsels, but there was usually sufficient picking for the ravens' little crops. They had found a suitable cave high up in the great cliffs of granite behind our den.

We were beginning to be quite friendly. My Eskimo companions ascribed to the birds almost human qualities and they talked to them reverently, thereby displaying their hearts' desire. The secrets of the future were all entrusted to their consideration. Would the "too-loo-ah" go to Eskimo Lands and deliver their messages? The raven said "ka-ah" (yes).

Etuq said, "Go and take the tears from An-na-do-a's eyes; tell her that I am alive and well and will come to her soon. Tell Pan-ic-pa [his father] that I am in Ah-ming-ma-noona [Musk-Ox Land]. Bring us some powder to blacken the bear's snout." "Ka-ah, ka-ah," said two ravens at once.

Wela began an appeal to drive off the bears and to set the raven spirits as guardians of our blubber caches. This was uttered in shrill shouts, and then, in a low trembling voice, he said: "Dry the tears of Mother's cheeks and tell her that we are in a land of todnu [tallow]."

"Ka-ah," replied the raven.

"Then go to Ser-wah; tell her not to marry that lazy

gull, Ta-tamh; tell her that Wela's skin is still flushed with thoughts of her, that he is well and will return to claim her in the first moon after sunrise."

"Ka-ah, ka-ah, ka-ah," said the raven, and rose as if to deliver the messages.

For the balance of that day we saw only three ravens. The two had certainly started for the Greenland shore. The other three, after an engorgement, rose to their cave and went to sleep for the night as we thought. No more was seen of them until the dawn of the following year.

A few days later we also made other acquaintances. They were the most interesting bits of life that crossed our trail, and in the dying effort to seek animal companionship our soured tempers were sweetened somewhat by four-footed joys.

A noise had been heard for several successive days at eleven o'clock. This was the time chosen by the bears for their daily exercise along our footpath, and we were usually all awake with a knife or a lance in hand, not because there was any real danger, for our house cemented by ice was as secure as a fort, but because we all felt more comfortable in a battle attitude. Through the peep-hole we saw them marching up and down along the footpath tramped down by our daily spells of leg-stretching.

They were feasting on the aroma of our footprints, and when they left it was usually safe for us to venture out. Noises, however, continued within the walls of the den. It was evident that there was something alive at close range.

We were lonely enough to have felt a certain delight in shaking hands even with Bruin if the theft of our blubber had not threatened the very foundation of our existence. For in the night we could not augment our supplies; and without fat, fire and water were impossible. No! there was not room for man and bear at Cape Sparbo. Without ammunition, however, we were nearly helpless.

But noises continued after Bruin's steps came with a decreasing metallic ring from distant snows. There was a scraping and a scratching within the very walls of our den. We had a neighbor and a companion. Who or what could it be? We were kept in suspense for some time. When all was quiet at the time which we chose to call midnight, a little blue rat came out and began to tear the bark from our willow lamp-trimmer.

I was on watch, awake, and punched Etuq without moving my head. His eyes opened with surprise on the busy rodent, and Wela was kicked. He turned over and the thing jumped into a rock crevasse.

The next day we risked the discomfort of Bruin's interview and dug up an abundance of willow roots for our new tenant. These were arranged in appetizing display and the rat came out very soon and helped himself, but he permitted no familiarity. We learned to love the creature, however, all the more because of its shyness. By alternate jumps from the roots to seclusion it managed to fill up with all it could carry. Then it disappeared as suddenly as it came.

In the course of two days it came back with a companion, its mate. They were beautiful little creatures, a little larger than mice. They had soft fluffy fur of a pearl-blue color, with pink eyes. They had no tails. Their dainty little feet were furred to the claw-tips with silky hair. They made a picture of animal delight which really aroused us from stupor to little spasms of enthusiasm. A few days were spent in testing our intentions. Then they arranged a berth just above my head and became steady boarders.

Their confidence and trust flattered our vanity and we treated them as royal guests. No trouble was too great for us to provide them with suitable delicacies. We ventured into the darkness and storms for hours to dig up savory roots and mosses. A little stage was arranged every day with the suitable footlights. In our eagerness to prolong the rodent theatricals, we fed the little things over and over, until they became too fat and too lazy to creep from their berths.

They were good, clean, orderly camp fellows, always kept in their places, and never ventured to borrow our bed furs, nor did they disturb our eatables. With a keen sense of justice, and an aristocratic air, they passed our plates of carnivorous foods without venturing a taste, and went to their herbivorous piles of sod delicacies. About ten days before midnight they went to sleep and did not wake for more than a month. Again we were alone. Now even the bears deserted us.

In the dull days of blackness which followed, few incidents seemed to mark time. The cold increased. Storms were more continuous and came with greater force. We were cooped up in our underground den with only a peep-hole through the silk of our old tent to watch the sooty nocturnal bluster. We were face to face with a spiritual famine. With little recreation, no amusements, no interfering work, no reading matter, with nothing to talk about, the six hours of a watch were spread out to weeks.

We had no sugar, no coffee, not a particle of civilized food. We had meat and blubber, good and wholesome food at that. But the stomach wearied of its never-changing carnivorous stuffing. The dark den, with its walls of pelt and bone, its floor decked with frosted tears of ice, gave no excuse for cheer. Insanity, abject madness, could only be avoided by busy hands and long sleep.

My life in this underground place was, I suppose, like that of a man in the Stone Age. The interior was damp and cold and dark; with our pitiable lamps burning, the temperature at the top was fairly moderate, but at the bottom it was below zero. Our bed was a platform of rocks wide enough for three prostrate men. Its forward edge was our seat when awake. Before this was a space where a deeper hole in the earth permitted us to stand upright, one at a time. There, one by one, we dressed and occasionally stood to move our stiff and aching limbs.[15]

On either side of this standing space was half a tin plate in which musk-ox fat was burned, with moss as a wick. These lights were kept burning day and night; it was a futile, imperceptible sort of heat they gave. Except when we got close to the light, it was impossible to see one another's faces.

We ate twice daily—without enjoyment. We had few matches, and in fear of darkness tended our lamps diligently. There was no food except meat and tallow; most of the meat, by choice, was eaten raw and frozen. Night and morning we boiled a small pot of meat for broth; but we had no salt to season it. Stooped and cramped, day by day, I found occasional relief from the haunting horror of this life by rewriting the almost illegible notes made on our journey.

My most important duty was the preparation of my notes and observations for publication. This would afford useful occupation and save months of time afterwards. But I had no paper. My three notebooks were full, and there remained only a small pad of prescription blanks and two miniature memorandum books.[16] I resolved, however, to try to work out the outline of my narrative in chapters in these. I had four good pencils and one eraser. These served a valuable purpose. With sharp points I shaped the words in small letters. When the skeleton of the book was ready I was surprised to find how much could be crowded onto a few small pages. By a liberal use of the eraser many parts of pages were cleared of unnecessary notes. Entire lines were written between all the lines of the notebooks, the pages thus carrying two narrations of series of notes.

By the use of abbreviations and dashes, I devised a kind of shorthand. My art of space economy complete, I began to write, literally developing the very useful habit of carefully shaping every idea before an attempt was made to use the pencil. In this way my entire book and several articles were written. Charts, films, and advertisement boxes were covered. In all 150,000 words were written, and absolute despair, which in idleness opens the door to madness, was averted.

Our needs were still urgent enough to enforce much other work. Drift threatened to close the entrance to our dungeon and this required frequent cleaning. Blubber for the lamp was sliced and pounded every day. The meat corner was occasionally stocked, for it required several days to thaw out the icy musk-ox quarters. Ice was daily gathered and placed within reach to keep the water pots full. The frost which was condensed out of our breaths made slabs of ice on the floor, and this required occasional removal. The snow under our bed furs, which had a similar origin, was brushed out now and then.

Soot from the lamps, a result of bad housekeeping, which a proud Eskimo woman would not have tolerated for a minute, was scraped from the bone rafters about once a week. With a difference of 100 degrees between the breathing air of the den and that outside, there was a rushing, interchanging breeze through every pinhole and crevice. The ventilation was good. The camp cleanliness could almost have been called hygienic, although only one bath had been indulged in for six months, and that only by an unavoidable, undesirable accident.

Much had still to be done to prepare for our homegoing in the remote period beyond the night. It was necessary to plan and make a new equipment. The sledge, the clothing, the camp outfit, all the things which had been used in the previous campaign, were worn out. Something could be done by judicious repairing, but nearly everything required reconstruction. In the new arrangement we were to take the place of the dogs at the traces and the sledge loads must be prepared accordingly. There was before us an unknown line of trouble for 300 miles before we could step on Greenland shores. It was only the hope of homegoing which gave some mental strength in the night of gloom. Musk-ox meat was now cut into strips and dried over the lamps. Tallow was prepared and molded in portable form for fuel.

But in spite of all efforts we gradually sank to the lowest depths of the Arctic midnight. The little midday glimmer on the southern sky became indiscernible. Only the swing of the Great Dipper and other stars told the time of the day or night. We had fancied that the persistent wind ruffled our tempers. But now it was still; not a breath of air moved the heavy blackness. In that very stillness we found reasons for complaint. Storms were preferable to the dead silence; anything was desirable to stir the spirits to action.

Still, the silence was only apparent. Wind noises floated in the frosty distance; cracking rocks, exploding glaciers, and tumbling avalanches kept up a muffled rumbling which the ear detected only when it rested on the floor rock of our bed. The temperature was $-48°$ F.—so low that at times the very air seemed to crack. Every creature of the wild had been buried in drift; all nature was asleep. In our dungeon all was a mental blank.

Shortly after black midnight descended, I began to experience a curious psychological phenomenon. The stupor of the days of travel wore away, and I began to see myself as in a mirror. I can explain this no better. It is said that a man falling from a great height usually has a picture of his life flashed through his brain in the short period of descent. I saw a similar cycle of events.

The panorama began with incidents of childhood, and it seems curious now with what infinite detail I saw people whom I had long forgotten, and went through the most trivial experiences. In successive stages every phase of life appeared and was minutely examined; every hidden recess of gray matter was opened to interpret the biographies of self-analysis. The hopes of my childhood and the discouragements of my youth filled me with emotion; feelings of pleasure and sadness came as each little thought picture took definite shape; it seemed hardly possible that so many things, potent for good and bad, could have been done in so few years. I saw myself, not as a voluntary being, but rather as a resistless atom, predestined in its course, being carried on by an inexorable fate.

Meanwhile our preparations for returning were being accomplished. This work had kept us busy during all of the wakeful spells of the night. Much still remained to be done.

Not until two weeks after midnight did we awake to a proper consciousness of life. The faint brightness of the southern skies at noon opened the eye to spiritual dawn. The sullen stupor and deathlike stillness vanished.

Although real pleasure followed all our efforts at physical labor, the balking muscles required considerable urging. Musk-ox meat was cut into portable blocks, candles were made, fur skins were dressed and chewed, boots, stockings, pants, shirts, sleeping bags were made. The sledge was re-lashed, things were packed in bags. All was ready about three weeks before sunrise. Although the fingers and the jaws were thus kept busy, the mind and also the heart were left free to wander.

In the face of all our efforts to ward aside the ill effects of the night, we gradually became its victims. Our skin paled, our strength failed, the nerves weakened, and the mind ultimately became a blank. The most notable physical effect, however, was the alarming irregularity of the heart.

In the locomotion of human machinery the heart is the motor. Like all good motors it has a governor which requires some adjustment. In the Arctic, where the need of regulation is greatest, the facilities for adjustment are withdrawn. In normal conditions, as the machine of life pumps the blood which drives all, its force and its regularity are governed by the never-erring sunbeams. When these are withdrawn, as they are in the long night, the heart pulsations become irregular; at times slow, at other times spasmodic.

Light seems to be as necessary to the animal as to the plant. A diet of fresh meat, healthful hygienic surroundings, play for the mind, recreation for the body, and strong heat from open fires, will help; but only the return of the heaven-given sun will properly adjust the motor of man.

20

NIGHT INTROSPECTION DURING WINTER INTERLUDE

Self-analysis had been a part of our plan of action whenever peace of mind and ease of stomach-desires afforded time for reveries but, during the long night, outward observations were so limited that inward inspection became a natural tendency. Part of this has appeared in previous pages. Here I attempt to give the state of mind peculiar to the physical effects of prolonged night darkness in Zero-land. To my companions the gloom of dayless nights was absorbed in the tendency of self-abnegation enforced by their habitat. To me it was ever new and ever a mystery. I had previously wintered in the Arctic and in the Antarctic but each polar night had produced a different effect.

Now, however, I could see that the differently appraised influences were but changes in the degrees of inward retreat of interest, the result of more or less human contact with the extent of borrowed light from others. Light and life are so closely related that even the penetrating science of our day has been unable to separate the life stream from celestial rays.

This vital relation between light and life is most easily grasped in the struggle of the mental powers for a working medium, during the long polar night. The problem gets its first elucidation if we regard the body as a universe of marine cells, enclosed within the sphere of the skin in a saline sea. Animal life and plant life in this respect differ very little. All life, it seems, came at the beginning out of saline water and in this life-producing water, single cells represented the first forms. The immense variation we see now is the result of cellular association and adaptation to new conditions. Each cell is in itself a planetary unit composed of atoms and molecules wherein electromagnetic energy is the basic source of all which life implies. A cell, therefore, is a capsule of confined light. The human body thus considered is in effect a Milky Way in the immensity of the universe of life, acquiring, generating, and giving off light and energy.

How can such frail tissue-confined power subsist when light fails as it does during the polar night? The answer must be that darkness and all seemingly dead things like rocks and frozen water contain and radiate some light. Invisible perhaps is this transmission of light, but it is the substance which keeps atoms and molecules and cells in power to transform within their respective spheres. Absolute darkness, like absolute zero in temperature, is perhaps never a condition on earth. How could it be? Night is but a shadow of the earth against the sun. This shadow has limits in degree of lightlessness and in its extent skyward. How far up from the earth is the end of night? is a question which can be figured out relatively. Beyond is celestial space where there is no night at any time. There millions of stars serving as suns radiate into celestial expanse, penetrating our seeming darkness and night at all times. Some life-giving light is thus at all times accessible during the polar winter of darkness. Furthermore, the food we eat, the water we drink, the air we breathe, the people we meet, every contact we make, offer a supply of light or its transformed energy. Because the accessible supply thus delivered during the Arctic night is limited, the cells become doubly hungry and stingy. This inadequate supply and overt economy of life power is the grave condition we have to meet in trying to conserve health while invading the ice world.

The symptoms of deficient light intake are not easily detected or appraised, by those who themselves become abnormal by such influence. This must explain the wide difference of opinion among explorers as to the effect of polar nights. Those who attain physical comfort, breathe fresh air, drink liberally of good water and eat food little cooked suffer least, but under the best possible hygienic conditions, some disastrous changes must be endured during the long night. The extent of this degeneration is too complex to outline here. Suffice it to say that all who must endure the blackness of the Arctic night must pay the price in disordered functions. This is true even of the Eskimos who are born with hereditary fitness, and acquire better enduring capacity with each generation.

The earliest effects become manifest in the mental realm. The physical changes become evident slowly, often not at all until near the end or at sunrise of the next year. Long-continued storms, with intervening periods of dark cloudy skies precede the passing of the sun in its final stages of descent for the long doom of blackness. At this time the native women become explosive in temperament and hysterical in cycles of weird activity. The men, though excitable, do not reach a climax of despair until the first weeks of night have passed. We did not feel the disaster of mental storm until about midnight. Being in a desperate environment, we were largely hiding our peculiarities from one another because we were trying to prevent discouragement.

Each of us, however, had very grave worries which were prolonged and intensified into hallucinations. Wela had a sweetheart. She was the temporary wife by a trial marriage to another man. In this theme there was the usual triangle of trouble. We tried to ease his animosity and fears by citing the beauty and love and capacity for happiness of another girl of whose sweetness Wela often sang in words of praise. But we found all love advice was bitter to him, so much so that he tried to evade mating subjects altogether.

Etuq felt that we were anchored at our present camp, that we could not get to Greenland as we had planned out of Jones Sound, and then along the coast northward. His forefathers had tried that and most of them had perished en route. The dead bodies were eaten to keep the few survivors alive. This brought to him the thought of eating human flesh and how he detested this calamity!

My own special type of worry related generally to home relations and specifically to our failing mental powers, which would perhaps make us incapable of sufficient good judgment to enable a return. My companions by conversation did so many crazy things that I felt we were all crazy, or would be if we ever reached Greenland.

I tried to direct the stream of conversation out of these ditches of self-imposed damnation and soon discovered that much could be done in this way by arousing new interest, or by introducing old themes of thought which I knew to be only partially lost in the fading ideas. The more gruesome the theme the more intense became the interest in these first experiments of thought entertainment.

Since Etuq talked of eating the dead who had starved or were frozen, and indicated that we might eventually be forced to do the same, I temporarily encouraged this trend of conversation as a means to eliminate the topic. "How does it feel to freeze? When people starve, what thought and action precede death? What does human flesh taste like?" This trend of conversation became increasingly exciting for some time and when it had played with our senses long enough we were in better spirits.

Though the Eskimo does not often mention death, and seldom speaks by name of those who have passed, the common tragedies of life are ever a common subject for discussion. In the expressions which follow, my companions quoted mostly the lines from ancient tales and traditions. These sentiments had become a part of their outlook on life. Said Etuq, "When people freeze, the fires within lack fuel. Men well fed seldom die of cold. When an individual feels death, it begins in the fingers and toes. This is why we always guard and protect the ends first. We bare our stomachs and backs to extreme cold but never the hands and feet if we can prevent it. Cold first dulls the feeling of the skin. Then the eyes, the ears and nose fail. After that the head gets dark and then the end is not far off."

Wela, in his description of the freezing body, gave much the same analysis as did Etuq, but added that his father had told him that after the arms and legs became too cold, the spirits began to leave the body and then suddenly the heart stopped.

How well these young men were posted on the symptoms of danger from extreme cold! They were, of course, informed about this because it was important in their ultimate survival, but how many men of their age among us would have so much important information as grounded intelligence ready for use?

Now for the next question: "When people starve, what thought and action precede death?" The Eskimo in his death-appeal seldom applies for a place in heaven or for special consideration in a future destiny. His gods are seemingly for earth-rule rather than for the heavens. It is necessary to state this and also to say that a natural death by disease as with us is not so often the end. Here men as a rule die in the act of hunting. The prospect of death by starvation and by freezing are brought to mind in the general run of the hardships of nature. They will often go for a week without food and for months with barely enough to keep going. In the long winter struggle, when left stranded and isolated by storms, the blueness of a freezing death is familiar in part to all, and because by experience and tradition this is so, they have an intelligent grasp of life's tragic dangers in the open contest with icy elements.

Wela offered the first description of the slow end by

famine. Said he, "It is in the nature of our people to be hopeful. Hunting luck is always a hazard, but in our worst failure we blame ourselves and expect better fortunes tomorrow. We obey taboos to please our gods, and with their aid we become better hunters, or the game is sent our way. This is the plan of thought and the plan of action until we are so weakened by starvation that only a wonder-worker can help. Then we call the Angekok, our spiritual adviser. He had perhaps advised us before. If so, we now consult the old men and the old women, for advice. Until now all of our neighborhood men have distributed their supply of meat. At last we are all starving. It is then important that the best hunter be kept well fed. Unless this is done, even if game returns, all will be too weak to fight. The dogs are now eaten. Some people will die. The old and the young die first; their bodies are eaten. Perhaps before many die all will quarrel and some will be killed in this crazy scramble. These bodies are divided for food among the favored few. All animal dung is eaten or burned. At last some game is secured. The season is advanced, and all survivors are saved. If not, and if escape by migration is not possible, the entire village becomes annihilated."

Etuq followed the same line of description, but he did it by giving specific examples, referring at last to his own people with tears in his eyes. Then he said, "So long as hunger persists, it dominates all thought and capacity for action; but hunger in time departs and then people become indifferent in their outlook on life and its future, if no food at all is eaten for four or five days. Thereafter there is no real desire for food. If a little food and plenty of water is supplied, men can long live without losing the urge of hunger. In the last days of starvation, as in the last days of freezing, the head becomes dark. There is then no pain, no thought, and no feeling. Mechtoshu was in that state. They hit him over the head, put his eye out in efforts to kill and eat him, but he was awakened by the blows and escaped. He still lived and can see more with one eye than most men can with two."

"What does human flesh taste like?" Both hesitated to give an answer, and implied by round-about remarks that an answer implied that they had eaten of a body. After some silence, Wela said, "Man flesh tastes like that of dogs and wolves and foxes and gulls and ravens. Even the flesh of the bear has a human aroma and taste."

In my reply I suggested that each of these creatures had meat distinctive in flavor for life of its kind. "Yes," said Wela, "this is as you say, but the meat of all these is smeary when cooked and sticky when raw, while the fat is like ours." "How do you know this?" said I. There was no answer. And thus our inquisition ended on that day. It was now time to eat, but we were not hungry.

Friendship and the brotherhood of good fellowship, also the sacredness of filial relations, are as well understood by savages as among us. Here it seemed to me was a theme to bring out the inner feelings. So I said, "What to you is the importance of friendship and home relations?" With this, as with other subjects, we led to the central theme gradually. Every Eskimo boy has a boy friend and a girl pal, perhaps two or three. We first discussed the alluring character of these companions, and then led to the abstract themes implied by the above question. During the introductory conversation Etuq said, "My father has always urged me to learn to befriend myself, and that men who did not acquire the pleasure of self-companionship died without friends and without helpful relatives."

This ancient philosophy of Etuq's antecedents gave the basis for a good sermon, so we drifted along on the borderland of his thought. Direct questions seldom bring good answers from primitive people, until the subject matter becomes elucidated from every side in open talk. What beautiful sentiments of friendship followed in the brief Eskimo manner of expression! "Friendship supplies the mental meat" was perhaps the most concrete and most potent wording. To me friendship is as diverse in quality as the fruits of the earth. During life, enduring friendships must stand as the bank account of the wealth of our relations to others. At the end friendship is the greatest value left behind. Among ourselves, where hardship, suffering, danger, grief, and hunger tested interdependent fellowship daily, friendship supplied the very essence, the attar of what is best in manhood.

We drifted from deep subjects to the superficial effervescence of daily events. Much of this talk might be interesting to others, but we can here treat only a few themes of the conversational drift. With interest centered in ourselves we became resigned introverts, but that part of the earth about us was in effect ever a part of our inner selves. One day we talked about the end of the earth's surface. The Eskimo, like most primitives, believes that the earth is flat. While this theme was up for discussion, I determined to prove to my companions once for all that the earth was round. I had been to the top and to the bottom of the globe and fairly all around it, and felt confident that the globular theory of the earth could be substantiated if I took the time to prepare the ground for the information to be given.

By way of a prelude, I told of my voyages of exploration and said that our present system of investigation was a part of this same desire to find out how and of what the world is made. I described the earth as a big ball "adrift in that same space you see above. It floats like the stars about the blue of space. It is round. You see no flat or square or angular forms in the heavens. Why should the earth in form be an exception?"

To this there was respectful listening but no reply and no questions, from which I concluded that my arguments were accepted.

I next drew an outline of our world as a globe and set in roughly the continental masses, giving the lands nearest the Pole considerable detail.

"Now," I said, "let us sit down and go over half of the full ball of the earth." About the Arctic I described the habitat of other Eskimos and the land of red Indians. This pleased them very much. Then I came down along the Atlantic Shore to New York, and to Florida, describing the people, the animals and plants, and then to Central and to South America, with similar information, but emphasizing the torrid conditions and black men. All this was received with intense interest. Then I presented the undersurface of the earth with the South Pole, but giving most attention to life and conditions about the southern point of South America.

Here they began to ask questions. "Did people and animals live here? Did birds fly about? Did big ships like our steamers sail over the sea?" Yes, I told them, people and animals and plants live there as they do here. "But how do they hold on?" asked Wela. "I can see how plants can root in and thus stick to the earth, but men and moving creatures without hooks on their feet would fall off the earth. There, if the world is a ball as you say, heads would be down, feet up. Men, rocks and water—everything would fall off. How could birds fly upside down? How could ships sail bottom side up? Here we stand on the earth. Our weight holds us down. There on the undersurface of your earth ball we would fall off. No, the earth is flat and because we can walk on it, no other idea of its shape is understandable by us."

Etuq now took the stage in defense of Eskimo beliefs in a flat earth. I afforded him a respectful hearing with few questions, for I must be at least as gracious and patient with their beliefs as they had been to me. Etuq began with what is known to ethnologists as the Sedna Myth. According to this legend, there was a time in the remote past when the only fire and the only light on earth were created by man. Said Etuq, "A beautiful maid was alone in an igloo awaiting her lover. It was dark and cold. There was no lamp burning. A man came, pretended he was her man. When too late she discovered that her lover was her brother. She screamed and ran out. He followed. The chase continued for a long time. At last they arrived at the end of the earth. She stepped off into space and winged the air. He still followed. In time she became the sun and he became the moon. The chase is still on. This proves to us that the earth is flat."

I saw that no argument of mine could counter this ancient belief. With a few compliments, I tried to change the subject, but then Wela took the stage by word action. He told how other people had left the earth—some by accident as did the sun maid, others to escape great floods and icy ages of storm, still others on hunting adventures—and these became the star groups of the heavens. The myth world to the Eskimo is to them more real than the Bible is to us.

In another daydream, in efforts to break the fetters of night, we discussed the relative qualities of men. My companions were, from my conversation, somewhat posted on the races of humans who wander over the earth. We discussed color and racial characteristics, food, occupation and home relations, but the greatest interest in time was focused on the beginners, the first men on earth. The Eskimo is a pygmy—the only yellow dwarf among pygmy races—and instead of feeling inferior because of his small size, he estimates his compact smallness as a superior advantage. This decision has come mainly in the Eskimo observation of unfitness of big white men in the Arctic. Many of the explorers under observation had been six feet or over, and their unwieldy cumbersomeness was not only a tragedy but a source of comic mental pictures. Those big men froze their noses. Frosted hands and feet resulted in lost toes and fingers. Furthermore, they withstood cold and hardship badly and could not on the whole deliver an enduring strength equal to the little five-foot Eskimo. I was compelled to agree with this in so far as Arctic pioneering gave examples. When I carried the thought a step further, the coming of a Pygmy Age seemed a necessary future tendency. In civilization the days for horsepower have passed. The machine age which now rules the world calls for men to press buttons and move levers. This can be done by a midget of four feet with ample head power better and at less expense than by the six-foot pride of our day with an excess baggage of unused fat and muscle.

In looking to the future in an effort to appraise the relative value of man power, I was compelled to admit the Eskimo was right. Evolution in machine ages to come will probably give us pygmy races.

Our changing sense of night perception came up often for illuminating remarks. During the first weeks of the long night, coming as we did from the snowy glare of the summer day, we had difficulty in seeing anything. Slowly our senses sharpened. The defect of eyesight in darkness was to some extent counteracted by better hearing, better nose perception, and better all-around feeling methods to find our way. In time, however, even the eye became more sensitive to light and color earlier invisible. This is best explained if we concede that the optic nerve becomes more sensitive to the longer and shorter rays at the end of the spectrum which ordinarily do not come into use. But perhaps the gain in sense acuteness was close to our urgent need of intelligence which must be gained somehow. In other words, we learned to feel the unseen as does the blind man.

The subject matter to enter this chapter is so vast and complex in extent that it calls for space of book length. But here we are forced to deal with the theme briefly as a suggestion of our peculiar efforts to escape the despair engendered by our mental desolation.

We were in effect wild men wandering over wild places to find our way back to a better human wilderness. Much was new to us. Within and without we were dealing with borders of the unknown, where novelty of endeavor becomes the daily inspiration. After all, there is perhaps nothing really new to men coming and going, except the first bar of light to the infant. That light is the beginning and perhaps ultimately the divining end of all intelligence, but that first ray is promptly affixed to the sense of form and color, then to heat, cold, sound, pain and so on. In that first sunbeam the little one plants and transplants all his later life, and because this is so all men are planters. We were, with infantile simplicity, trying to find our way out of the night of death by giving light and form and color to passing beams of the light memory. Memory travels backward, imagination is telescopic. When the two brain qualities combine it is possible to transcribe the future, but at its best this is only a halo of the past. To us for the time all was halo.

In this drift of brainstorms, with the searchlight directed inward, mirages were perhaps too often taken as real thought forms, and in this strain I will close with an epic from an old planter, one of my father's forefathers, out of Schleswig.

"Early life must always be a planting season. To continue working and waiting while the plants of destiny get ready to bring forth fruit will always be wearisome, but it must be done with patient anticipation. Those who gather green fruits cheat themselves. Autumn precedes the winter in nature with a definite purpose. Middle age precedes the winter of old age with a similar purpose. If you would live long and enjoy the pleasure of your own prudence, eat only ripe fruit and plant the seeds." To this even an Eskimo will subscribe, for Pan-ic-pa, Etuq's father, often said, "Every boy is the father of his own manhood and must mother his offspring to plant a better type of people."

n

↑

21

POLAR DAWN

      I think I can understand the feelings of Adam when, suddenly in full manhood and alone, he looked over a world unknown. The dawn which blends the polar night with the coming day illustrates as nothing else can the loneliness, the isolation, the mental emptiness of man at the beginning of creation. And above all, polar dawn impresses the thought that contrast and opposition are most important to fire the embers of life.

In mid-January, following a few weak displays of aurora borealis, the south at noon was a little brighter than the other parts of the horizon. A few pale lemon-colored rays ran over the night blue of the winter sky.

The night blackness of noon now paled and colored more each day. I think there is some doubt as to the reliability of the color sense in those passing through this long night. I had noted this among trained artists on previous expeditions. I had not sufficient command of Eskimo to discuss the unique color blends coming over the south. To me the charm was intoxicating. Nature's paint brush, which heretofore had worked with black and blue and gray, now exchanged gray for the magic glow of flame. Green also began to appear and at times liquid violet seemed to ooze from the heavens. The dawn thus gave a night's splendor to noon, which brightened and doubled in duration every day, but the hard earth with its crystal covering of icy death remained cold, silent, and unresponsive to animation.

The aurora borealis, in our experience, pales and becomes less evident as we go north of the Magnetic Pole. In the region now under observation, geographically about 300 miles northeast of the Magnetic Pole, it was always difficult to distinguish auroral displays from moon and star brightness, also from the afterglow and pre-glow of passing or coming glimmer of day, when motion or an influence upon the compass was likely to be auroral and was observed and noted as such. A phenomenon of this kind was seen at 3 A.M., when we were excited about the coming sun. A few cloudlike strata of seemingly frozen vapor appeared in the south, where we were expecting the sun to come near the horizon on the following day. The first appearance was a commonplace glimmer like that of an electric glow over a distant city at night.

Was it the moon?

"No," said Etuq, "it is the working light of the people in the heavens above, who are seeking a way to eternal rest."

Wela was trying to find words to express an idea when suddenly the picture changed. The background darkened, the clouds split into a thousand ragged films and shot to the zenith in pale pink flashes. Though the luminous parts were narrow, all was rapidly changing, and of short duration. The entire heavens, including the atmosphere, seemed animated. After a brief period, the pink faded to flashes in lines of silver-gray and then short wobbly bars appeared in a peculiar green. These were so numerous and in controlled cloudlike masses that a rain of luminous green worms seemed imminent. Suddenly all disappeared with an almost inaudible series of sounds, and a little later we noted an aroma in the atmosphere and a taste in the air we breathed. The entire body was influenced, but the feeling came and went so rapidly that little attention was paid to the general influence. I had witnessed many more brilliant auroral displays in the Arctic and in the Antarctic, but none which so much influenced the senses.

Wela said, "It is a dance of the people in heaven," and this best expresses the sentiments engendered in us.

Though each served a six-hour duty of regular watch, two were usually awake at a time and, when something unusual attracted attention, all were awake. The aurora had excited us a good deal. We went out frequently to observe the entire heavens and the ground of the horizon. From within our cave we watched through the peep-holes in the window and continued thus occupied for long hours until the flush of dawn. In spite of a diligent watch we were unable to determine when the seemingly electric glow of the aurora merged with the pre-glow of dawn.

Now as we looked from sea to land and from land to the

heavenly source of light, there was the gross aspect of a
gruesome glory which words will ever fail fully to picture.
The silence seemed at the command of a divine hush. No living thing by sound or motion, no moving air, no rustling
snows or cracking ice interrupted the stillness. The dead
earth was flushed by a liquid blue which seemed bright to
our night-dulled eyes, but the light was so feeble that we
could not see footprints in the snow.

With the brain so little occupied during the long sleep of
the long winter night, we were now hypersensitive to every
incoming mental impression. The idle ovens of thought were
being duly fired.

In this pre-glow of the coming day of Arctic gladness,
our minds rose to the heights in explosive passions. We
longed to break the frozen silence by wild shouts, but when
we gave vent to a voice long unused to producing violent
sounds, there was no echo. The earth had become sound-
proof, under aged blankets of winter snow. Sound, like light
and heat, was absorbed and lost in the downy covering of
frozen celestial vapor on the ground. There was happiness
to us as the eye engaged new aspects in the ever-widening
horizon. Though the gloom of the night of months was but
briefly broken at noon, we realized that day follows dawn.
In that long day of months to follow there was a promise
which meant much to us now. We were aroused and en-
thusiastic with pleasant anticipation and yet all about was a
cold, lifeless desert. We think of the world as a mass coming
originally out of heavenly space, hot and covered with vapor before the first forms of earth life began. That part of
the world about was another phase of creation in the making. It was also covered with vapor, but it was frozen vapor,

the rock form of water. In this cheerless desert of crystal vapor we found cheer, not so much from its favor as from the favor of intelligence carried from life to other parts of the sphere. I wonder if one came down from heaven knowing nothing of the good of nature elsewhere, how would this dominion of zero world appear?

Our experience has taught us that in no part of the world is one so near the Creator and His methods as in the seeming chaos of polar regions.

Time was never long in our icy isolation. Day after day we would now have breath-taking spells of splendors at noon; for, because of some elemental effect, as quickly as the south light blued to the even blueness of the night skies, a wind emerged from somewhere, and clouds came and went, followed by an ugly mingling of colors. Nature, it seemed, was jealous of these few moments of undisturbed nothingness in the mystery of pre-creation—the secrets of the handiwork of God in transformation of celestial energy in ages of the earth's beginning.

As the approaching day brightened to a few hours of twilight at midday, we developed a mood for animal companionship. A little purple was now thrown on the blackened snows. The weather was good. All the usual sounds of nature were suspended, but unusual sounds came with a weird thunder. The very earth began to shake in an effort to break the seal of frost. For several days nothing moved into our horizon which could be imagined alive.

About two weeks before sunrise the rats woke and began to shake their beautiful blue fur in graceful little dances, but they were not really alive and awake in a rat sense for several days. At about the same time, the ravens began to descend from their hiding place and screamed for food. There were only three; two were still conversing with the Eskimo maidens far away, as my companions thought.

In my subsequent strolls I found the raven den and to my horror discovered that the two were frozen. I did not deprive Etuq and Wela of their poetic dream; the sad news of raven bereavement was never told.

The foxes now began to bark from a safe distance and advanced to get their share of the camp spoils. Ptarmigan shouted from near-by rocks. Wolves were heard away in the musk-ox fields, but they did not venture to pay us a visit.

The bear that had shadowed us everywhere before midnight was the last to claim our friendship at dawn. There were good reasons for this which we did not learn until later. The bear stork had arrived. But really we had changed heart even toward the bear. Long before he returned we were prepared to give him a welcome reception. In our new and philosophical turn of mind we thought better of Bruin. In our greatest distress during the previous summer he had kept us alive. In our future adventures he might perform a similar mission. After all he had no sporting proclivities; he did not hurt or trouble us for the mere fun of our discomfort or the chase. His aim in life was the very serious business of getting food. Could we blame him? Had we not a similar necessity?

A survey of our caches proved that we were still rich in the coin of the land. There remained meat and blubber sufficient for all our needs, with considerable to spare for other empty stomachs. So, to feed the bear, meat was piled up in heaps for his delight.

The new aroma rose into the bleaching night air. We

peeped with eager eyes through our ports to spot results. The next day at eleven, footsteps were heard. The noise indicated caution and shyness instead of the bold quick step which we knew so well. There was room for only one eye and only one man at a time at the peep-hole, and so we took turns. Soon the bear was sighted, proceeding with the utmost caution behind some banks and rocks. The blue of the snows, with yellow light, dyed his fur to an ugly green. He was thin and gaunt and ghostly. There was the stealth and the cunning of the fox in his movements. But he could not get his breakfast, the first after a fast of weeks, without coming squarely into our view.

The den was buried under the winter snows and did not disturb the creature, but the size of the pile of meat did disturb his curiosity. When within twenty-five yards, he made a few sudden leaps, and his ponderous claws came down on a musk-ox shoulder. His teeth began to grind like a stonecutter. For an hour the bear stood there and displayed himself to good advantage. Our hatred of the creature entirely vanished.

Five days passed before that bear returned. In the meantime we longed for him to come back. We had unconsciously developed quite a brotherly bear interest. In the period which followed we learned that eleven o'clock was the hour, and that five days was the period between meals. The bear calendar and the clock were consulted with mathematical precision.

We also learned that our acquaintance was a parent. By a little exploration in February we discovered the bear den, in a snow-covered cave, less than a mile west. In it were two saucy little Teddies in pelts of white silk that would have gladdened the heart of any child. The mother was not at home at the time, and we were not certain enough of her friendship, or of her whereabouts, to play with the twins.

With a clearing horizon and a wider circle of friendship, our den now seemed a cheerful home. Our spirits awakened as the gloom of the night was quickly lost in the new glitter of day.

On the eleventh of February the snow-covered slopes of North Devon glowed with the sunrise of 1909. The sun had burst nature's dungeon. Cape Sparbo glowed with golden light. The frozen sea glittered with hills of shimmering lilac. We escaped to a joyous freedom. With a reconstructed sled, new equipment and newly-acquired energy we were ready to pursue the return journey to Greenland and fight the last battle of the polar campaign.

n

↑

22

FINAL DASH ON
THE POLAR PACK

As the polar dawn permanently gave place to a long brilliant twilight of color, physical action was in part suspended to permit the brain to drink the fresh blood of a world anew.

On February 18, 1909, the reconstructed sledge was taken beyond the ice fort and loaded for the home run. We had given up the idea of journeying to Lancaster Sound to await the whalers. There were no Eskimos on the American side nearer than Pond's Inlet. It was somewhat farther to our headquarters on the Greenland shores, but all interests would be best served by a return to Annoatok.

During the night we had fixed all of our attention upon the return journey, and had prepared a new equipment with the limited means at our command; but, traveling in the coldest season of the year, it was necessary to carry a cumbersome outfit of furs, and furthermore, since we were to take the place of the dogs in the traces, we could not expect to transport supplies for more than thirty days. In this time, however, we hoped to reach Cape Sabine, where Etuq's father had been told to place a cache of food for us.

Starting so soon after sunrise, the actual daylight proved very brief, but a brilliant twilight gave a remarkable illumination from eight to four. The light of dawn and that of the afterglow was tossed to and fro in the heavens, from reflecting surfaces of glitter, for four hours preceding and following midday. To use this play of light to the best advantage, it was necessary to begin preparations early by starlight; and thus, when the dim purple glow from the northeast brightened the dull gray-blue of night, the start was made for Greenland shores and for home.

We were dressed in heavy furs. The temperature was −49°. A light air brushed the frozen mist out of Jones Sound, and cut our sooty faces. The sled was overloaded, and the exertion required for its movement over the groaning snow was tremendous. A false, almost hysterical, enthusiasm lighted our faces, but the muscles were not yet equal to the task set for them.

Profuse perspiration came with the first hours of dog work, and our heavy fur coats were exchanged for the lighter sealskin *nitshas*. At noon the snows were fired and the eastern skies burned in great lines of flame. But there was no sun. We sat on the sledge for a prolonged period, gasping for breath and drinking the new celestial glory so long absent from our outlook. As the joy of color was lost in the cold purple of half-light, our shoulders were braced more vigorously into the traces. The ice proved good, but the limit of strength placed camp in a snowhouse ten miles from our winter den. With the new equipment, our camp life now was not like that of the polar campaign. Dried musk-ox meat and strips of musk fat made a steady diet. Molded tallow served as fuel in a crescent-shaped dish of tin, with a carefully prepared moss wick. Over this primitive fire we managed to melt enough ice to quench thirst, and also to make an occasional pot of broth as a luxury. While the drink was liquefying, the chill of the snow igloo was also moderated, and we crept into the bags of musk-ox skins, where agreeable repose and dreams of home made us forget the cry of the stomach and the torment of the cold.

At the end of eight days of forced marches we reached Cape Tennyson. The disadvantage of man power, when compared to dog motive force, was clearly shown in this effort. The ice was free of pressure troubles and the weather was endurable. Still, with the best of luck, we had averaged only about seven miles daily. With dogs, the entire run would have been made easily in two days.

As we neared the land two small islands were discovered. Both were about 1,000 feet high, with precipitous sea walls, and were on a line about two miles east of Cape Tennyson. The more easterly was about one and a half miles long, east to west, with a cross-section, north to south, of about three-quarters of a mile. About half a mile to the west of this was a much smaller island. There was no visible vegetation, and no life was seen, although hare and fox tracks were crossed on the ice. I decided to call the larger island Etuq and the smaller Wela. These rocks will stand as monuments to the memory of my faithful savage comrades when all else is forgotten.

From Cape Tennyson to Cape Isabella the coast of Ellesmere Land was charted, in the middle of the last century, by ships at a great distance from land. Little has been added since. The wide belt of pack thrown against the coast made further exploration from the ship very difficult, but in our northward march over the sea ice it was hoped that we might keep close enough to the shores to examine the land carefully.

A few Eskimos had, about fifty years previously, wandered along this ice from Pond's Inlet to the Greenland camps. They left the American shores because famine, followed by forced cannibalism, threatened to exterminate the tribe. A winter camp had been placed on Coburg Island. Here many walruses and bears were secured during the winter, while in summer, from Kent Island, many guillemots were secured. In moving from these northward, by skin boat and kayak, they noted myriads of guillemots, or "acpas," off the southeast point of the mainland. There being no name in the Eskimo vocabulary for this land, it was called "Acpohon," or "The Home of Guillemots." The Greenland Eskimos had previously called the country "Ah-ming-mah Noons" or "Musk-Ox Land" but they also adopted the name of Acpohon, and so we have taken the liberty of spreading the name over the entire island as a general name for the most northern land west of Greenland. In pushing northward, many of the Eskimos starved, and the survivors had a bitter fight for subsistence. Our experience was similar.

Near Cape Paget those ancient Eskimos had made a second winter camp. Here narwhals and bears were secured, and through Talbot's Fjord a short pass was discovered over Ellesmere Land to the musk-ox country of the west shores. The Eskimos who survived the second winter reached the Greenland shores during the third summer. There they introduced the kayak, and also the bow and arrow. Their descendants are today the most intelligent of the most northern Eskimos.

To my companions the environment of the new land which we were passing was in the nature of digging up ancient history. Several old camp sites were located, and Etuq, whose grandfather was one of the old pioneers, was able to tell us the incidents of each camp with remarkable detail.

As a rule, however, it was very difficult to get near the land. Deep snows, huge pressure lines of ice, and protruding glaciers forced our line of march far from the Eskimo ruins which we wished to examine. From Cape Tennyson to Cape Clarence the ice near the open water proved fairly smooth, but the humid saline surface offered a great resistance to the metal plates of the sled. (Here ivory or bone plates would have lessened the friction very much.) A persistent northerly wind also brought the ice and the humid discomfort of our breath back to our faces with painful results. During several days of successive storms we were imprisoned in the domes of snow. By enforced idleness we were compelled to use a precious store of food and fuel, without making any necessary advance.

Serious difficulties were encountered in moving from Cape Clarence to Cape Faraday. Here the ice was tumbled into mountains of trouble. Tremendous snowdrifts and persistent gales from the west made traveling next to impossible, and with no game and no food supply in prospect, I knew that to remain idle would be suicidal. The sledge load was lightened, and every scrap of fur which was not absolutely necessary was thrown away. The humid boots, stockings, and sealskin coats could not be dried out, for fuel was more precious than clothing. All of this was discarded, and with light sleds and reduced rations, we forced along over hummocks and drifts. In all of our polar march we had seen no ice which offered so much hardship as did this so near home shores. The winds again cut gashes across our faces. With overwork and insufficient food, our furs hung on bony eminences over shriveled skins.

At the end of thirty-five days of almost ceaseless toil, we managed to reach Cape Faraday. Our food was gone. We were face to face with the most desperate problem which had fallen to us in our long run of hard luck. Famine confronted us. We were far from the haunts of game; we had seen no living thing for a month. Every fiber of our bodies quivered with cold and hunger. In desperation we ate bits of skin and chewed tough walrus lines. A half candle and three cups of hot water served for several meals. Some tough walrus hide was boiled and eaten with relish. While trying to masticate this, I broke some of my teeth. It was hard on the teeth, but easy on the stomach, and it had the great advantage of dispelling for prolonged periods the pangs of hunger. But only a few strips of walrus line were left after this was used.

Traveling, as we must, in a circuitous route, there was still a distance of 100 miles between us and Cape Sabine, and the distance to Greenland might, by open water, be spread to 200 miles. This unknown line of trouble could not be worked out in less than a month. Where, I asked in desperation, were we to obtain subsistence for that last thirty days?

To the eastward, a line of black vapors indicated open water about twenty-five miles off shore. There were no seals on the ice. There were no encouraging signs of life; only old imprints of bears and foxes were left on the surface of the cheerless snows at each camp. For a number of days we had placed our last meat as bait to attract the bears, but none had ventured to pay us a visit. The offshore wind and the nearness of the open water gave us some life from this point.

Staggering along one day, we suddenly saw a bear track. These mute marks, seen in the half-dark of the snow, filled us with a wild resurgence of hope for life. On the evening of March 20 we prepared cautiously for the coming of the bear.

A snowhouse was built, somewhat stronger than usual; before it a shelf was arranged with blocks of snow, and on this shelf attractive bits of skin were arranged to imitate the dark outline of a recumbent seal. Over this was placed a looped line, through which the head and neck must go in order to get the bait. Other loops were arranged to entangle the feet. All the lines were securely fastened to solid ice. Peepholes were cut in all sides of the house, and a rear port was cut, from which we might escape or make an attack. Our lances and knives were now carefully sharpened. When all was ready, one of us remained on watch while the others sought a needed sleep. We had not long to wait. Soon a crackling sound on the snows gave the battle call, and with a little black nose extended from a long neck, a vicious creature advanced.

Through our little eye-opening he appeared gigantic. Apparently as hungry as we were, he came in straight rushes for the bait. The run port was opened. Wela and Etuq emerged, one with a lance, the other with a spiked harpoon shaft. Our lance, our looped line, our bow and arrow, I knew, however, would be futile.

During the previous summer, when I foresaw a time of famine, I had taken my last four cartridges and hid them in my clothing. Of the existence of these, the two boys knew nothing. These were to be used at the last stage of hunger, to kill something—or ourselves. That desperate time had not arrived till now.

The bear approached in slow, measured steps, smelling the ground where the skin lay.

I jerked the line. The loop tightened about the bear's neck. At the same moment the lance and the spike were driven into the growling creature.

A fierce struggle ensued. I withdrew one of the precious cartridges from my pocket, placed it in my gun, and gave the gun to Wela, who took aim and fired. When the smoke cleared, the bleeding bear lay on the ground.

We skinned the animal, and devoured the warm, steaming flesh. Strength revived. Here were food and fuel in abundance. We were saved! With the success of this encounter, we could sit down and live comfortably for a month; and before that time should elapse, seals would seek the ice for sun baths, and when seals arrived, the acquisition of food for the march to Greenland would be easy.

n

↑

23

HOMEWARD IN THE SHADOW OF DEATH

At no time of all our dangerous adventure were we so near the end of our earthly stay as when the sight of the home shores of Greenland gladdened our hearts. Failing to sit down and wait when the immediate outlook was bad had been the chief cause of failure in our various efforts to escape with least trouble. It was again our failing now. In looking backward over our desperate predicaments it now seems that much suffering might have been overcome in watchful waiting periods. "Sit down and wait," was my inner command. But we did not sit down. Greenland was in sight; and to an Eskimo, Greenland, with all of its icy discomforts, has attractions not promised in heaven. In this belief, as in most others, I was Eskimo by this time. With very little delay, the stomach was spread with bear chops, and we stretched to a gluttonous sleep, only to awake with appetites that permitted of prolonged stuffing. It was a matter of economy to fill up and thus make the sled load lighter. When more eating was impossible we began to move for home shores, dragging a sled overloaded with the life-saving prize.

A life of trouble, however, lay before us. Successive storms, mountains of jammed ice, and deep snow, interrupted our progress and lengthened the course over circuitous wastes of snowdrifts. Here the gloom of storm again blackened our horizon. When, after prodigious efforts with long delays, we reached Cape Sabine, our food supply was again exhausted.

Here an old seal was found. It had been caught a year before and cached and marked with upturned stones by Panic-pa, Etuq's father. With it was found a rude drawing spotted with sooty tears. This told us the story of a loving father's fruitless search for his son and friends. The seal meat had the aroma of Limburger cheese, and age had changed its flavor; but, with no other food possible, our palates were easily satisfied. In an oil-soaked bag was found about a pound of salt. We ate this as sugar, for no salt had passed over our withered tongues for over a year.

The skin, blubber, and meat were devoured with a relish. Every eatable part of the animal was packed on the sled as we left the American shore.

Smith Sound was free of ice, and open water extended sixty miles northward. A long detour was necessary to reach the opposite shores, but the Greenland shores were temptingly near. With light hearts and cheering contemplations of home, we pushed along Bache Peninsula to a point near Cape Louis Napoleon. The horizon was now cleared of trouble. The ascending sun had dispelled the winter gloom of the land. Leaping streams cut out through crystal gorges. The ice moved; the sea began to breathe. The snows sparkled with the promise of double days and midnight suns.

Life's buds had opened to full blossom. On the opposite shores, which now seemed near, Nature's incubators had long worked overtime to start the little ones of the wilds. Tiny bears danced to their mothers' call; baby seals sunned in down pelts. Little foxes were squinting at school in learning the art of sight. In the wave of germinating joys, our suppressed nocturnal passions rose with surprise anew. We were emotionally raised to the joys of an Arctic paradise.

As it lay in prospect, Greenland had the charm of Eden. There were the homes of my savage companions. It was a stepping-stone to my home, still very far off. It was a land where man had a fighting chance for his life.

In reality, we were now in the most desperate throes of the grip of famine which we had encountered during all of our hard experience. Greenland was only thirty miles away. But we were separated from it by impossible open water—a hopeless stormy deep. To this moment I do not know why we did not sit down and allow the blood to cool with famine and cold. We had no good reason to hope that we could cross, but again hope—the stuff that goes to make dreams— kept our eyes open.

I preferred not to think of the tragic events which history had stamped on the visible headlands of the horizon in the ages of trouble that had preceded our adventure. At or near every cape was the site of a death camp. Here in an effort similar to ours Eskimos had starved and died and the dead bodies had been eaten by the few who survived. About the barren rocks of Cape Sabine General Greely had wintered. There nineteen of his twenty-seven men had starved and the dead bodies had been used as bait to secure shrimp to feed the survivors. Graves of white men and of Eskimos were under slabs of rocks all along the coast on all sides. Suppress as I would the calamity thus expressed on the frozen face of Mother Earth, I could not escape seeing the possibility of three other graves.

But we started with forced courage to tread the seeming road of death.

We were as thin as it is possible for men to be. The scraps of meat, viscera, and skin of the seal, buried for a year, were now our sole diet. We traveled the first two days northward over savage uplifts of hummocks and deep snows, tripping and stumbling over blocks of ice like wounded animals. Then we reached good, smooth ice, but open water forced us northward, ever northward from the cheering cliffs under which our Greenland homes and abundant supplies were located. No longer necessary to lift the feet, we dragged the ice-sheeted boots step after step over smooth young ice. This eased our tired, withered legs, and long distances were covered. The days were prolonged, the decayed seal food ran low. To secure drinkable water was almost impossible. Life no longer seemed worth living. We had eaten the strips of meat and frozen seal cautiously. We had eaten other things not to be mentioned here—our very boots and leather lashings went down as a last resort.

We reached the land-adhering ice about twenty miles north of Annoatok. The high sky line of cliffs behind our old camp through the clear air seemed but a few miles off. Underestimating our strength, we started along with double speed to reach home that day. New-fallen snow made traveling difficult and soon so tired us that we sat down in a cold sweat to rest and reconsider. A straight course was not possible. The rocky land was unsuited to travel. Excited, and in desperate straits for food and water, we decided to risk all by going light. The sled with its load was cached on land under a big rock. With the ice ax, the lance, the harpoon and line as our only equipment, we made another start. Each thus had an ice-testing staff and a line to safeguard us over dangerous crevasses. Thus stripped of burden, we made good progress for a while, but when the first spasm of home-nearing excitement was over, muscles became limp and legs refused to step. We lay down in the snow for a brief rest. When the heart action became regular again, our courage returned, but with each renewed effort to make progress we became weaker. Strength was leaving us in the critical moment of seemingly sure relief. Could we endure the strain of these last few miles? Frankly, to me there was some doubt about that, though I never admitted it. A gable-topped iceberg of considerable height and easy slopes was a mile or two ahead. If we could reach this berg, we might climb to the top and from there give a signal of distress which the keen-eyed Eskimos at Annoatok might perceive. Another strong effort was made, but we kept close together; for with blue lips and failing legs, we knew that for each our physical end was near.

With chattering teeth, Wela said, "Perhaps the camp is

deserted—if so, this is the end." I then saw two graves and one unburied, and wondered who would be first to bury, and where to find the rocks, but did not answer. So weak that we had to climb on hands and knees, we reached the top of the iceberg and from there we saw Annoatok with a few jets of vapor and some smoke above igloos not visible to the naked eye. The picture of death now receded into the background.

We had agreed to raise a signal flag of distress, but it was hardly necessary. As soon as our gaunt dark bodies arrayed in fur rags were silhouetted against the snowy realm of the beyond, we were recognized as men in need of help. Dark figures began to dart over the spotted snow near camp. Dogs were gathered and hitched to sleds and then a dog train bounced from the land and over the pack-ice for our position. We were glad. However, gladness was expressed not in cheers but in frosty tears. We slid down from the berg on worn fur trousers, on seats free of hair, and stood at attention to meet our friends.

We had long been given up as dead, and were not recognized individually until the dogs halted. Then we recognized one after another of the dog drivers.

Among them was a tall blond stranger. Who was he? Hardly had we put the question when the man took the lead, came up and extended his hand.

"I am Harry Whitney. We feel honored to greet you."

The other Eskimos by this time had posted Whitney, for they knew us. We had not met Whitney before.

After a round of greetings and a little vague conversation, I instructed an Eskimo to get the sled we had left behind in our dire distress, and then we jumped on the sleds with prancing dogs eager to rush back to camp with us as visitors. There was little conversation on this return dash. We had found a new grip on our slipping energy with the excitement of new companionship. My home camp, the old box house was still there, but it had been moved and reconstructed.

"You have been away fourteen months [17] with food for two months. How have you done this?" This was Whitney's first question. I answered but have no memory of my reply. Indeed, before I could make an adequate reply, the shore was reached and there I was introduced to two other white men [18] in my camp. Their presence and that of Whitney was not to me fully explained for more than twenty-four hours. The thin, bony specimens of starving men entered the house of plenty. We wanted for the time only sleep and food, but the popping eyes of human kindness from our savage friends seemed useful brain food to start a new day of life for us.

For a while we grunted as the Eskimo does as an introduction to conversation. In the meantime, all were busy inside and outside. Messengers were sent along the coast to distribute the news. The fires were forced. The pots were boiling. The aroma of tasty food told better news to our waiting emptiness than words. For me there was first coffee with fresh biscuits and butter. For my companions, meat broth with a few slices of liver. And then a long wait for a few hours with needful rest and sleep, for we knew that starving men must not take nourishment too fast. During this restful period I did not sleep, could not close my eyes.

Whitney came along and said, "Doctor, you are the dirtiest man I ever saw. We have a bath ready for you—a tub of hot water, plenty of soap and brushes and big clean towels."

What a luxury to one who had not had a real cleansing bath for more than a year!

I scrubbed myself in soapsuds with a stiff brush for a half hour. Then another tub of hot water to rinse off, but the water was still black. I thought now I was clean. At any rate I had too little flesh on my bony body to continue the rough scraping without pain. Resting for a while between blankets, I dozed off exhausted. When I awoke, Whitney was at my side as a nurse.

He said, "Doctor, either you have turned black in ugly spots, or you are still very dirty."

I said, "Yes, but on with the food. This bathing must be taken on the installment plan. I have not enough strength to continue."

Etuq and Wela also took a tub scrubbing, but then they went to an igloo to be anointed by fresh seal blubber, after which the skin was polished with corn meal and finished off with hare forepaw, in the hands of a friend. Their bathing had a scientific purpose—rapid rehabilitation. Mine was not so good in its immediate effect upon the skin.

The world now seemed brighter. The most potent factor in the change was food and more food—a bath and another bath—clean clothes, and the new human contact with its sudden inspiration.

Were we happy? For a time, yes, but soon came the urge to be up and doing and going and seeing and feeling the strangeness of the strange world out of which we had just emerged. Greenland, though a border of the abysmal unknown beyond, was too familiar to us to excite our attention. The memory of hardship, of starvation, of isolation, of near-death from starvation and stilling zero weather was soon only the background to a wild adventure of thrilling experience. Etuq and Wela had excited their listeners and were ready to go back to colonize the new world, so full of trouble to us. And half of their friends were ready to follow. I was nearly in the same humor. We were as eager, as enraptured by inquisitiveness as are animals who linger and wander about in the neighborhood of traps which they know will snap sure death by close familiarity.

It would take a long time to describe fully the slow change in the rehabilitation which now followed, and this might not interest others. We had been so long in the chill of impending death that, compared to Whitney and to the Eskimos about, we were but half alive. Something like a resurrection from suspended life was in us again in progress. Normal existence had for more than a year been submerged under a sea of trouble. Here our book should close, but in a few lines I must place on record some of the mental and physical transformations, for the interest and benefit of others in seemingly terminal experiences who near the world's end as we did.

After the thrill of news and new human contacts had passed, the most notable change in the personality of each was a strange foreign feeling to changing surroundings. We had become exotic. This, with us, was to be a more or less permanent quality. Henceforth we were native to Nowhere. We were strange to ourselves and strange to others. Having borrowed from each other all ideas that could be used in a long-continued hermit life, we acquired unconsciously merged personalities. From this acquisition the result should be in each a uniform similarity to the reactions of life. The result, however, was quite the opposite. We differed from each other in common thought and tastes and habits more than we did at the beginning of our long isolation. Having studied ourselves as men seldom do, a set plan for future existence had become a definite rule for action. Most pronounced in this self-law was the grounded resolution that in all future journeys we would see a way back before a start was made.

We had aged twenty years in our manner of thought and in general behavior. Within this aging effect there was some rejuvenation. Our bodies were so thin and mental storage was so reduced that in the process of renovation and rebuilding now in progress, we became new men in tissue also, as in methods and vigor of thought. Against this withering, our senses in many respects had become doubly keen. We had acquired some instincts of the creature of the wilds, in that we sensed more intelligence through eyes aided by nose and ear. The sense of feeling, instead of being less, was greatly increased. We had learned that animal instincts can deliver a high order of co-ordinated knowledge.

We were now to go back to our respective fields finding a new thrill in life. To each there comes often the question, "Was the desperate battle against famine and frost worth the price?" The first answer must always be that for us there was little choice. We were suspended on the bridge between life and death. Were we to abandon the urge to live for the abysmal depths of the beyond? We had gained a wealth of useful experience, had learned to exchange interdependence for independence, and had under dire need become efficient. Even as invaders of a new realm of snowy deserts we had learned that opportunity or lack of opportunity, the make and break of daily events, gave spark and time to the engines of life. Our all-important discovery must be noted in that we found the greatest mystery, the greatest unknown, is not that beyond the frontiers of knowledge but that unknown capacity in the spirit within the inner man of self. In other words, all lasting good must be planted and nursed in that garden of life between the ears and behind the eyes. Therein is the greatest field for exploration. To have suffered the tortures and to have become resigned to the aspects of death as we did—to learn this is experience which no gold can buy. The shadow of death had given new horizons, new frontiers to life.

n

EPILOGUE

Life is sweetest when death seems nearest. How often, when too late, does this engrossing thought come to passing men? How little do we appreciate the job of living until the end becomes merged with the gloom of the final darkness? It is perhaps advantageous to remember that death is in the background of every picture of life.

In the adventure which these pages have recorded, the coming of the long night with premonitions of nearing death was for months a daily thought which we could not escape. To this was added the suffering of breathtaking storms, the bite of piercing cold, the blight of slow but progressive starvation, combined with the apparent hopelessness and the isolation of a bleak Arctic Sahara of desolation. It was an adventure perhaps best described as misadventure, but such is the inescapable result of trail-blazing.

And yet there was pleasing inspiration in the actual hardship of our threatened existence. We had become accustomed to suffering and deprivation. In brief spells between darkness and gloom there were darting sunbeams burning in snow crystals of the frozen desert. Sparkling icy embers engaged the eye and gladdened the heart. Though half-starved for much of the time, with bodies stripped of all excess tissues, there was also delight in the natural exercise of the poverty of our strength. Hunger and cold, with the awareness of impending death, clear the brain for action as nothing else can. That we survived at all must be credited largely to this advantage.

Brotherhood is a far-reaching emotion, and to a brotherly interdependence more than to any other social trait must be ascribed our eventual success. Here we have dealt with primitive life of the cave-man days. My two companions were but a generation or two above the Stone Age. They rose to an emergency requiring a high order of intelligence. I reverted and reacted to the basic urgency of the primitive. Together we suffered and worked as brothers to feed and shelter and protect each other. We speak of the brotherhood of man, but only among savages is this love and helpfulness most effectually expended. Individual greed in civilization has exchanged human brotherhood for that cupidity in man's inhumanity to man, which embitters the social order of our day.

The most enduring and the most agreeable memories which linger with me to the winter of life from this journey to the End of North, center in the splendor of co-ordinated brotherly love of my two savage companions. If there had not been this cordial spirit between us not one would have returned alive.

We do not credit savage people with inventive genius or originality, or with capacity to become explorers and pioneers, but the working brain of modern man was conditioned by primitives and the terrestrial expanse as now in use was discovered and explored and re-explored during thousands of years before the Bible was written. My two savage companions taught me more than I could ever teach them. Being aborigines, they must daily generate original ideas to find subsistence. Like the polar bear, they were terraqueous in their habitat, living with equal ease on land or sea, and therefore pioneering of the first order was to them a daily study; while my attention was forced for much of the time on a conservation of mental and physical vigor, on efforts to adapt the best of primitive genius to scientific principles and thus to prevent our utter annihilation in a region where death is easier than a fully supplied life.

Perhaps all intelligence and all knowledge is the result of exploration. We enter the realm of discovery with elation the moment baby eyes open to light, and this urging verve never entirely leaves us. If childhood could explain its psychic awakening while its world was being explored in the freshness of first impressions, it would be a dreamland story not easily grasped, and only partly believed by adults. We usually find it hard fully to credit unusual experiences which we have forgotten or never felt, and because this is so, no amount of explanation gives a correct picture of what is envisioned by others in strange lands. In this direction the reader may have found it difficult to grasp the other-world life here presented. We had hardships and dangers to overcome greater than the wilderness folk of the caves in the Stone Age, but became so accustomed to the vital tax that only short sentences entered the daily notes. One must live such a life to find suitable words for its expression, and then after the feeling is phrased in the impulse of action, the background has still to be supplied. Language is still a defective vehicle to move passions beyond the borderland of accustomed living routine. In travel books it often becomes necessary to explore the explorer's text to digest the knowledge presented.

To the average man accustomed to the comfort and security of a modern home it is not easy to convey the driving spirit of polar exploration. The effort seems to him like inviting suicide, but it must be remembered that those engaged in pioneering are imbued with an interest daily freshened.

The wealth and aesthetic glory of the United States and of all modern empires is and was the result of forgotten pioneering with unbelievable hardship. History pages this twilight of our beginning and it attempts to give voice to those long under the sod, but it seldom gives personal feeling to individuals or races in the passing. This must be read between the lines. The urge of the primitive in those engaged in pioneering through any wilderness gives surprising repercussions to fire interest with lasting enthusiasm and enduring inspiration. The spirit thus generated dispels the outlook of danger and the inward suffering from lack of comfort and from long-continued deprivation. In the polar wilderness, to live we must react to the urge of aborigines, and this gives new power with the pleasures of forgotten ages existing close to nature. In this aspect research work becomes bridgework to span the wide reach between primitive existence and that of modern culture. On the one side is the sum total of human endeavor, out of which our knowledge has arisen. On the other side is impending death—beyond the dark unknown. On this suspension between the past and the future, the experience that has been related was enacted as a part of the hunger for a better understanding of the remote blanks on our maps of this sphere. When we work for the benefit of all mankind, the risk of suicide to one is but small expense.

All reports of pioneer efforts are subject to errors in judgment by the writer and by the reader, and to misunderstanding in passing systems of expression. These mistakes are also in part due to errors in self-understanding.

The explorer cannot escape the usual tendency of all writers in that his reflections are influenced by a glimmer from the mirror of self. Since we narrate observations out of personal experience, since all which intelligence implies must first be put through the writer's brain, self-assertion and self-expression and self-reflection thus become mingled in the stream of thought as it pours down on the written page. All this is subject to discount and amplification by the reader, as is all individual opinion. In a final analysis the book maker uses an art, the art of self-expression. This is all he has to deliver.

n

↑

NOTES

1. In using the term "magnetic meridian" Dr. Cook was under an erroneous conception. There is no north-south line between the North Pole and the North Magnetic Pole along which the variation of the compass is 180°. But he was logically correct on his return journey in following the pointing of the compass, with corrections for estimated lateral drift. Ultimately the compass would have brought him to the area of the Magnetic Pole, as it very nearly did.

2. Boothia Felix, where the North Magnetic Pole formerly was believed to be located, is far south of Prince of Wales Island, and Prince of Wales Island is as far south of Grinnell Peninsula as Grinnell Peninsula is distant from the northern end of Axel Heiberg Island. It now seems fairly well established that the North Magnetic

Pole has been moving in the past half century somewhat west of
north at the rate of about four and a half miles a year. It was believed to be on Boothia Peninsula in 1829, and some years after the
time of Dr. Cook's Arctic journey it was believed to be located on
Prince of Wales Island. Chart 1706 of the Hydrographic Office,
U. S. Navy, compiled from comprehensive analysis of world-wide
magnetic observations since 1905, shows the variation of the compass for the year 1945, and locates the North Magnetic Pole on
Bathurst Island, west of Grinnell Peninsula. "Actually, in the general area [of the North Magnetic Pole] there are many magnetic
poles. . . . Since the compass does not point toward any of these
poles, save by accident, they would be very hard to find even if
they were stationary. The direction and strength of the magnetic
field are ever changing, and the magnetic poles are always moving
about. . . . The North Magnetic Polar Area is not a circle—it is
decidedly elongated in the direction NNW-SSE." (H. Herbert
Howe, *Magnetic Poles and the Compass*. U. S. Department of Com-
merce, Coast and Geodetic Survey, Serial 726.) Scientists did not
know and do not now know with certainty where the North Magnetic Pole was located during the year of Dr. Cook's journey, nor
did anyone know nor does anyone now know the exact variation of
the compass during the year 1908 along Dr. Cook's route after he
passed the Ringnes Islands. It is likely that for at least the latter part
of his return journey from the Pole to Crown Prince Gustav Sea,
Dr. Cook was close to the line of compass variation of about 180°.

3. Dr. Cook's seven expeditions from 1891 to 1907 were four into
or toward the Arctic, one into the Antarctic, and two to Mount
McKinley near the Arctic Circle.

4. Annoatok is Dr. Cook's spelling. The name is also variously
spelled Anoritok, Anoratok, Anonitok, Annootok, etc.

5. Of his choice of route, Dr. Cook wrote (*My Attainment of the
Pole*, pp. 79-80): "I aimed to reach the top of the globe in the angle
between Alaska and Greenland, a promising route through a new

and lonesome region which had not been tried, abandoning what has come to be called the 'American Route.' I should strike westward and then northward, working new trails. . . . I knew from the general reports of the natives, and from the explorations of Sverdrup, that the beginning of the intended route offered abundant game, and the indications were that further food would likewise be found as we advanced." What Dr. Cook had learned from the explorations of Sverdrup is to be found in a paper read in 1903 by Captain Otto Sverdrup ("The Second Norwegian Polar Expedition in the 'Fram,' 1898-1902," *Scottish Geographical Magazine*, Vol. 19, 1903, pp. 337-53). He says: "In many parts of the newly discovered lands there would appear to exist an abundance of animal life, especially musk oxen and smaller game, such as hares and ptarmigan, as well as foxes and wolves. . . . On the western side of Axel Heiberg [Is]land we again saw numerous traces of reindeer, but no indication of musk oxen. All the same, I do not doubt that musk oxen would be found by proceeding a little way up the fjords, for we had abundant evidence that animals of all kinds were plentiful enough throughout the whole of the east coast of that land. . . . Bears also were pretty numerous in certain localities, both in Jones Sound and all the way along the coast of King Oscar Land northward from Eureka Sound."

6. Dr. Cook's renewal of acquaintance with his Eskimo friends was in 1901 and again in 1907. His original contact with the Smith Sound Eskimos was in 1891-2.

7. Water sky is sky over open water, and is not so white as sky over gleaming snow and ice.

8. "Five suns all at once"—a parhelion.

9. Dr. Cook's experience with an exclusively meat diet, mostly raw, without salt or vegetables, was nothing new to him. He wrote ("Medical Observations Among the Esquimaux," *New York Journal of Gynaecology and Obstetrics*, Vol. 4, March, 1894): "These

people live on an absolute meat diet, two-thirds raw and frozen, one-third cooked, because in this way the blood is extracted; this forms their only drink except water." He said their teeth were in good condition, and: "We did not need any antiscorbutic remedies." His description of the virtues of a meat diet was substantiated in 1921 by Dr. Vilhjalmur Stefansson (*The Friendly Arctic*). Dr. Stefansson's observations were met with such incredulity that he proceeded to prove the antiscorbutic quality of such a diet under conditions of controlled medical observation in New York City in 1928. There had been repeated instances of healthy survival in the Arctic on an exclusively meat diet, mostly raw, ever since the days of Queen Elizabeth, when three men marooned on Spitzbergen lived for a winter on whale meat and blubber. But civilized men, and especially the medical profession, had ignored the facts until Dr. Stefansson convinced the scientific world of what Dr. Cook and others had demonstrated.

10. "Where Franklin and other explorers, bleached and blued in scurvy, had died with shiploads of supplies . . . we lived in the thrill of native luxury." This attitude condemned Dr. Cook in the eyes of many of the explorers and patrons of explorers of his day. With so little equipment, they reasoned, he should not have been successful, and therefore he could not have been. Dr. Cook failed to meet orthodox expectations. He should have had an unending struggle with ceaseless suffering all the way to the Pole and back; but while he did experience hours and days of hardship and danger, he also had days of intense enjoyment.

11. An oogzuk (ugruk or ugyuk) seal is bearded and four times the size of ordinary seals. Eskimos consider the skin of the bearded seal almost indispensable for boot soles, umiak covers, and rawhide rope. (Vilhjalmur Stefansson, *My Life with the Eskimos*, pp. 267-9, 526-7.)

12. "Intelligence begins and ends in the mental format of the savage." Professor H. P. Steensby wrote (*Fortnightly Review*,

November, 1909, p. 891): "Dr. Cook, who knows children of nature from several other regions, does not conceal the fact that he considers the polar Eskimos and some of their Arctic kinsmen to be perhaps the most intelligent of the untutored mankind. In all that concerns their peculiar means of obtaining a livelihood, and in all the connection of life which common sense can throw light on, their intelligence is highly developed." Steensby added (p. 893): "I conceived the greatest admiration for his [Dr. Cook's] fine grasp of the moral as well as the material culture of the tribes." Dr. Cook wrote (*Century Magazine*, March, 1900): "The lesson of ages to untutored man has impressed upon him a prescription of moral direction, which is quite as good as, and far more appropriate for him than, the white man's code of ethics." Pertinent also to Dr. Cook's comment on the intelligence of the savage, in contrast with the culture of civilization, is the statement by Harry Payne Whitney (*Hunting with the Eskimos*, 1911, p. 46): "No matter how conventional [or] wedded to luxury, somewhere in his innermost soul a man harbors the primordial instinct, an inheritance from savage ancestors. A white man is transformed into an Indian very quickly, but to transform an Indian into a white man is a process of evolution that requires generations."

13. The compass was an unreliable timepiece. The needle does not point toward either of the magnetic poles, but is always parallel to the line of the magnetic force at the locality where the compass is. Dr. Cook had no means of knowing the variation of the compass with any precision. For all he knew, the compass might point south or west or anywhere between, in the region of Grinnell Peninsula. For example, in 1945 in Queen's Channel west of Grinnell Peninsula, the compass pointed 150° west of north, or 30° west of south. The compass could not have been an accurate instrument for Dr. Cook to rely upon to determine when the sun stood directly to the south at noon.

14. If the principle of protective coloration were the primary factor operative among Arctic animals, those animals would have

lighter colored fur against the background of gleaming snow and ice in the summer sun, and darker fur against the dark background of the winter twilight and night. As Dr. Cook observed, the contrary is the fact.

15. Dr. Cook wrote ("The People of the Farthest North," *Everybody's Magazine*, January, 1902): "We could not understand how human beings could subsist and extricate anything worth living for in an irregular dungeon, less than ten feet in its longest diameter, hardly affording standing room, and with bits of stone and ice for furniture. The luxurious Caucasian loses all sense of proportion as he first views this home, but after he is compelled to undergo the life of hardship and suffering which is the lot of his Eskimo friends, he learns to regard this dark chamber as a kind of paradise. He forgets his own palatial home, and feels real comfort and spiritual elation, snugly tucked under furs, as the freezing wind and snow rush over his head. After all, everything in life is good or bad by comparison." These cheerful sentences were written six years before the winter in the den at Cape Sparbo forced him to eat his romantic words.

16. One of Dr. Cook's notebooks is 4½ by 6¾ inches; entries in it are dated from March 20, 1908. One of the memorandum books, with entries from September 1, 1908, to April 30, 1909, is 2⅝ by 4¾ inches. On some pages of his notebooks, Dr. Cook wrote legibly twelve lines to the inch.

17. Dr. Cook's handwriting became irregular from March 1 to April 12. The entry for April 15 indicates arrival at Annoatok. Actually, he returned to Annoatok on April 18, 1909. He had lost three days in his reckoning of the time during the fourteen months of his absence. It is interesting to read an entry for February 16, 1908, while he was preparing for the polar dash: "About once a month Rudolph [Francke] gets a notion that we have lost a day and so we watch with eager interest the phases of the moon to keep

tally on our date, for if we should gain or lose a day, it would be a serious business in determining our positions."

18. The other two white men in Dr. Cook's camp at Annoatok were Bo's'n Murphy and the cabin boy Pritchard of Peary's expedition ship *Roosevelt*.

BIBLIOGRAPHY

ADAMS, CYRUS C., "North Pole at Last." *Review of Reviews*, 40: 420-6, October, 1909.

AHLEFELDT, RALPH SHAINWALD VON, manuscript letter to Franklin Delano Roosevelt, May 20, 1940.

AMUNDSEN, ROALD, "Close Calls in My Life as an Explorer." *World's Work*, Vol. 54, No. 2, June, 1927, pp. 170-83.

—— "Amundsen Answers His Critics." *World's Work*, Vol. 54, No. 3, July, 1927, pp. 281-93.

ARCTIC CLUB OF AMERICA, Bulletin of Information, July 30, 1908, and February 27, 1909.

—— Program and menu for banquet in honor of Frederick Albert Cook, September 23, 1909.

BALCH, EDWIN SWIFT, *The North Pole and Bradley Land*. Campion & Company, Philadelphia, 1913.

—— *Mount McKinley and Mountain Climbers' Proofs*. Campion & Company, Philadelphia, 1914.

—— "Present Status of the North Pole Question." *Scientific American*, 114:301, March 18, 1916.

—— "North Pole Questions." *Independent*, 115:575-6, 593, November 21, 1925; 115:607-8, 624, November 28, 1925; 116:255, February 27, 1926.

BALDWIN, EVELYN B., letter to editor. *New York Times*, December 29, 1913.

BARNES, J. K., *World's Work*, 45:611-8, April, 1923.

BARTLETT, ROBERT ABRAM, *The Log of "Bob" Bartlett*. G. P. Putnam's Sons, New York, 1928.

BATES, ROBERT H., *American Alpine Journal*, Vol. 5, 1943, No. 1, pp. 1-13.

BORUP, GEORGE, *A Tenderfoot with Peary*. Frederick A. Stokes Company, New York, 1911.

BRADLEY, J. R., "My Knowledge of Dr. Cook's Polar Expedition." *Independent*, 67:636-40, September 16, 1909.

BRIDGES, E. LUCAS, *Uttermost Part of the Earth*. Hodder & Stoughton, Ltd., London, 1948.

BRIDGMAN, HERBERT L., "The Dash to the Pole." *Independent*, 67:571-4, September 9, 1909.

—— "Commander Peary." *Independent*, 67:633-6, September 16, 1909.

BROWNE, BELMORE, *The Conquest of Mount McKinley*. G. P. Putnam's Sons, New York, 1913.

CHAMBERLIN, J., "Battle of the Pole; When the Peary-Cook Controversy Stirred the Nation." *Reader's Digest*, 35:79-83, August, 1939.

Congressional Record, Sixty-Third Congress, Third Session. Vol. 52, No. 16, December 23, 1914, pp. 637-9; Vol. 52, No. 56, February 10, 1915, pp. 3874-84; Vol. 52, No. 78, March 4, 1915, pp. 6279-86; Vol. 52, No. 80, Part 2, March 15, 1915, pp. 6515-20.

—— Sixty-Fourth Congress, First Session. Vol. 53, No. 44, February 12, 1916, pp. 2793-852.

Cook, Dr. Frederick Albert, magazine articles, 1894-1909.

—— *Through the First Antarctic Night.* Doubleday & McClure Company, New York, 1900.

—— Notebooks and diaries, 1907-1909.

—— *To the Top of the Continent.* Doubleday, Page & Company, New York, 1908.

—— "Statement on Peary." Unpublished manuscript, undated.

—— *My Attainment of the Pole.* The Polar Publishing Company, New York, 1911.

—— Letter to editor. *Time*, Vol. 27, No. 13, April 30, 1936, p. 4.

Current Literature, 47:353-64, October, 1909; 47:683-5, December, 1909; 50:18-20, January, 1911.

Decker, Karl, "Dr. Frederick A. Cook—Faker." *Metropolitan Magazine*, Vol. 31, No. 4, January 1910, pp. 417-35.

Diebitsch-Peary, Josephine, *My Arctic Journal.* Contemporary Publishing Company, New York, 1893.

Dunn, Robert, *The Shameless Diary of an Explorer.* Outing Publishing Company, New York, 1907.

Egan, Maurice Francis, "The Witnesses for Dr. Cook." *Rosary Magazine*, Vol. 35, No. 5, November, 1909.

Everett, Marshall, *The True Story of the Cook and Peary Discovery of the North Pole.* Educational Company, Chicago, 1909.

Franke, Rudolph, *Erlebnisse eines Deutschen im hohen Norden.* Alfred Janssen, Hamburg, 1914.

Furlong, Col. Charles Wellington, obituary of Lucas Bridges. *Geographical Journal*, Vol. 114, December, 1949, pp. 240-1.

Gibbs, Philip, "How I Exposed Dr. Cook's Polar Fraud." *World's Work*, 45:478-86, March, 1923.

—— *Adventures in Journalism.* Harper and Brothers, New York, 1923.

Gibson, Rex, "Mount McKinley in War Time." *Canadian Alpine Journal*, Vol. 28, 1943, pp. 147-58.

Greely, Maj. Gen. A. W., "Dr. Cook's North Polar Discoveries." *Independent*, 67:641-3, September 16, 1909.

—— *Handbook of Polar Discoveries.* Fourth edition, Little, Brown & Company, Boston, 1909.

330

—— "Reluctant Peary Doubter." *Independent,* 115:442, October 17, 1925.

HALL, THOMAS F., *Has the North Pole Been Discovered?* Vol. 1, R. G. Badger, Boston, 1917. Vol. 2, Supplement, privately printed, Omaha, 1920.

Hampton's Magazine, 26:51-66, 162-76, 295-308, 493-502, January-April, 1911.

Harper's Weekly, 53:5, September 11, 1909; 53:6, November 20, 1909.

HARRIS, ROLLIN ARTHUR, "Arctic Tides." *Scottish Geographical Magazine,* Vol. 27, August, 1911, pp. 433-4.

—— "Undiscovered Land in the Arctic Ocean." *American Museum Journal,* Vol. 13, No. 2, February, 1913, pp. 56-61.

HAYES, JAMES GORDON, *Robert Edwin Peary.* G. Richards & H. Toulmin, London, 1929.

—— *The Conquest of the North Pole.* Thornton Butterworth, Ltd., London, 1934.

HENSON, MATTHEW ALEXANDER, "The Negro at the North Pole." *World's Work,* 19:12825-37, April, 1910.

—— *A Negro Explorer at the North Pole.* Frederick A. Stokes Company, New York, 1912.

HIGH, FRED, *The Case of Dr. Cook; Its Appeal to Congress and to the American People.* Privately printed, Chicago, 1914.

—— "New Light on an Historical Episode Never Before Published." *Waynesburg (Pa.) Republic,* November 10, 1932.

HOBBS, WILLIAM HERBERT, *Peary.* Macmillan Company, New York, 1936.

HOUBEN, H. H., *Call of the North.* E. Mathews & Marrot, London, 1932.

HUBBARD, ELBERT, "Fair Play and Dr. Cook." Short article, undated.

HUBER, LOUIS R., "The Incredible Conquest of Mount McKinley." *Natural History,* Vol. 43, No. 10, December, 1949, pp. 440-6.

HUSSEY, E. FOUNTAIN, *Independent,* 67:1081-3, November 11, 1909.

Independent, 67:623-4, September 16, 1909; 67:815-20, October 7, 1909; 67:936-7, October 21, 1909; 67:1513-4, December 30, 1909; 116:255, February 27, 1926.

INGERSOLL, ERNEST, *The Conquest of the North; an Authentic Account of the Finding of the North Pole by Dr. Frederick A. Cook::Commander Robert E. Peary, U.S.N., Together with Biographies of the Explorers and a Brief History of Arctic Discovery.* C. S. Hammond & Company, New York, 1909.

JOHNSON, WILLIAM N., *Did Commander Peary "Achieve" the North Pole?* Dvorak & Weiser, Chicago, 1915.

KENNAN, GEORGE, "Commander Peary's Return." *Outlook*, 93:252-5, October 2, 1909; 93:339, October 16, 1909.

LECOINTE, GEORGES, *Au Pays des Manchots. Recit du Voyage de la Belgica.* Expédition Antarctique Belge, Brussels, 1904.

LEITZELL, TED, "Peary's Conspiracy Against Dr. Cook," "The North Pole Boomerang," "What Is the True Story of Robert Peary?" and "Who Stole the North Pole?" *Real America*, October, 1935-January, 1936.

LEVIN, HUGO, *Adventure Magazine*, May, 1938, pp. 127-32.

LEWELS, MAXIMILIAN, *Dr. Cook und der Nordpol.* Katholisches Lyzeum, Hamburg, 1916.

LEWIN, WALTER HENRY, *The Great North Pole Fraud.* C. W. Daniel Co., Ltd., London, 1935.

Literary Digest, "Peary, Who Carried the American Flag to the North Pole." 64:52-8, March 13, 1920.

—— "Living 'Off the Country' on an Ice Cake and Never Missing a Meal." 66:68-74, August 7, 1920.

—— 79:10-1, December 8, 1923; 99:48-61, October 16, 1926; 104:36, 38, 40, February 1, 1930.

Living Age, 263:44-61, October, 1909; 274:28-36, July 6, 1912.

LONSDALE, WALTER, "The Real Story of Dr. Cook and the North Pole." *Travel Magazine*, May-June, 1910.

LYON, H. M., "When Cook Came to Copenhagen; the Brooklyn Explorer Gets the Third Degree from British and Danish Reporters." *Collier's*, 44:22, September 25, 1909.

MACMILLAN, DONALD B., "New Evidence that Cook Did Not Reach the Pole." *Geographical Review*, Vol. 5, 1918, pp. 140-1.

—— "Peary as a Leader." *National Geographic*, 37:293-317, April, 1921.

—— *How Peary Reached the Pole.* Houghton Mifflin Company, Boston, 1934.

McAree, J. V., "Was Peary the Faker?" *Toronto Globe and Mail,* August 4, 1938.

McConnell, Burt M., "The Peary Side of the North Pole Controversy; an Interview with Vilhjalmur Stefansson." *Independent,* 116:384-6, April 3, 1926.

Metcalfe, Gertrude, "Mount McKinley and the Mazama Expedition." *Pacific Monthly,* September, 1910, pp. 255-65.

Miller, Edwin, "Killer Mountain." *Argosy,* Vol. 325, No. 2, August, 1947, pp. 12-15, 106-7.

Miller, James Martin, *Discovery of the North Pole: Dr. Frederick A. Cook's Own Story of How He Reached the North Pole April 21, 1908, and the Story of Commander Robert E. Peary's Discovery April 6, 1909.* Copyright by J. T. Moss, Chicago (?), 1909.

Mirsky, Jeannette, *To the North! The Story of Arctic Exploration from Earliest Times to the Present.* Viking Press, Inc., New York, 1934.

Nation, 89:373-4, October 21, 1909; 89:616, December 23, 1909; 89:591-2, December 16, 1909; 90:255-6, March 17, 1910; 93:411-2, November 2, 1911; 117:624, December 5, 1923.

National Geographic, November, 1909, p. 916.

Nature, 81:306-8, September 9, 1909.

Newsweek, Vol. 4, No. 19, November 10, 1934; Vol. 16, No. 54, August 12, 1940.

New York Herald, September 2, 1909, ff.

New York Herald Tribune, May 5, 1940; August 8, 1940.

New York Times, September 2, 1909, ff.

New York Journal of Gynaecology and Obstetrics, Vol. 4, March, 1894, pp. 287-9.

Osbon, Capt. B. S., "Cook and Peary." *Tourist Magazine,* August-November, 1910, pp. 184-5, 208-16, 309-18, 342-4, 443-56.

Outlook, 93:361-2, October 23, 1909; 93:844-6, December 18, 1909; 94:1-2, January 1, 1910; 135:575, December 5, 1923; 142:216-9, February 10, 1926; 154:454, March 19, 1930.

PARADYNE, HENRY, "Dr. Cook's Achievements." *Harper's Weekly*, 53:11-2, September 25, 1909.

PEARY, ROBERT EDWIN, "The North Greenland Expedition of 1891-92." Address delivered December 31, 1892.

—— *Northward Over the "Great Ice."* Frederick A. Stokes Company, New York, 1898, 2 vols.

—— "The Last Years of Arctic Work." *McClure's*, February, 1903.

—— *Nearest the Pole. A Narrative of the Polar Expedition of the Peary Arctic Club in the S.S. Roosevelt, 1905-1906*. Doubleday, Page & Company, New York, 1907.

—— *The North Pole; Its Discovery in 1909*. Frederick A. Stokes Company, New York, 1910.

PHELPS, WILLIAM LYON, *Good Housekeeping*, 114:39, January, 1942.

Photo-Era Magazine, 64:215, April, 1930.

Polar Record, 8:134-5, July, 1934.

QUERVAIN, DR. ALFRED DE, and STOLBERG, DR. A., *Durch Grönlands Eiswüste. Reise der Deutsch-Schweizerischen Grönlandexpedition 1909 auf das Inlandeis*. J. Singer, Strassburg, 1911.

Review of Reviews, 40:515-8, November, 1909.

ROBINSON, BRADLEY, *Dark Companion*. Robert M. McBride & Company, New York, 1947.

ROOD, HENRY E., "The Coming of Cook." *Saturday Evening Post*, April 16, 1910.

ROST, ERNEST CHRISTIAN, *Mount McKinley, Its Bearing on the Polar Controversy*. Milans & Sons, Washington, D.C., 1914.

RUSK, C. E., "On the Trail of Dr. Cook." *Pacific Monthly*, October, 1910, pp. 430-42; November, 1910, pp. 472-86.

Scientific American, 95:445-6, December 15, 1906; 101:183, September 11, 1909; 104:404-5, April 22, 1911; 113:286, October 2, 1915; 113:359, October 23, 1915; 114:296, March 18, 1916.

SHEA, WILLIAM E., "Is the North Pole Still Undiscovered? Contradictions in Admiral Peary's Story." *Independent*, 115:205-7, August 22, 1925.

—— "Did Peary Touch the Pole?" *Independent*, 116:680-2, June 12, 1926.

334

STANTON, THEODORE, "Dr. Cook at Copenhagen." *Independent*, 67:815-20, October 7, 1909.

STEAD, W. T., "Character Sketch and Interview of Dr. Frederick A. Cook and of Robert E. Peary." *Review of Reviews* (London), 40:323-39, 341-2, 420, October, 1909.

STEENSBY, PHIL. H. P., "The Polar Eskimos and the Polar Expeditions." *Fortnightly Review*, November, 1909, pp. 891-902.

STEFANSSON, VILHJALMUR, *My Life with the Eskimo*. Macmillan Company, New York, 1913. Also, *My Life with the Eskimos*, (the former book abridged). Macmillan Company, New York, 1927.

—— "Solving the Problem of the Arctic." *Harper's*, Vol. 138, October, 1919.

—— "Peary." *New Republic*, 22:27-8, March 3, 1920.

—— *The Friendly Arctic*. Macmillan Company, New York, 1921.

—— "The Problem of Meighen Island." Unpublished, privately printed, New York, 1939.

—— *Not by Bread Alone*, Macmillan Company, New York, 1946.

STUCK, HUDSON, "The Ascent of Denali." *Scribner's Magazine*, Vol. 54, No. 5, November, 1913, pp. 531-52.

—— *Ten Thousand Miles with a Dog Sled*. Charles Scribner's Sons, New York, 1916.

SVERDRUP, OTTO NEUMANN, "The Second Norwegian Polar Expedition in the 'Fram,' 1898-1902." *Scottish Geographical Magazine*, Vol. 19, 1903, pp. 337-53.

—— *New Land—Four Years in the Arctic Regions*. Longmans, Green & Company, New York, 1904.

Time, Vol. 27, No. 11, March 16, 1936, p. 41; Vol. 27, No. 15, April 13, 1936, pp. 8, 10; Vol. 34, No. 23, December 4, 1939, p. 34.

VIDAL, NUMA F., "Who Climbed Mount McKinley?" *Saturday Evening Post*, February 18, 1950.

WALSH, HENRY COLLINS, *The Last Cruise of the Miranda*. Transatlantic Publishing Company, New York, 1896.

WASHBURN, BRADFORD, "Mount McKinley from the North and West." *American Alpine Journal*, Vol. 6, No. 3, 1947, pp. 283-93.

WEIR, HUGH C., "The Conquest of the North Pole." *World Today*, 17:1020-6, October, 1909.

WHITNEY, CASPAR, "Who's the Liar?" *Collier's*, 44:15, October 16, 1909.

WHITNEY, HARRY PAYNE, "Hunting in the Arctic." *Outing*, 55:258-80, December, 1909.

—— *Hunting with the Eskimos*. Century Company, New York, 1911.

WILKINS, SIR GEORGE HUBERT, and SHERMAN, HAROLD M., *Thoughts Through Space*. Creative Age Press, New York, 1942.

World's Work, 18:12071, October, 1909; 45:611-8, April, 1923.